MEDIÆVAL SCOTTISH POETRY

Edited by GEORGE EYRE-TODD, 1862 ~

MEDIÆVAL SCOTTISH POETRY

KING JAMES THE FIRST
ROBERT HENRYSON
WILLIAM DUNBAR
GAVIN DOUGLAS

821.208

GREENWOOD PRESS, PUBLISHERS
WESTPORT, CONNECTICUT

Originally published in 1892
by William Hodge & Company, Glasgow

Reprinted from an original copy in the collections
of the George Peabody Branch of the Enoch Pratt Free Library

First Greenwood Reprinting 1971

Library of Congress Catalogue Card Number 70-98754

SBN 8371-3095-6

Printed in the United States of America

NOTE.

THE mediæval poetry of Scotland, equally with the earliest Scottish poetry, has hitherto been all but inaccessible to the general reader. The difficulties in the way of anything like a popular study of poets such as James I., Henryson, Dunbar, and Douglas may be gathered from the fact that the works of these four, when found, are scarcely to be had together for a smaller sum than five guineas. The present volume is an attempt to overcome these difficulties, and to render available the flower of mediæval Scottish poetry. In all cases, excepting the more voluminous works of Gavin Douglas, the poems included are printed complete.

CONTENTS.

CONTENTS.

MEDIÆVAL SCOTTISH POETRY.

THE history of Scottish poetry divides itself
naturally into certain strongly marked periods
corresponding to periods in the political history
of the country. The most interesting of these
poetic periods in many respects is that in which
the mediæval spirit reached its highest
expression. Almost the sole subject of the
country's early muse had been the deeds of
arms and heroes. After the great struggle with
England there had ensued the century of the
chronicler-poets, and in their hands Scottish
verse had drawn its inspiration entirely from the
national patriotism. James I., however, among
other advantages, brought home with him from
his captivity a new poetic influence—the
influence of Petrarch and Chaucer. From that
time, beginning with James' own kingly com-
position, a fresh life seemed to be abroad in
Scottish poetry. It was as if a soft summer
wind had come blowing out of the south. In
the heart of the north there began to throb new

pulses of thought and desire. Imagination stirred again and woke. Beside the old stem of heroic narrative sprang new poetic forms—pastoral, allegory, satire, ballad. And presently, passionate, rich, and exuberant, this later poesy of the Middle Ages burst into prodigal flower.

In the fifteenth century there was passing over Europe one of those great waves of vitality which from time to time have made and marked the eras of history. A later wave of the same sort, yet unnamed, made its political mark in the French Revolution, and finding early expression in Scotland in the poetry of Burns, gave birth to the romantic genius of Byron, Scott, Balzac, and Goethe, and the world of modern thought. The moving event in the fifteenth century, perhaps, was the capture of Constantinople by the Turks in 1453. For hundreds of years the ancient capital of the Eastern Empire had been the chief repository of the traditions of Greek literature and civilization; and the scattering of Byzantine scholarship over Europe upon the fall of the city largely helped to bring about that revival of thought and art which in the south took the form of the Renaissance and in the north of the Reformation.

The Scottish poets of the last decades of the fifteenth and the first of the sixteenth century cannot, it is true, be reckoned singers of the new era. There is about the work of Henryson, Dunbar, and Douglas a mournful note that betokens it of an age about to pass away. They are not the prophets of a morning-time, and the soul that shines in their verse has the splendid weariness of full experience, not the hot enthusiasm of an epoch's youth. It would seem, however, as if a breath of the coming life had touched the air, and to the ripeness of the older time had added a flush of colour and strength. There is reason to believe that all the great Scottish poets of the period had visited the Continent, and there, it is probable, they had felt something of the quickening of the new era that was about to dawn. At any rate it is certain that the poetry of mediæval Scotland found its fullest and richest expression at the last, when feudalism in church and state had reached its climax, and when, before the kindling of the Reformation, the old order was about to disappear.

The political circumstances of the period in Scotland throw their own light upon the subject.

In the history of every nation which has perfected a national life there can be distinguished a golden era. Athens had her time of Pericles, Rome her Augustan age, Later Italy her Renaissance, England her reign of Elizabeth. A regular likeness may be noticed in the circumstances of all these periods. When a Philosophy of History, Aristotle's ambitious dream, at last is written, the phenomena of national growth and decay may be discovered to be as regular, even to minute details, as the growth, flourish, and decay of the forest oaks. It is enough here to remark that, after an infancy of obscure development and a youth of storm and struggle, there appears always to come a national manhood of exuberant spirit and strength. A new sense of power seems to awaken. While conquest flushes the country's arms, and wealth floats in upon a flowing tide, the national genius of poetry and art breaks into splendid fire.

Scotland reached this era of her history towards the end of the fifteenth century. Out of its Celtic, Saxon, Cymric, and Norman elements the nation had been born into a new existence amid the early Wars of Independence. Afterwards, for one hundred and fifty years, the Stewarts had been making their way from the position of little more than party leaders among a turbulent nobility to the actual sovereignty of the state. But towards the close of the fifteenth century the royal house had at last secured for itself unquestioned power. A firm, strong government was established under the sceptre of James IV. To its more ancient acquisitions of the Western Isles and the Isle of Man the crown had lately added the isles Orkney and Shetland. By the rapid increase of the country's maritime enterprise possibilities of wealth had recently developed to an extent before unknown. And in the eyes of Europe just then, chiefly because of the foothold she afforded for checkmating the movements of Henry VII., Scotland had assumed a position of large consideration.

These were the greater political influences at work to bring about the ripeness of the time. Some minor circumstances were perhaps not less important.

James IV. had inherited the hoarded wealth of his unfortunate father, as Augustus Cæsar inherited the wealth of the dead Julius; and, like Augustus, the Scottish king sought by all available means to encourage the arts of civilization in his realm. James himself was no mean scholar, speaking Latin, French, German, Flemish, Italian, Spanish, and Gaelic, besides his native Scottish, and his tastes and his policy alike were towards refinement.* Never before

* These and other particulars of James and of Scotland at that time are to be found in a letter dated London, 25th July, 1498, from Don Pedro de Ayala, Spanish ambassador to Scotland, to his master, Ferdinand, contained in the *Calendar of Spanish State Papers*, edited by Mr. Bergenroth (1862-8). See also for a view of the reign an interesting little volume, *The Days of James IV.*, arranged in extracts from contemporary writers by G. Gregory Smith, M.A., 1890.

had there been so brilliant a court in Scotland, and never was there to be so brilliant a court again. For the fourth time a Scottish king had married an English princess, and for the fourth time a consequent wave of civilization seemed to pass across the country.* Gay tournaments, huntings, feastings, were the pursuits of the nobility; and amid the quickening of social life the arts that elevate and the arts that charm rose into high esteem. At the same time—as great an influence, perhaps, of another sort—the discovery of printing was introduced into Scotland during the reign of James IV.

It was in circumstances like these—the national pulse beating with its fullest life, and the fortunes of the country a rising flood—that the national poetry might be expected to put forth its brightest blossoms. This in fact was what came to pass. Fifty years earlier than the great revival of letters in the southern half of the island the golden age of her poetry arrived in Scotland.

* Malcolm Canmore had married the sister of Edgar Atheling, Alexander III. the daughter of Henry III., James I. the niece of Henry IV., and the reign of each of these kings had marked a distinct advance in the cultivation of the arts of peace in Scotland.

KING JAMES THE FIRST.

KING JAMES THE FIRST.

WITH James I. there appeared in Scottish history at once the genius which inspired and the tragedy which haunted the ill-starred Stewart race. His grandfather, Robert II., had not lacked energy in his youth. It was in great part owing to him that the tide of English conquest had been rolled back in the minority of David II. But he was fifty-five years of age when he ascended the throne, and his day for brilliance in kingly parts was over. Robert III. also had been past his first vigour when the sceptre came to his hand, and besides, in some early tournament the kick of a horse had lamed and unfitted him for the part of a leader in that active and warlike age. But in James I., perhaps the most accomplished knight and statesman of his time, to say nothing of his poetic gifts, shone forth again with larger lustre the spirit of that gallant Walter Stewart who fought at Bannock-burn and Berwick, and whose marriage with the daughter of Bruce brought to his house the inheritance of the Scottish crown. And the deeds and fate of James form a fitting prelude to the reign of a race whose chivalry and misfortunes for three hundred

years, till its final eclipse at Culloden, have made
Scottish history read like a romance.

The second son of Robert III. and his queen
Annabella, daughter of Sir John Drummond of
Stobhall, James was born at Dunfermline in July,
1394. Singularly unfortunate in those who should
have been his strongest support, he was indebted for
the tragic events which respectively gave him the
throne and ended his life to his two uncles, Robert
Stewart, Duke of Albany, and Walter Stewart, Earl of
Athole. King Robert III. (whose baptismal name,
John, had been considered unfortunate for a monarch),
incapacitated by disposition and infirmity for strong
government, had entrusted the affairs of state to his
brother Albany. This nobleman, as bold and
ambitious as the king was easy and weak, had not
been slow to perceive the possibility thus afforded of
carving his own way to the throne. Recently in simi-
lar circumstances in England he had seen Richard II.
deposed by Henry of Lancaster, and it was more
than possible that a like effort would be attended with
like success in the north. It was only by a slip in
the second step of his enterprise that his calculations
defeated their own ends.

Between him and the crown stood the king's elder
son, David, Duke of Rothesay, and the young prince
James, Earl of Carrick. Upon a plea of dissipation
and extravagance, the former, while travelling quietly
in Fife, was seized and thrown into Albany's tower
of Falkland, where, in spite of the pitying efforts of
a poor woman, who, it is said, fed him for a time

through the bars with thin barley cakes and milk from her own bosom, he died horribly of starvation in March, 1402.

Fearful, after this, for the safety of his remaining son, the king first entrusted James to the care of Henry Wardlaw, Bishop of St. Andrews, and afterwards, upon the plea of securing better education, arranged to send him to the court of Charles VI. of France. It illustrates alike the fierceness of the times and the power of the king's brother, that though Albany made no effort to arrest James on his way to the Bass, yet, for a political revenge of his own, he had the prince's escort and kinsman, Sir David Fleming of Cumbernauld, waylaid and slain on returning towards Edinburgh.

Tytler in his *Lives of Scottish Worthies* has left small doubt that Albany intrigued with Henry IV. of England for the capture of the prince at sea. Possibly he calculated upon the perpetual confinement and ultimate death of James. It is known that on his own side he had a strong inducement to offer the English king for the effecting of his purpose. Though the death of Richard II. at Pomfret had been announced, it was rumoured that the deposed king had been recognized in the outer isles of Scotland. The story is one of the last told by Wyntoun. A baron's daughter of Ireland, who had seen Richard in that country, and had married a brother of the Lord of the Isles, had recognized the monarch in the person of a poor wanderer seated by the kitchen fire in her castle. This individual was now at the Scottish court, and his safe-keeping, or even removal, could be used to bribe or control the action of Henry IV. Albany's intrigue, however, succeeded only in part.

Sailing from the Bass with the second Earl of Orkney and others on board, the prince's ship, though it was in time of truce, was taken by the English off Flamborough Head on Palm Sunday, the 12th of April, 1405. But James was neither slain in the action nor ill-treated afterwards. Though a prisoner, he was furnished with all the education befitting a prince, and in the keeping of Henry was safer by far than he could have been under the wardship of his uncle Albany. The possession of James was valuable to the English king in several ways. By producing him at any time the latter could annul in a day the power of the Scottish regent; the possibility of his doing this could always be used to prevent any exploiting of the claims of Richard II. by Albany; and the retention of the prince in English hands might even be made to minimise Scottish succours to the enemy in the war with France.

It is true that Robert III. died slowly of grief after the news of his son's capture; but to James himself nothing but profit can be said to have accrued from his detention in the south. Imprisoned successively in the Tower, in Nottingham Castle, and at Windsor, his studies were ably supervised by Sir John Pelham, and full opportunity was afforded him of attaining perfection in all the knightly accomplishments of the time. Practice even in the art of war formed part of his curriculum; for, carried by Henry V. to France in

1421, he commanded the English at the siege of Dreux, and it is recorded that by his energy he reduced the town in six weeks. Literature, in particular, is indebted to his imprisonment for the opportunity it afforded of studying the works of the English poets, and for the occasion it furnished for the production of his own greatest poem.

By his own account he had been a captive nearly eighteen years when one morning, looking from his prison lattice into the castle garden at Windsor, he beheld the Lady Jane Beaufort, daughter of the Earl of Somerset, and niece of Henry IV., who became successively the inspiration of his verse, the means of his liberation, and the partner of his throne.

Meanwhile in Scotland the organism of the state and society had been rapidly going to wreck. Albany's policy had been to conciliate the great barons upon whose support he calculated for the retention of power. To this end their gravest misdeeds were overlooked, and in order that they might have no inducement for the restoration of James they were granted large possessions out of the crown lands and revenues. Upon the death of Albany in 1419 the regency descended to the weak hands of his son Murdach, and the state of affairs, already grievous, fast became intolerable. Bands of feudal marauders overran the country, industry was at a standstill, and no man's life was safe. Far from being able to govern the kingdom, the regent appeared unable to control his own sons, and it is said that a gross insult from one of them finally determined him to seek the return of the king. To the offender he is reported to have said, "Since thou wilt give me neither reverence nor obedience, I will fetch home one whom we must all obey."

This had lately become an easy matter. No English purpose could now be served by the prince's detention. The fear of Richard II. had passed away, and the presence of James on the English side did not prevent the Scottish auxiliaries fighting for France. On the other hand an alliance with the English royal house in the person of the Lady Jane appeared to offer sufficient security for the goodwill of the monarch. Accordingly a ransom of £40,000 in name of maintenance was arranged to be paid; on 2nd February, 1424, the young lovers were married in the church of St. Mary Overy, keeping their wedding feast in the Bishop of Winchester's palace close by; on 1st April they entered Scotland amid great rejoicings; and on 21st May James was crowned at Scone.

Thirty years of age, the king is described as of middle height, with chest broad and full, strong but light in build, an adept in horsemanship, swords-manship, and all knightly accomplishments, and a master of music, painting, and poetry, while history shows him to have been as resolute in mind as he was active in physique. The historians of that century fill pages with the records of his versatility, and it is known that the fame of his accomplishments spread even to the south of Europe.

Strangely momentous must have been his thoughts

as he came northwards to require an account at the
hands of his regent.   News of his brother's terrible
death must have been one of his earliest impressions.
His own seizure and his father's consequent decease,
as well as the nineteen years' captivity without attempt
at ransom, could not but be burning in his mind.
He found the crown all but bankrupt, its revenues
plundered, its estates given away.   He found Scotland
in a state of anarchy, misrule, and licentiousness, the
church laid waste, the nobles at war.   There was a
long account to settle, but the barons, swollen in
power, and long accustomed to their own pleasure,
were likely ill to brook the interference of a master.

For ten months he waited, unsuspected by the
half-contemptuous nobles, silently informing himself
of the polity of the country and assuring himself of
the support of friends.   In order to ascertain the
condition of the common people he is even said
to have moved about incognito.   Then on 12th
March, 1425, he summoned a parliament at Perth,
and the blow fell.   By a sudden mandate were
arrested the Duke of Albany and his two sons, with
his father-in-law, the Earl of Lennox.   These were
tried by their peers at Stirling on the 24th and
25th May, convicted of high treason, and forthwith
executed on the Heading Hill.

It is greatly to the credit of James that almost by
these four executions alone he reduced the country
from lawlessness to obedience.   Had he been less
prompt in action Scotland could scarcely have escaped
the horrors of civil war.   As it was, his resolution

struck terror to the hearts of the lawless barons, and soon made apparent what he himself declared at Perth, that "no longer were authority, honesty, and virtue to be accounted idle names, nor that reckoned right which was gained and kept by stroke of sword." The Highlands, it is true, continued for some time to give trouble; but even there the king's sharp energy quickly made itself felt, and after overwhelming defeat in a marsh of Lochaber, Alaster Macdonald, Lord of the Isles, was finally reduced to appear, half-naked, in Holyrood Church on an Easter Day and throw himself unreservedly on the monarch's mercy.

It had soon become evident that James had vigorous ideas on the duties of government, and that he meant to carry them out. On coming to Scotland he had vowed that though he himself should lead the life of a dog he would make "the key keep the castle and the bush the cow," and resolutely he kept his word. For thirteen years Scotland enjoyed such justice as had not been known since the regency of Randolph. Arts were promoted, circuit courts were established, and law everywhere impartially administered, while much was done to reform the clergy. Once more as in the days of Malcolm Canmore, in strikingly similar circumstances, civilization had begun to make a fresh growth in the country, when the clouds suddenly darkened round the head of the king.

James had not established law and order without offending many whose license he curtailed. The discontent among these, chiefly the barons, grew in silence for some time. Murmurs, however, at length began to be heard, and in the parliament of 1435 Sir Robert Graham, whose nephew had been deprived by James of the earldom of Strathearn, is said actually to have laid hands on the king. He was instantly arrested and thrown into prison, but escaping and fleeing to "the country of the wild Scots," he sent a letter to James renouncing his allegiance and swearing mortal revenge whenever this should be in his power. The king in the end of the following year was prosecuting the siege of Roxburgh, then in English hands, when the queen came suddenly to the camp bringing tidings of danger. Her exact information is unrecorded, but it is now known that the old Earl of Athole had become the head of a formidable conspiracy which promised to set his son, Sir Robert Stewart, on the throne. At the queen's tidings James raised the siege of Roxburgh and, mistakenly perhaps, disbanded his army. Resolving to spend Christmas at Perth, he was about to cross the Forth, when a Highland "prophetess" suddenly appeared and warned him that if he crossed that water he should never return alive. The king seemed startled for a moment, and paused, but the warning was finally disregarded. The rest of the story is tragic enough.

The evening of the 20th February, 1437, had been spent gaily by the court in the Blackfriars Monastery at Perth. Music, chess, and the reading of romances had been kept up till a late hour, and the Earl of Athole and his son, Sir Robert Stewart, were among the last courtiers to retire. Before the gates closed the Highland woman had again appeared to seek an

audience of the king, had forced her way even to the
chamber door, but had been refused admission by the
usher. At midnight, James, in his nightgown and
slippers, was standing before the fire chatting
pleasantly with the queen and her ladies. Just then
a sudden clashing of armour was heard in the garden
below, and great flashes of torchlight were cast up
against the casements of the windows. At once the
king remembered Sir Robert Graham and the warning
of the Highland prophetess. There was no time for
escape, the assassins were already on their way, and
as the king wrenched up the flooring with the tongs
and leaped into a sewer-vault below, Catherine
Douglas sprang to the door and for lack of a bolt
thrust her own arm into the empty staples. All,
however, was in vain. The door was burst open,
the king's hiding-place discovered, the queen wounded,
and James, weaponless, after a terrific struggle with
the two first ruffians who leaped down upon him,
stabbed and hacked to death by Graham.

Of succeeding events little need be said. Notwith-
standing the death of the king the throne remained
unshaken. Forty days later, so swift was the queen's
pursuit, all the conspirators were captured and put to
death with fearful tortures.

Such, in barest outline, is the life of King James I.
of Scotland, a life that for romantic and tragic incident
and for the illustration of a resolute, lofty, and finished
character, has not been surpassed by poetic invention.
As a king he proved himself, what the Stewarts not
always were, entirely capable for his place and time,

and as a civilizing influence he sowed seeds which have
been bearing gentle fruit in the national life for nearly
five hundred years. Were it for nothing more than his
effect upon the national music he must be entitled to
grateful remembrance, many of the sweetest Scottish
airs sung to the present day in castle and clachan, being
owed, it is believed, to him. But above his fame as a
composer and even as a statesman towers his reputa-
tion in another realm. King James is likely to remain
best known to the world by his work as a poet.

In 1783 Tytler first printed *The Kingis Quair*, or
Book, from the only known copy, the Selden MS. in
the Bodleian Library at Oxford. His edition, however,
though it made the poem available, proved somewhat
inaccurate, the transcription having been entrusted to
" an ingenious young gentleman," a student of Oxford.
The various editions which followed were more or less
merely reprints of Tytler's text, and it is to Professor
Skeat, in his edition for the Scottish Text Society in
1883, that the first reliable version of the poem is owed.
The Kingis Quair is in Chaucer's seven-line stanza,
called from this use of it Rime Royal. It celebrates
the love of the captive prince for the Lady Jane
Beaufort, and is understood to have been written by
James at Windsor in 1423, the year before his release.
Mair in his History of Scotland states that it was
written before the king's marriage. From stanza 10,
in which the poet speaks of Fortune having been first
his foe and afterwards his friend, it is probable that
the exact date of composition was soon after the
successful issue of his suit.

In the last stanza James acknowledges Chaucer and Gower as his masters in verse, and it is certain that he imbibed from these masters an influence which, carried by his work into the north, was to exert a far-reaching effect upon Scottish poetry. The green branch of southern poesy which James engrafted on the grey bardic stem of Scotland flourished luxuriantly for more than a hundred years, and was hardly all cut down even by the stern pruning-knife of the Reformation. There was more in the royal poet, however, than he got from his masters. They as well as he may be said in the words of one critic to " breathe the romantic and elegant grace which the immense popularity of Petrarch had at that time made the universal pattern throughout Europe." The father of English verse, moreover, was monarch of realms into which the Scottish poet never sought to enter. But, as Mr. Stopford Brooke has said, in *The Kingis Quair* "the natural description is more varied, the colour is more vivid, and there is a modern self-reflective quality which does not belong to Chaucer at all"; and the same writer must be listened to when he declares the work of James to be "sweeter, tenderer, and purer than any verse till we come to Spenser." The allegoric form in which a great part of the poem is written has passed away, it is true, from modern taste; but *The Kingis Quair* possesses perennial qualities which remain as fresh yet as when the verses were penned by the royal prisoner. No poet has ever painted love-longing and the dawn of love more delicately or with subtler artistic touch ; no poet has given a more exquisite impression of the sweet awe and loveliness of womanhood.

As it stands, *The Kingis Quair* places James in the gallery of the world's immortal lovers. Beside Petrarch penning his sonnets to Laura, and the pale Dante gazing on his dead Beatrice, must remain the picture of the captive prince looking forth from his lattice in the tower of Windsor, while below in the garden alleys there lingers for a space, half-consciously, the maid of "beautee eneuch to mak a world to dote."

This, nevertheless, was not the only poem composed by James I. First of all, Mair, who wrote about the year 1500, says that besides "the book concerning the queen," and many songs still popular in his own day, James had written other two compositions beginning respectively with the words "Yas sen" and "At Beltayn." Then, in Bannatyne's MS., written in 1568, the poem of *Christ's Kirk on the Green* has the note appended "Quod K. James the First." And still further, both Dr. Irving and Mr. Skeat print a poem of three stanzas, whose authenticity can hardly be questioned, as it is ascribed to James I. in *The Gude and Godlie Ballates* of 1578, and in *Ane compentiovs Booke of godly and spiritual Songs*, printed in 1621.

The last of these poems is included in the present volume, but regarding the identity and authenticity of the first three—the compositions beginning with "Yas sen" and "At Beltayn," and the poem of *Christ's Kirk*—grave doubts have been expressed. The only clue to the first two are the words given by Mair, but,

on the strength of these, two compositions printed in
Pinkerton's *Ancient Scottish Poems* have been attri-
buted to James—a *Song on Absence* beginning :

> Sen that [the] eyne that workis my weilfare
> Dois no moir on me glance ;

and the well-known *Peblis to the Play*, which begins
with :

> At Beltane quhen ilk bodie bownis
> To Peblis to the Play.

Of *Christ's Kirk on the Green,* printed in the same
collection, the only suggestion of James' authorship is
Bannatyne's note.

Against the authenticity of the *Song on Absence* and
Peblis to the Play is remarked the slightness of Mair's
evidence. The first words of the former have to be
transposed to fit his quotation, while regarding the
latter he distinctly affirms that as the king's poem was
not accessible, several substitutes had been made ;
the opening "At Beltayn," therefore, may be under-
stood to have become hackneyed. Against James'
authorship of *Christ's Kirk on the Green* it is observed
that the sole authority, Bannatyne, appears to have
been careless or confused enough to make a mistake.
The next poem but one in his collection he ascribes
to "James the Fyift," or as some read it, "the Fyrst,"
in mistake for James the Fourth, and it is supposed
he may have made a similar error with *Christ's Kirk.*
Further, it is averred that common tradition previous
to the discovery of the Bannatyne MS. invariably
ascribed the poem to James V. This tradition is
supported by the usage of the early writers, Dempster

in the beginning of the seventeenth century, Bishop Gibson in 1691, and James Watson in 1706. Sibbald in his *Chronicle of Scottish Poetry* may be quoted: " James V. certainly was a writer of verses, as we know from the undoubted testimony of Lindsay, and it appears safer upon the whole in this instance to trust to vulgar tradition than to the *ipse dixit* of Bannatyne, who seems to have had but an indistinct notion of our different kings of the name of James." It has been pointed out that the style and strain of humour both of *Peblis to the Play* and of *Christ's Kirk* are exactly the same as those of *The Gaberlunzieman,* which has always been attributed to James V.; while on the other hand one writer, Guest, in his *English Rhythms,* has said: "One can hardly suppose those critics serious who attribute this song *(Christ's Kirk)* to the moral and sententious James I." Finally, Professor Skeat declares that "if we are to have any regard at all to the language, style, and metre of these poems, we cannot make them earlier than half-a-century or more after 1437." It would seem most fair, therefore, to follow the example of critics like Percy, Warton, Ritson, and Stopford Brooke, and assign the probable authorship both of *Peblis to the Play* and *Christ's Kirk on the Green* to James the Fifth.

It is upon his *Kingis Quair* that the poetic fame of James the First must ultimately depend. By it he is sufficiently proved to be, in the words of Dr. Irving, " a royal poet upon whose character royalty itself could scarcely confer any additional splendour."

ON the plea that *The Kingis Quair* was written in an imitation of Chaucer's dialect, and that the language of the poem therefore was technically imperfect, Mr. Skeat undertook to regulate the lines by addition of words and syllables where he considered requisite. As absolute regularity of rhythm, however, may not have been the poet's intention, only such additions are here inserted (in brackets) as seem necessary for the sense. For most of these, and for the light which its notes frequently cast on the text, indebtedness has to be acknowledged to Mr. Skeat's edition. The poem is here printed complete.

THE KINGIS QUAIR.

Maid be King Iames of Scotland the First quhen his Maiestie wes in Ingland.

HEIGH in the hevynnis figure circulere
　　The rody sterres twynklyng as the fyre;
　　And, in Aquary, Cynthia[1] the clere　　　　[1] MS. Citherea.
Rynsid hir tressis like the goldin wyre,
That late tofore, in fair and fresche atyre,
Through Capricorn heved hir hornis bright,
North northward approchit the myd-nyght;

Quhen as I lay in bed allone waking,
　　New partit out of slepe a lyte tofore[2],　　　[2] a little before.
Fell me to mynd of many diuerse thing,
　　Off this and that; can I noght say quharfore,
　　Bot slepe for craft in erth myght I no more;
For quhich as tho[3] coude I no better wyle,　　[3] then.
Bot toke a boke to rede apon a quhile:

Off quhich the name is clepit[4] properly　　　　[4] called.
　　Boece, eftere him that was the compiloure,
Schewing [the] counsele of philosophye,
　　Compilit by that noble senatoure
　　Off Rome, quhilom[5] that was the warldis floure,　[5] formerly.
And from estatë by fortune a quhile
Foriugit[6] was to pouert[7] in exile:　　　　　　[6] Condemned.
　　　　　　　　　　　　　　　　　　　　　　[7] poverty.

And there to here this worthy lord and clerk,
His metir suete, full of moralitee ;
His flourit pen so fair he set a-werk,
1 Describing.   Discryving[1] first of his prosperitee,
And out of that his infelicitee ;
2 poetic narra-   And than how he, in his poetly report[2],
tive.
3 began.   In philosophy can[3] him to confort.

4 though.   For quhich, thoght[4] I in purpose, at my boke,
5 that.   To borowe a slepe at thilkë[5] tyme began,
6 stopped.   Or euer I stent[6], my best was more to loke
Vpon the writing of this noble man,
That in him-self the full recouer wan
Off his infortune, pouert, and distresse,
7 true security.   And in tham set his verray sekernesse[7].

And so the vertew of his youth before
Was in his age the ground of his delytis :
Fortune the bak him turnyt, and therfore
He maketh ioye and confort, that he quit is
8 these uncertain. Off thir vnsekir[8] warldis appetitis ;
MS. theire.
9 worthily.   And so aworth[9] he takith his penance,
And of his vertew maid it suffisance :

With mony a noble resoun, as him likit,
Enditing in his fairë Latyne tong,
10 rhetorically   So full of fruyte, and rethorikly pykit[10],
culled.
11 skull, head.   Quhich to declare my scole[11] is ouer yong ;
Therefore I lat him pas, and, in my tong[12],
12 tongue,   Procede I will agayn to my sentence
language.
Off my mater, and leue all incidence.

The long nyght beholding, as I saide,
  Myn eyne gan to smert for studying;
My buke I schet, and at my hede it laide;
  And doune I lay bot[1] ony tarying,   1 without.
  This matere new in my mynd rolling;
This is to seynë[2], how that eche estate,   2 say.
As Fortune lykith, thame will [oft] translate.

For sothe it is, that, on hir tolter[3] quhele,   3 unstable.
  Euery wight cleuerith in his stage[4],   4 clambers in his rank.
And failyng foting oft, quhen hir lest rele,
  Sum vp, sum doune, is none estate nor age
  Ensured, more the pryncë than the page:
So vncouthly hir werdes[5] sche deuidith,   5 So strangely her fates.
Namly[6] in youth, that seildin ought prouidith.   6 Especially.

Among thir[7] thoughtis rolling to and fro,   7 these.
  Fell me to mynd of my fortune and vre[8];   8 chance.
In tender youth how sche was first my fo,
  And eft[9] my frende, and how I gat recure   9 afterwards.
  Off my distresse, and all myn auenture
I gan oure-hayle[10], that langer slepe ne rest   10 overhaul.
Ne myght I nat, so were my wittis wrest.

For-wakit and for-walowit[11], thus musing,   11 Sore waking and sore tossing.
  Wery, forlyin[12], I lestnyt sodaynlye,   12 tired with lying.
And sone I herd the bell to matynes ryng,
  And vp I rase, no langer wald I lye:
  Bot now, how trowe ye? suich a fantasye
Fell me to mynd, that ay me-thoght the bell
Said to me, "Tell on, man, quhat the befell."

¹ then.

Thoght I tho¹ to my-self, "Quhat may this be?
This is myn awin ymagynacioun;

² person.

It is no lyf² that spekis vnto me;
It is a bell, or that impressioun
Off my thoght causith this illusioun,

³ maketh me think so foolishly.

That dooth me think so nycely³ in this wise;"
And so befell as I schall you deuise.

Determyt furth therewith in myn entent,
Sen I thus haue ymagynit of this soune,
And in my tyme more ink and paper spent
To lyte effect, I tuke conclusioun
Sum new thing to write; I set me doun,
And furth-with-all my pen in hand I tuke,

⁴ began.

And maid a ✚, and thus begouth⁴ my buke.

⁵ innocent.
⁶ crude.

Thou [sely]⁵ youth, of nature indegest⁶,
    Vnrypit fruyte with windis variable;
Like to the bird that fed is on the nest,
    And can noght flee; of wit wayke and vnstable,

⁷ liable.

    To fortune both and to infortune hable⁷;
Wist thou thy payne to cum and thy trauaille,
For sorow and drede wele myght thou wepe and
        waille.

⁸ stands.

Thus stant⁸ thy confort in vnsekernesse,

⁹ guide.

    And wantis it that suld the reule and gye⁹:

¹⁰ helmless.

Ryght as the schip that sailith sterëles¹⁰

¹¹ must hie to harm.
¹² help.

    Vpon the rok[kis] most to harmes hye¹¹,
    For lak of it that suld bene hir supplye¹²;
So standis thou here in this warldis rage,
And wantis that suld gyde all thy viage.

I mene this by my-self, as in partye[1];
   Though nature gave me suffisance in youth[2],
The rypenesse of resoun lak[it] I,
   To gouerne with my will; so lyte I couth[3],
   Quhen sterëles to trauaile I begouth[4],
Amang the wawis of this warld to driue;
And how the case, anone I will discriue.

[1] lament this regarding myself, as participator.
[2] sufficient reason for a youth.
[3] so little I could.
[4] began.

With doutfull hert, amang the rokkis blake,
   My feble bote full fast to stere and rowe,
Helples allone, the wynter nyght I wake,
   To wayte[5] the wynd that furthward suld me throwe.
   O empti saile! quhare is the wynd suld blowe
Me to the port, quhar gynneth all my game?
Help, Calyope, and wynd, in Marye name!

[5] ascertain.

The rokkis clepe[6] I the prolixitee
   Off doubtfulnesse[7] that doith[8] my wittis pall:
The lak of wynd is the deficultee
   In enditing of this lytill trety small:
   The bote I clepe the mater hole of all:
My wit vnto the saile that now I wynd,
To seke connyng[9], though I bot lytill fynd.

[6] name.
[7] MS. doubilnesse.
[8] maketh.

[9] skill.

At my begynnyng first I clepe and call
   To yow, Cleo[10], and to yow, Polymye[11],
With Thesiphone[12], goddis and sistris all,
   In nowmer ix., as bokis specifye;
   In this processe my wilsum[13] wittis gye;
And with your bryght lanternis wele conuoye
My pen, to write my turment and my ioye!

[10] Clio, Muse of History.
[11] Polyhymnia, Muse of Song, &c.
[12] Tisiphone, a Fury mist. perh. for a Muse.
[13] wilful.

1 spring.

In vere[1], that full of vertu is and gude,
  Quhen Nature first begynneth hir enprise,
That quhilum was be cruell frost and flude
  And schouris scharp opprest in many wyse,

2 Cynthius.
  And Synthius[2] [be]gynneth to aryse

3 morning.
Heigh in the est, a morow[3] soft and suete,
  Vpward his course to driue in Ariete:

4 degrees exactly (*i.e.* one hour). MS. Passit bot midday.
Passit mydday bot fourë greis evin[4],
  Off lenth and brede his angel wingis bryght
He spred vpon the ground doune fro the hevin;
  That, for gladnesse and confort of the sight,
  And with the tiklyng of his hete and light,
The tender flouris opnyt thame and sprad;
And, in thaire nature, thankit him for glad.

Noght fer passit the state of innocence,

5 *i.e.* nearly ten years old.
  Bot nere about the nowmer of yeris thre[5],
Were it causit throu hevinly influence
  Off goddis will, or othir casualtee,
  Can I noght say; bot out of my contree,
By thaire avise that had of me the cure,
Be see to pas, tuke I myn auenture.

Puruait of all that was vs necessarye,
  With wynd at will, vp airly by the morowe,
Streight vnto schip, no longere wold we tarye,

6 before.
  The way we tuke, the tyme I tald to-forowe[6];
  With mony "fare wele" and "Sanct Iohne to

7 be your security.
      borowe[7]"
Off falowe and frende; and thus with one assent
We pullit vp saile, and furth oure wayis went.

Vpon the wawis weltering to and fro,
 So infortunate was vs that fremyt[1] day,   [1] unlucky.
That maugre, playnly, quhethir we wold or no,
 With strong hand, by forse, schortly to say,
 Off inymyis takin and led away
We weren all, and broght in thaire contree;
Fortune it schupe[2] none othir wayis to be.   [2] destined.

Quhare as in strayte ward and in strong prisoun,
 So fer forth[3] of my lyf the heuy lyne,   [3] far forward.
Without confort, in sorowe abandoune,
 The secund sistere lukit hath to twyne[4],   [4] *i.e.* Lachesis, spinner of life's thread, has seen to it to cut in twain.
 Nere by the space of yeris twise nyne;
Till Iupiter his merci list aduert[5],   [5] pleased to turn.
And send confort in relesche[6] of my smert.   [6] relief.

Quhare as in ward full oft I wold bewaille
 My dedely lyf, full of peyne and penance,
Saing ryght thus, "Quhat haue I gilt to faille[7]   [7] done ill to lose.
 My fredome in this warld and my plesance?
 Sen euery wight has thereof suffisance,
That I behold, and I a creature
Put from all this—hard is myn auenture!

The bird, the beste, the fisch eke in the see,
 They lyve in fredome euerich[8] in his kynd;   [8] every one.
And I a man, and lakkith libertee;
 Quhat schall I seyne[9], quhat resoun may I fynd, [9] say.
 That Fortune suld do so?" Thus in my mynd
My folk I wold argewe[10], bot all for noght;   [10] *i.e.* argue with.
Was none that myght, that on my peynes rought.

Than wold I say, "Gif God me had deuisit
To lyve my lyf in thraldome thus and pyne[1],
Quhat was the cause that he [me] more comprisit
Than othir folk to lyve in suich ruyne[2]?
I suffer allone amang the figuris nyne[3],
Ane wofull wrecche that to no wight may spede[4],
And yit of euery lyvis[5] help hath nede."

The long dayes and the nyghtis eke
I wold bewaille my fortune in this wise,
For quhich, agane distresse confort to seke,
My custum was on mornis for to ryse
Airly as day; O happy excercise!
By the come I to ioye out of turment.
Bot now to purpose of my first entent :—

Bewailing in my chamber thus allone,
Despeired of all ioye and remedye,
For-tirit[6] of my thoght, and wo-begone,
Unto[7] the wyndow gan I walk in hye[8],
To se the warld and folk that went forby;
As for the tyme, though I of mirthis fude
Myght haue no more, to luke it did me gude.

Now was there maid fast by the touris wall
A gardyn faire, and in the corneris set
Ane herbere[9] grene, with wandis long and small
Railit about; and so with treis set
Was all the place, and hawthorn hegis knet,
That lyf[10] was none walking there forby[11],
That myght within scarse ony wight aspye.

[1] pain.
[2] ruin.
[3] *i.e.* when alone, as cipher among the nine numerals.
[4] give help.
[5] person's.
[6] Full weary.
[7] MS. And to.
[8] haste.
[9] shrubbery.
[10] person.
[11] past.

So thik the bewis[1] and the leues grene
   Beschadit all the aleyes that there were,
And myddis euery herbere myght be sene
   The scharp grenë suetë ienepere,
   Growing so faire with branchis here and there,
That, as it semyt to a lyf without,
The bewis spred the herbere all about;

And on the small grenë twistis[2] sat   2 twigs.
   The lytill suetë nyghtingale, and song
So loud and clere, the ympnis[3] consecrat   3 hymns.
   Off lufis vse, now soft, now lowd among[4],   4 at times.
   That all the gardyng and the wallis rong
Ryght of thaire song and of the copill[5] next   5 couplet. MS.
                                      on the copill.
Off thaire suete armony, and lo the text:

[CANTUS.]
" Worschippë, ye that loueris bene, this May,
   For of your blisse the kalendis are begonne,
And sing with vs, away, Winter, away!
   Cum, Somer, cum, the suete sesoun and sonne!
   Awake for schame! that haue your hevynnis wonne,
And amorously lift vp your hedis all,
Thank Lufe that list[6] you to his merci call."   6 is pleased.

Quhen thai this song had song a lytill thrawe[7],   7 space.
   Thai stent[8] a quhile, and therewith vnaffraid,   8 stopped.
As I beheld and kest myn eyne a-lawe[9],   9 below.
   From beugh to beugh thay hippit and thai plaid,
   And freschly in thaire birdis kynd arraid
Thaire fetheris new, and fret thame in the sonne,
And thankit Lufe, that had thaire makis[10] wonne.   10 mates.

This was the planë ditee of thaire note,
  And there-with-all vnto my-self I thoght,

¹ way of life.

" Quhat lyf¹ is this, that makis birdis dote?
  Quhat may this be, how cummyth it of ought?
  Quhat nedith it to be so dere ybought?
It is nothing, trowe I, bot feynit chere,
And that men list to counterfeten chere."

² Afterwards.

Eft² wald I think; "O Lord, quhat may this be?
  That Lufe is of so noble myght and kynde,
Lufing his folk, and suich prosperitee
  Is it of him, as we in bukis fynd?

³ make fast.

  May he oure hertes setten³ and vnbynd?
Hath he vpon oure hertis suich maistrye?
Or all this is bot feynyt fantasye!

For gif he be of so grete excellence,
  That he of euery wight hath cure and charge,
Quhat haue I gilt to him or doon offense,
  That I am thrall, and birdis gone at large,

⁴ Since.

  Sen⁴ him to serue he myght set my corage?

⁵ say.

And gif he be noght so, than may I seyne⁵,
Quhat makis folk to iangill of him in veyne?

Can I noght elles fynd, bot gif that he
  Be lord, and as a god may lyue and regne,
To bynd and louse, and maken thrallis free,
  Than wold I pray his blisfull grace benigne,

⁶ fit.
⁷ worthy.

  To hable⁶ me vnto his seruice digne⁷;
And euermore for to be one of tho
Him trewly for to serue in wele and wo.

And there-with kest I doune myn eye ageyne,
   Quhare as I sawe, walking vnder the toure,
Full secretly, new cummyn hir to pleyne[1],   1 play.
   The fairest or the freschest yong floure
   That euer I sawe, me-thoght, before that houre,
For quhich sodayn abate, anone astert
The blude of all my body to my hert.

And though I stude abaisit tho a lyte[2],   2 then a little.
   No wonder was; for quhy, my wittis all
Were so ouercome with plesance and delyte,
   Onely throu latting of myn eyën fall,
   That sudaynly my hert became hir thrall
For euer, of free wyll; for of manace
There was no takyn[3] in hir suetë face.   3 token.

And in my hede I drewe ryght hastily,
   And eft-sonës[4] I lent it forth ageyne,   4 soon after.
And sawe hir walk, that verray womanly,
   With no wight mo, bot onely wommen tueyne.
   Than gan I studye in my-self, and seyne,
"A! suete, ar ye a warldly creature,
Or hevinly thing in likenesse of nature?

Or ar ye god Cupidis owin princesse,
   And cummyn are to louse me out of band?
Or ar ye verray[5] Nature the goddesse,   5 truly.
   That haue depayntit with your hevinly hand
   This gardyn full of flouris, as they stand?
Quhat sall I think, allace! quhat reuerence
Sall I minister[6] to your excellence?   6 MS. minster.

Gif ye a goddesse be, and that ye like

1 avoid.   To do me payne, I may it noght astert[1];

2 maketh me sigh. Gif ye be warldly wight, that dooth me sike[2],

3 Why pleased.   Quhy lest[3] God mak you so, my derrest hert,

4 innocent.   To do a sely[4] prisoner thus smert,

5 knows.   That lufis yow all, and wote[5] of noght bot wo?

    And therefor, merci, suete! sen it is so."

6 while.   Quhen I a lytill thrawe[6] had maid my moon,

    Bewailling myn infortune and my chance,

Vnknawin how or quhat was best to doon,

    So ferre i-fallyng into lufis dance,

    That sodeynly my wit, my contenance,

My hert, my will, my nature, and my mynd,

Was changit clene ryght in ane-othir kynd.

Off hir array the forme gif I sall write,

    Toward hir goldin haire and rich atyre

7 trimmed. In fret-wise couchit[7] [was] with perllis quhite

8 Balassian rubies glowing.   And gretë balas lemyng[8] as the fyre,

    With mony ane emeraut and faire saphire;

And on hir hede a chaplet fresch of hewe,

Off plumys partit rede, and quhite, and blewe;

Full of quaking spangis bryght as gold,

9 forget-me-not(?)   Forgit of schap like to the amorettis[9],

    So new, so fresch, so plesant to behold,

10 great St. John's-wort flower.   The plumys eke like to the floure-ionettis[10],

11 "a sort of curled tuft." MS. repeats "floure-ionettis."   And othir of schap like to the [round crokettis],[11]

And, aboue all this, there was, wele I wote,

    Beautee eneuch to mak a world to dote.

About hir nek, quhite as the fyre amaille[1],
   A gudely cheyne of smale orfeuerye[2],
Quhareby there hang a ruby, without faille,
   Lyke to ane hert schapin verily,
   That, as a sperk of lowe[3], so wantonely
Semyt birnyng vpon hir quhytë throte;
Now gif there was gud partye[4], God it wote!

And for to walk that freschë Mayes morowe,
   Ane huke[5] sche had vpon hir tissew[6] quhite,
That gudeliare had noght bene sene toforowe[7],
   As I suppose; and girt sche was a lyte.
   Thus halflyng[8] louse for haste, to suich delyte
It was to see hir youth in gudelihede,
That for rudenes to speke thereof I drede.

In hir was youth, beautee, with humble aport[9],
   Bountee, richesse, and wommanly facture[10],
God better wote than my pen can report.
   Wisedome, largesse, estate, and connyng[11] sure
   In euery poynt so guydit hir mesure,
In word, in dede, in schap, in contenance,
That nature myght no more hir childe auance.

Throw quhich anone I knew and vnderstude
   Wele, that sche was a warldly creature;
On quhom to rest myn eyë, so mich gude
   It did my wofull hert, I yow assure,
   That it was to me ioye without mesure;
And, at the last, my luke vnto the hevin
I threwe furthwith, and said thir versis[12] sevin:

---

[1] enamel made by fire.
[2] gold work.
[3] flame.
[4] a good partner. Fr. *partie.*
[5] loose upper dress.
[6] thin under-garment.
[7] before.
[8] partly.
[9] demeanour.
[10] fashioning.
[11] skill.
[12] these lines.

"O Venus clere! of goddis stellifyit[1]!
   To quhom I yelde homage and sacrifise,
Fro this day forth your grace be magnifyit,
   That me ressauit haue in suich [a] wise,
   To lyve vnder your law and do seruise;
Now help me furth, and for your merci lede
My hert to rest, that deis nere for drede."

Quhen I with gude entent this orisoun
   Thus endit had, I stynt a lytill stound[2];
And eft[3] myn eye full pitously adoune
   I kest, behalding vnto hir lytill hound,
   That with his bellis playit on the ground;
Than wold I say, and sigh there-with a lyte,
"A! wele were him that now were in thy plyte!"

Ane-othir quhile the lytill nyghtingale,
   That sat apon the twiggis, wold I chide,
And say ryght thus, "Quhare are thy notis smale,
   That thou of loue has song this morowe-tyde?
   Seis thou noght hire that sittis the besyde?
For Venus sake, the blisfull goddesse clere,
Sing on agane, and mak my lady chere.

And eke I pray, for all the paynes grete,
   That, for the loue of Proigne[4] thy sister dere,
Thou sufferit quhilom, quhen thy brestis wete
   Were with the teres of thyne eyën clere,
   All bludy ronne; that pitee was to here
The crueltee of that vnknyghtly dede,
Quhare was fro the bereft thy maidenhede,

Lift vp thyne hert, and sing with gude entent;
   And in thy notis suete the tresone telle,
That to thy sister trewe and innocent
   Was kythit[1] by hir husband false and fell;   1 shown.
   For quhois gilt, as it is worthy wel,
Chide thir husbandis that are false, I say,
And bid thame mend, in the twenty deuil way[2].   2 *i.e.* in every possible way. MS. xxty.

O lytill wrecch, allace! maist thou noght se
   Quho commyth yond? Is it now tyme to wring[3]?   3 grieve.
Quhat sory thoght is fallin vpon the?
   Opyn thy throte; hastow no lest[4] to sing?   4 hast thou no desire.
   Allace! sen thou of resone had felyng,
Now, suetë bird, say ones to me 'pepe:'
I dee for wo; me-think thou gynnis slepe.

Hastow no mynde of lufe? Quhare is thy make?
   Or artow seke, or smyt with ielousye?
Or is sche dede, or hath sche the forsake?
   Quhat is the cause of thy malancolye,
   That thou no more list[5] maken melodye?   5 art pleased to.
Sluggart, for schame! lo here thy goldin houre,
That worth were hale[6] all thy lyvis laboure!   6 wholly.

Gyf thou suld sing wele euer in thy lyve,
   Here is, in fay[7], the tyme, and eke the space: 7 in faith.
Quhat wostow than[8]? sum bird may cum and stryve   8 What knowest thou then?
   In song with the, the maistry to purchace.
   Suld thou than cesse, it were grete schame, allace!
And here, to wyn gree[9] happily for euer,   9 degree, superiority.
Here is the tyme to syng, or ellis neuer."

I thoght eke thus, gif I my handis clap,

[1] throw forth (a sound).

    Or gif I cast[1], than will sche flee away;

And gif I hald my pes, than will sche nap:

[2] knows.

    And gif I crye, sche wate[2] noght quhat I say:

    Thus, quhat is best, wate I noght be this day:

Bot, blawe wynd, blawe, and do the leuis schake,

That sum twig may wag, and mak hir to wake.

[3] MS. he.

With that anone ryght sche[3] toke vp a sang,

    Quhare come anone mo birdis and alight;

Bot than, to here the mirth was thame amang,

[4] Above that too.

    Ouer that to[4], to see the suetë sicht

    Off hyr ymage, my spirit was so light,

Me-thoght I flawe for ioye without arest,

[5] bound all too fast.

So were my wittis boundin all to fest[5].

And to the notis of the philomene,

[6] Which.

    Quhilkis[6] sche sang, the ditee there I maid

Direct to hire that was my hertis quene,

    Withoutin quhom no songis may me glade;

    And to that sanct, [there] walking in the schade,

My bedis thus, with humble hert entere,

Deuotly [than] I said on this manere.

[7] have pity.

" Quhen sall your merci rew[7] vpon your man,

[8] unknown.

    Quhois seruice is yit vncouth[8] vnto yow?

[9] Since.
[10] then.

Sen[9], quhen ye go, ther is noght ellis than[10]

[11] that.
[12] may not go through.

    Bot, 'Hert! quhere as[11] the body may noght throu[12],

[13] *i.e.* thou, O heart!

    Folow thy hevin! Quho suld be glad bot thou[13],

That suich a gyde to folow has vndertake?

[14] refuse thou not.

Were it throu hell, the way thou noght forsake[14]!'"

And efter this the birdis euerichone[1]
  Tuke vp ane-othir sang full loud and clere,
And with a voce said, "Wele is vs begone[2],
  That with oure makis[3] are togider here;
  We proyne[4] and play without dout and dangere,
All clothit in a soyte[5] full fresch and newe,
In lufis seruice besy, glad, and trewe.

[1] every one.
[2] Well has it happed with us.
[3] mates.
[4] preen.
[5] in one suit.

And ye, fresche May, ay mercifull to bridis,
  Now welcum be ye, floure of monethis all;
For noght onely your grace vpon vs bydis[6],
  Bot all the warld to witnes this we call,
  That strowit hath so playnly ouer all
With new freschë suete and tender grene,
Oure lyf, oure lust[7], oure gouernoure, oure quene."

[6] abides.
[7] delight.

This was thair song, as semyt me full heye[8],
  With full mony vncouth suete note and schill[9],
And therewith-all that faire[10] vpward hir eye
  Wold cast amang[11], as it was Goddis will,
  Quhare I myght se, standing allane full still,
The faire facture[12] that nature, for maistrye[13],
In hir visage wroght had full lufingly.

[8] loud.
[9] shrill.
[10] fair one.
[11] at times.
[12] workmanship.
[13] as a master-piece.

And, quhen sche walkit had a lytill thrawe[14]
  Vnder the suetë grenë bewis bent[15],
Hir faire fresche face, as quhite as ony snawe,
  Scho turnyt has, and furth hir wayis went;
  Bot tho[16] began myn axis[17] and turment,
To sene hir part[18], and folowe I na myght;
Me-thoght the day was turnyt into nyght.

[14] while.
[15] bended boughs.
[16] then.
[17] fever.
[18] see her depart.

Than said I thus, "Quhare-to lyve I langer?
 Wofullest wicht, and subiect vnto peyne!
Of peyne? no! God wote, ya[1]: for thay no stranger
 May wirken[2] ony wight, I dare wele seyne.
 How may this be, that deth and lyf, bothe tueyne,
Sall bothe atonis[3] in a creature
Togidder duell, and turment thus nature?

I may noght ellis done bot wepe and waile,
 With-in thir cald wallis thus i-lokin[4];
From hennsfurth my rest is my trauaile;
 My dryë thrist with teris sall I slokin,
 And on my-self bene al my harmys wrokin:
Thus bute[5] is none; bot[6] Venus, of hir grace,
Will schape[7] remede, or do my spirit pace[8].

As Tantalus I trauaile, ay but-les,
 That euer ylikë[9] hailith at the well
Water to draw with buket botemles,
 And may noght spede; quhois penance is ane hell:
 So by[10] my-self this tale I may wele telle,
For vnto hir that herith noght I pleyne;
Thus like to him my trauaile is in veyne."

So sore thus sighit I with my-self allone,
 That turnyt is my strenth in febilnesse,
My wele in wo, my frendis all in fone[11],
 My lyf in deth, my lyght into dirknesse,
 My hope in feer, in dout my sekirnesse[12];
Sen sche is gone: and God mote hir conuoye[13],
That me may gyde to turment and to ioye!

[1] God knows, yea.
[2] these (pains) no more strongly may afflict.
[3] at once.
[4] locked.
[5] remedy.
[6] unless.
[7] prepare.
[8] make my spirit pass.
[9] alike.
[10] regarding.
[11] foes.
[12] certainty.
[13] may God convoy her.

The long day thus gan I prye and poure,
  Till Phebus endit had his bemes bryght,
And bad go farewele euery lef and floure,
  This is to say, approch gan the nyght,
  And 'Esperus his lampis gan to light;
Quhen in the wyndow, still as any stone,
I bade¹ at lenth, and, kneling, maid my mone.   ¹ abode.

So lang till evin, for lak of myght and mynd,
  For-wepit and for-pleynit² pitously,   ² weary with
Ourset so sorow had bothe hert and mynd,   weeping and
  That to the cold stone my hede on wrye³   plaining.
  I laid, and lent, amaisit verily,   ³ awry.
Half sleping and half suoune, in suich a wise:
And quhat I met, I will you now deuise⁴.   ⁴ describe.

Me-thoght that thus all sodeynly a lyght
  In at the wyndow come quhare that I lent,
Off quhich the chambere-wyndow schone full bryght,
  And all my body so it hath ouerwent,
  That of my sicht the vertew hale iblent⁵;   ⁵ the whole power
And that with-all a voce vnto me saide,   was lost.
"I bring the confort and hele⁶, be noght affrayde." ⁶ healing.

And furth anone it passit sodeynly,
  Quher it come in, the ryght way ageyne,
And sone, me-thoght, furth at the dure in hye⁷   ⁷ haste.
  I went my weye, nas nothing me ageyne⁸;   ⁸ nor was there
  And hastily, by bothe the armes tueyne,   anything
I was araisit vp in-to the aire,   hindering me.
Clippit⁹ in a cloude of cristall clere and faire. ⁹ Embraced.

Ascending vpward ay fro spere to spere,
  Through aire and watere and the hotë fyre,
  Till that I come vnto the circle clere
  Off Signifere[1], quhare fairë, bryght, and schire[2],
  The signis schone; and in the glade empire
  Off blisfull Venus, [quhar] ane cryit now
  So sudaynly, almost I wist noght how.

Off quhich the place, quhen I come there nye,
  Was all, me-thoght, of cristall stonis wroght,
  And to the port I liftit was in hye,
  Quhare sodaynly, as quho sais at a thoght[3],
  It opnyt, and I was anon in broght
  Within a chamber, largë, rowm[4], and faire;
  And there I fand of peple grete repaire[5].

This is to seyne, that present in that place
  Me-thoght I sawe of euery nacioun
  Loueris that endit [had] thaire lyfis space
  In lovis seruice, mony a mylioun,
  Off quhois chancis[6] maid is mencioun
  In diuerse bukis, quho thame list to se;
  And therefore here thaire namys lat I be.

The quhois auenture and grete labouris
  Aboue thaire hedis writin there I fand;
  This is to seyne, martris and confessouris[7],
  Ech in his stage, and his make[8] in his hand;
  And therewith-all thir peple sawe I stand,
  With mony a solempnit[9] contenance,
  After as Lufe thame lykit to auance[10].

[1] *i.e.* the sphere of the zodiac.
[2] clear.
[3] *i.e.* in a trice, as one may say.
[4] spacious.
[5] concourse.
[6] adventures.
[7] *i.e.* for love.
[8] mate.
[9] MS. solempt.
[10] As Love chose to advance them.

Off gude folkis, that faire in lufe befill[1],
   There saw I sitt in order by thame one[2]
With hedis hore; and with thame stude Gude-will
   To talk and play. And after that anone
   Besyde thame and next there saw I gone[3]
Curage, amang the freschë folkis yong,
And with thame playit full merily and song.

1 befell.
2 by themselves.
3 go about.

And in ane-othir stage, endlong[4] the wall,
   There saw I stand, in capis wyde and lang,
A full grete nowmer; bot thaire hudis all,
   Wist I noght quhy, atoure[5] thair eyën hang;
   And ay to thame come Repentance amang[6],
And maid thame chere, degysit in his wede[7].
And dounward efter that yit I tuke hede.

4 along.
5 over.
6 at times.
7 disguised in dress.

Ryght ouerthwert[8] the chamber was there drawe
   A trevesse[9] thin and quhite, all of plesance,
The quhich behynd, standing, there I sawe
   A warld of folk, and by thaire contenance
   Thaire hertis semyt full of displesance,
With billis in thaire handis, of one assent
Vnto the iuge thaire playntis to present.

8 athwart.
9 curtain.

And there-with-all apperit vnto me
   A voce, and said, "Tak hede, man, and behold:
Yonder[10] thou seis the hiest stage and gree[11]
   Off agit folk, with hedis hore and olde;
   Yone were the folke that neuer changë wold
In lufe, bot trewly seruit him alway,
In euery age, vnto thaire ending-day.

10 MS. Yonder there.
11 degree.

For fro the tyme that thai coud vnderstand
The exercise, of lufis craft the cure[1],
Was none on lyve[2] that toke so moch on hand
For lufis sake, nor langer did endure
In lufis seruice; for, man, I the assure,
Quhen thay of youth ressauit had the fill,
Yit in thaire age thame lakkit no gude will.

Here bene also of suich as in counsailis
And all thar dedis, were to Venus trewe;
Here bene the princis, faucht the grete batailis,
In mynd[3] of quhom ar maid the bukis newe,
Here bene the poetis that the sciencis knewe,
Throwout the warld, of lufe in thaire suete layes,
Suich as Ouide and Omere in thaire dayes.

And efter thame downe in the next stage,
There as[4] thou seis the yong folkis pleye:
Lo! thise were thay that, in thaire myddill age,
Seruandis were to Lufe in mony weye,
And diuersely happinnit for to deye;
Sum soroufully, for wanting of thare makis[5],
And sum in armes for thaire ladyes sakis.

And othir eke by othir diuerse chance,
As happin folk all day, as ye may se;
Sum for dispaire, without recouerance;
Sum for desyre, surmounting thaire degree;
Sum for dispite and othir inmytee;
Sum for vnkyndënes without a quhy[6];
Sum for to moch[7], and sum for ielousye.

[1] The practice, the skill of the craft of love.
[2] alive.
[3] memory.
[4] where.
[5] mates.
[6] a why, a reason.
[7] *i.e.* too much love.

And efter this, vpon yone stage adoun[1],
  Tho that thou seis stond in capis wyde;
Yone were quhilum[2] folk of religioun,
    That from the warld thaire gouernance[3] did hide,
    And frely seruit lufe on euery syde
In secrete, with thaire bodyis and thaire gudis.
And lo! quhy so thai hingen doune thaire hudis:

For though that thai were hardy at assay[4],
  And did him seruice quhilum priuely,
Yit to the warldis eye it semyt nay;
    So was thaire seruice half [bot] cowardy:
    And for thay first forsuke him opynly,
And efter that thereof had repenting,
For schame thaire hudis oure thaire eyne thay hyng.

And seis thou now yone multitude, on rawe[5]
  Standing, behynd yone trauerse of delyte?
Sum bene of thame that haldin were full lawe,
    And take by frendis, nothing thay to wyte[6],
    In youth from lufe into the cloistere quite;
And for that cause are cummyn, recounsilit[7],
On thame to pleyne that so thame had begilit.

And othir bene amongis thame also,
  That cummyn ar to court, on Lufe to pleyne[8],
For he thaire bodyes had bestowit so,
    Quhare bothe thaire hertes gruchit[9] ther-ageyne;
    For quhich, in all thaire dayes, soth to seyne[10],
Quhen othir lyvit in ioye and [in] plesance,
Thaire lyf was noght bot care and repentance;

[1] MS. doun.

[2] once.

[3] conduct.

[4] stout in trial.

[5] in a row.

[6] blame.

[7] *i.e.* reunited to their mates.

[8] complain.

[9] repined. MS. gruch.

[10] truth to say.

And, quhare thaire hertis gevin were and set,
    Were coplit with othir that coud noght accord;

1 misdeed.   Thus were thai wrangit that did no forfet[1],

2 Separating.   Departing[2] thame that neuer wold discord.

    Off yong ladies faire, and mony lord,

3 driven from
their choice.   That thus by maistry were fro thair chose dryve[3],

    Full redy were thaire playntis there to gyve."

And othir also I sawe compleynyng there
    Vpon Fortune and hir grete variance,
That, quhere in loue so wele they coplit were,
    With thaire suete makis coplit in plesance,

4 MS. So.   Sche[4] sodeynly maid thaire disseuerance,
    And tuke thame of this warldis companye,

5 reason.   Withoutin cause, there was none othir quhy[5].

And in a chiere of estate besyde,
    With wingis bright, all plumyt, bot his face,
There sawe I sitt the blynd god Cupide,
    With bow in hand, that bent full redy was,
    And by him hang thre arowis in a cas,
Off quhich the hedis grundyn were full ryght,
Off diuerse metals forgit faire and bryght.

And with the first, that hedit is of gold,
    He smytis soft, and that has esy cure;
The secund was of siluer, mony-fold

6 Worse.   Wers[6] than the first, and harder auenture;

7 recovery.   The thrid, of stele, is schot without recure[7];

8 bright.   And on his long yalow lokkis schene[8]
    A chaplet had he all of levis grene.

And in a retrete lytill of compas,
  Depeyntit[1] all with sighis wonder sad,
Noght suich sighis as hertis doith manace[2],
  Bot suich as dooth lufaris to be glad,
  Fond I Venus vpon hir bed, that had
A mantill cast ouer hir schuldris quhite :
Thus clothit was the goddesse of delyte.

Stude at the dure Fair-calling, hir vschere,
  That coude his office doon in connyng wise,
And Secretee, hir thrifty chamberere,
  That besy was in tyme to do seruise,
  And othir mo that I can noght on avise[3];
And on hir hede, of rede rosis full suete,
A chapellet sche had, faire, fresch, and mete.

With quaking hert astonate of that sight,
  Vnnethis[4] wist I quhat that I suld seyne ;
Bot at the last febily, as I myght,
  With my handis on bothe my kneis tueyne,
  There I begouth my caris to compleyne ;
With ane humble and lamentable chere
Thus salute I that goddesse bryght and clere :

" Hye Quene of Lufe ! sterre of beneuolence !
  Pitouse princes, and planet merciable[5] !
Appesare of malice and violence !
  By vertew pure of your aspectis hable[6],
  Vnto youre grace lat now bene acceptable
My pure request, that can no forthir gone
To seken help, bot vnto yow allone !

[1] Painted.

[2] makes menace to hearts.

[3] more, of whom I cannot tell.

[4] Scarcely.

[5] merciful.

[6] powerful.

As ye that bene the socoure and suete well
　　Off remedye, of carefull hertes cure,
And, in the hugë weltering wawis fell
　　Off lufis rage, blisfull havin and sure ;
　　O anker and keye of our gude auenture,
Ye haue your man with his gude-will conquest[1] :
Merci, therefore, and bring his hert to rest !

[1] conquered.

Ye knaw the cause of all my peynes smert
　　Bet than my-self, and all myn auenture
Ye may conuoye, and as yow list, conuert
　　The hardest hert that formyt hath nature :
　　Sen in your handis all hale[2] lyith my cure,
Haue pitee now, O bryght blisfull goddesse,
Off your pure man[3], and rew[4] on his distresse !

[2] wholly.
[3] poor servant.
[4] have pity on.

And though I was vnto your lawis strange,
　　By ignorance, and noght by felonye,
And that your grace now likit hath to change
　　My hert, to seruen yow perpetualye,
　　Forgiue all this, and shapith[5] remedye
To sauen me of your benignë grace,
Or do me steruen[6] furth-with in this place.

[5] prepare.
[6] make me die.

And with the stremes of your percyng lyght
　　Conuoy my hert, that is so wo-begone,
Ageyne vnto that suetë hevinly sight,
　　That I, within the wallis cald as stone,
　　So suetly saw on morow[7] walk and gone,
Law in the gardyn, ryght tofore myn eye :
Now, merci, Quene ! and do me noght to deye."

[7] in the morning.

Thir wordis said, my spirit in dispaire,
  A quhile I stynt, abiding efter grace[1]:
And there-with-all hir cristall eyën faire
  Sche[2] kest asyde, and efter that a space,
  Benignëly sche turnyt has hir face
Towardis me full pleasantly conueide;
And vnto me ryght in this wise sche seide :

" Yong man, the cause of all thyne inward sorowe
  Is noght vnknawin to my deite,
And thy request, bothe now and eke toforowe[3],
  Quhen thou first maid professioun to me ;
  Sen of my grace I haue inspirit the
To knawe my lawe, contynew furth, for oft,
There as I mynt[4] full sore, I smyte bot soft.

Paciently thou tak thyne auenture,
  This will my sone Cupide, and so will I,
He can the stroke, to me langis[5] the cure
  Quhen I se tyme, and therefor humily
  Abyde, and serue, and lat Gude-hope the gye[6]:
Bot, for I haue thy forehede here present,
I will the schewe the more of myn entent.

This is to say, though it to me pertene
  In lufis lawe the septre to gouerne,
That the effectis of my bemes schene[7]
  Has thaire aspectis by ordynance eterne,
  With otheris bynden, mynes to discerne,
Quhilum in thingis bothe to cum and gone,
That langis noght to me, to writh allone[8];

[1] stopped, waiting to find grace.

[2] MS. Me.

[3] formerly.

[4] There where I aim.

[5] belongs.

[6] guide thee.

[7] bright.

[8] *i.e.* My means of discernment, past and future, are bound up with others' (powers); control belongs not to me alone. MS. bind and.

As in thyne awin case now may thou se,
For-quhy[1] lo, that [by] otheris influence[2]
Thy persone standis noght in libertee;
Quharefore, though I geve the beneuolence,
It standis noght yit in myn aduertence[3],
Till certeyne coursis endit be and ronne,
Quhill[4] of trew seruis thow have hir graice i-wone.

And yit, considering the nakitnesse
Bothe of thy wit, thy persone, and thy myght,
It is no mach, of thyne vnworthynesse
To hir hie birth, estate, and beautee bryght:
Als like ye bene, as day is to the nyght;
Or sek-cloth is vnto fyne cremesye[5];
Or doken to the freschë dayesye.

Vnlike the mone is to the sonnë schene[6];
Eke Ianuarye is vnlike to May[7];
Vnlike the cukkow to the phylomene;
Thaire tabartis[8] ar noght bothe maid of array[9];
Vnlike the crow is to the papë-iay[10];
Vnlike, in goldsmythis werk, a fischis eye
To peire[11] with perll, or maked be so heye.

As I haue said, vnto me belangith
Specialy the cure of thy seknesse;
Bot now thy matere so in balance hangith,
That it requerith, to thy sekernesse[12],
The help of othir mo that[13] bene goddes,
And haue in thame the menes and the lore,
In this matere to schorten with thy sore[14].

[1] For which reason.
[2] *i.e.* other planet's influence.
[3] control.
[4] Until.
[5] crimson cloth.
[6] bright.
[7] MS. like unto May.
[8] coats of arms.
[9] arrayed alike.
[10] parrot.
[11] compare. MS. pererese.
[12] assurance.
[13] MS. than.
[14] *i.e.* to shorten thy woe with.

And for thou sall se wele that I entend,
   Vn-to thy help, thy welefare to preserue,
The streight weye thy spirit will I send
   To the goddesse that clepit is Mynerue,
   And se that thou hir hestis wele conserue,
For in this case sche may be thy supplye[1],
And put thy hert in rest, als wele as I.

[1] help.

Bot, for the way is vncouth vnto the[2],
   There as hir duelling is and hir soiurne,
I will that Gude-hope seruand to the be,
   Youre alleris frend[3], to let the to murn[4],
   Be thy condyt and gyde till thou returne,
And hir besech that sche will, in thy nede,
Hir counsele geve to thy welefare and spede,

[2] unknown to thee.

[3] Friend of you all.
[4] to prevent thy mourning.

And that sche will, as langith hir office,
   Be thy gude lady, help and counseiloure,
And to the schewe hir rype and gude auise[5],
   Throw quhich thou may, be processe and laboure,
   Atteyne vnto that glad and goldyn floure,
That thou wald haue so fayn with all thy hart.
And forthir-more, sen thou hir seruand art,

[5] advice.

Quhen thou descendis doune to ground ageyne,
   Say to the men that there bene resident,
How long think thay to stand in my disdeyne,
   That in my lawis bene so negligent
   From day to day, and list thame noght repent,
Bot breken louse, and walken at thaire large?
Is nocht eft none[6] that thereof gevis charge?

[6] There is not even one.

And for," quod sche, " the angir and the smert
Off thaire vnkyndënesse dooth me constreyne,
My femynyne and wofull tender hert,
That than I wepe; and, to a token pleyne,
As of my teris cummyth all this reyne,
That ye se on the ground so fast ybete
Fro day to day, my turment is so grete.

¹ cease at another time. And quhen I wepe, and stynten othir quhile¹,
For pacience that is in womanhede,
Than all my wrath and rancoure I exile;
And of my cristall teris that bene schede,
The hony flouris growen vp and sprede,
² pray. That preyen² men, in thaire flouris wise,
Be trewe of lufe, and worschip my seruise.

And eke, in takin of this pitouse tale,
Quhen so my teris dropen on the ground,
In thaire nature the lytill birdis smale
3 space of time. Styntith thaire song, and murnyth for that stound³,
And all the lightis in the hevin round
4 compassion. Off my greuance haue suich compacience⁴,
That from the ground they hiden thaire presence.

And yit in tokenyng forthir of this thing,
Quhen flouris springis, and freschest bene of hewe,
And that the birdis on the twistis sing,
5 MS. to renew. At thilkë tyme ay gynnen folk renewe⁵
That seruis vnto loue, as ay is dewe,
Most commonely has ay his obseruance,
6 former. And of thaire sleuth tofore⁶ haue repentance.

Thus maist thou seyne, that myn effectis grete,
　　Vnto the quhich ye aughten maist weye[1],
No lyte offense, to sleuth is [al] forget[2]:
　　And therefore in this wisë to thame seye,
　　As I the here haue bidden[3], and conueye
The matere all the better tofore said[4];
Thus sall on the my chargë bene ilaid.

Say on than, ' Quhare is becummyn, for schame!
　　The songis new, the fresch carolis and dance,
The lusty lyf, the mony change of game,
　　The fresche array, the lusty contenance,
　　The besy awayte[5], the hertly obseruance,
That quhilum was amongis thame so ryf?
Bid thame repent in tyme, and mend thare lyf:

Or I sall, with my fader old Saturne,
　　And with al hale[6] oure hevinly alliance,
Oure glad aspectis from thame writh[7] and turne,
　　That all the warld sall waile[8] thaire gouernance.
　　Bid thame be-tyme that thai haue repentance,
And [with] thaire hertis hale renew my lawe;
And I my hand fro beting sall withdrawe.

This is to say, contynew in my seruise,
　　Worschip my law, and my name magnifye,
That am your hevin and your paradise;
　　And I your confort here sall multiplye,
　　And, for your meryt here, perpetualye
Ressaue I sall your saulis of my grace,
To lyve with me as goddis in this place.'"

[1] ought most to pay regard. MS. aught and.
[2] owing to sloth is all forgotten.
[3] MS. bid.
[4] said before.
[5] service (waiting upon).
[6] all whole.
[7] remove.
[8] bewail.

With humble thank, and all the reuerence

¹ skill.   That feble wit and connyng¹ may atteyne,
I tuke my leue; and from hir presence,
Gude-hope and I to-gider, bothë tueyne,

² shortly to say.   Departit are, and, schortly for to seyne²,
i.e. to be brief.
He hath me led [be] redy wayis ryght
Vnto Mineruis palace, faire and bryght.

³ gate.   Quhare as I fand, full redy at the yate³,
The maister portare, callit Pacience,
That frely lete vs in, vnquestionate;
And there we sawe the perfyte excellence,

⁴ The sober   The said renewe⁴, the state, the reuerence,
retinue (?)
⁵ dignified.   The strenth, the beautee, and the ordour digne⁵
Off hir court riall, noble and benigne.

And straught vnto the presence sodeynly
Off dame Minerue, the pacient goddesse,
Gude-hope my gydë led me redily;

⁶ timorous   To quhom anone, with dredefull humylnesse⁶,
humility.
Off my cummyng the cause I gan expresse,
And all the processe hole, vnto the end,
Off Venus charge, as likit hir to send.

Off quhich ryght thus hir ansuere was in bref:
" My sone, I haue wele herd, and vnderstond,
Be thy reherse, the matere of thy gref,

⁷ seek.   And thy request to procure, and to fonde⁷
Off thy pennance sum confort at my hond,
Be counsele of thy lady Venus clere,
To be with hir thyne help in this matere.

Bot in this case thou sall wele knawe and witt,
  Thou may thy hert ground on suich a wise,
That thy laboure will be bot lytill quit[1];
  And thou may set it in anothir wise[2],
  That wil be to the grete worschip and prise;
And gif thou durst vnto that way enclyne,
I will the geve my lore and disciplyne.

[1] requited.

[2] MS. in othir wise.

Lo, my gude sone, this is als mich to seyne[3],
  As, gif thy lufe [be] sett all-uterly
Of nycë lust[4], thy trauail is in veyne;
  And so the end sall turne of thy folye
  To payne and repentance; lo, wate thou quhy[5]!
Gif the ne list on lufe thy vertew set,
Vertu sall be the cause of thy forfet[6].

[3] as much as to say.

[4] On foolish desire.

[5] know thou why.

[6] disaster.

Tak Him before in all thy gouernance,
  That in His hand the stere[7] has of you all;
And pray vnto His hyë purueyance[8]
  Thy lufe to gye, and on Him traist and call,
  That corner-stone and ground is of the wall
That failis noght; and trust, withoutin drede,
Vnto thy purpose sone He sall the lede.

[7] control.

[8] providence.

For lo, the werk that first is foundit sure,
  May better bere a pace[9] and hyare be,
Than othir-wise, and langere sall endure,
  Be monyfald, this may thy resoun see,
  And stronger to defend[10] aduersitee:
Ground thy werk, therefore, vpon the stone,
And thy desire sall forthward with the gone.

[9] stage, storey.

[10] resist.

Be trewe, and meke, and stedfast in thy thoght,
    And diligent hir merci to procure,
Noght onely in thy word, for word is noght;
    Bot gif thy werk and all thy besy cure[1]
Accord thereto; and vtrid be mesure[2]
The place, the houre, the maner, and the wise;
Gif mercy sall admitten thy seruise.

All thing has tyme, thus sais Ecclesiaste;
    And wele is[3] him that his tyme wel abit[4].
Abyde thy time; for he that can bot haste
    Can noght of hap[5], the wisë man it writ;
    And oft gude fortune flourish with gude wit:
Quharefore, gif thou will be wele fortunyt,
Lat wisedome ay to thy will be iunyt[6].

Bot there be mony of so brukill[7] sort,
    That feynis treuth in lufë for a quhile,
And setten all thaire wittis and disport[8]
    The sely innocent woman to begyle,
    And so to wynne thaire lustis with a wile;
Suich feynit treuth is all bot trechorye,
Vnder the vmbre[9] of hid ypocrisye.

For as the foulere quhistlith in his throte
    Diuersëly, to counterfete the brid,
And feynis mony a suete and strangë note,
    That in the busk[10] for his desate[11] is hid,
    Till sche be fast lokin his net amyd;
Ryght so the fatoure[12], the false theif, I say,
With suete tresoun oft wynnith thus his pray.

---

[1] care.

[2] given forth by rule.

[3] well is it with.
[4] abideth. MS. wil abit.

[5] controls not fortune.

[6] joined.

[7] brittle, unreliable.

[8] sport, delight.

[9] shade.

[10] bush.
[11] deceit.

[12] deceiver.

Fy on all suich ! fy on thaire doubilnesse !
  Fy on thaire lust and bestly appetite !
Thaire wolfis hertis, in lambis liknesse ;
  Thaire thoughtis blak, hid vnder wordis quhite ;
  Fy on thaire laboure ! fy on thaire delyte !
That feynen outward all to hir honour,
And in thaire hert hir worschip wold deuoure.

So hard it is to trusten now on dayes
  The warld, it is so double and inconstant,
Off quhich the suth is kid[1] be mony assayes ;
  More pitee is ; for quhich the remanant,
  That menen wele, and ar noght variant,
For otheris gilt ar[2] suspect of vntreuth,
And hyndrit oft, and treuely that is reuth.

Bot gif the hert be groundit ferme and stable
  In Goddis law, thy purpose to atteyne,
Thy laboure is to me agreable ;
  And my full help, with counsele trew and pleyne,
  I will the schewe, and this is the certeyne ;
Opyn thy hert, therefore, and lat me se
Gif thy remede be pertynent to me."

" Madame," quod I, " sen it is your plesance
  That I declare the kynd of my loving,
Treuely and gude, withoutin variance,
  In lufe that floure abufe all othir thing ;
  And wold bene he that to hir worschipping
Myght ought auaile, be Him that starf on rude[3],
And nouthir spare for trauaile, lyf, nor gude[4].

[1] the truth is shown.

[2] MS. and.

[3] by Him that died on cross

[4] goods.

And forthirmore, as touching the nature
 Off my lufing, to worschip or to blame,
I darre wele say, and there-in me assure,
 For ony gold that ony wight can name

1 MS. Wald. Nold[1] I be he that suld of hir gude fame
 Be blamischere in ony point or wyse,
2 endure. For wele nor wo, quhill my lyfe may suffise[2].

3 MS. theffect. This is the effect[3] trewly of myn entent,
 Touching the suete that smertis me so sore,
4 feigned (fault?). Giff this be faynt[4], I can it noght repent,
 All-though my lyf suld forfaut be therefore,
 Blisful princes! I can seye you no more;
5 desire so com- Bot so desire my wittis dooth compace[5],
  passes my wits.
6 without. More ioy in erth kepe I noght bot[6] your grace."

7 I will not say it " Desire," quod sche, "I nyl it noght deny[7],
  nay.
 So thou it ground and set in Cristin wise;
 And therefore, sone, opyn thy hert playnly."
8 truly without "Madame," quod I, "trew withoutin fantise[8],
  deceit.
9 MS. That day That day sall neuer be I sall vp-rise[9]
  sall I never
  up-rise.
 For my delyte to couate[10] the plesance
10 covet.
11 honour. That may hir worschip[11] putten in balance[12].
12 jeopardy.

 For oure all thing, lo, this were my gladnesse,
 To sene the freschë beautee of hir face;
13 MS. it. And gif I[13] myght deseruë, be processe[14],
14 in course of
  time.
 For my grete lufe and treuth, to stond in grace,
15 Her honour Hir worschip sauf[15], lo, here the blisfull cace[16]
  safe.
16 lot. That I wold ask, and there-to attend,
 For my most ioye vnto my lyfis end."

"Now wele," quod sche, "and sen that it is so,
  That in vertew thy lufe is set with treuth,
To helpen the I will be one of tho
    From hensforth, and hertly without sleuth[1],
  Off thy distresse and excesse to haue reuth
That has thy hert; I will pray full faire
That Fortune be no more thereto contraire.

For suth it is, that all ye creaturis
  Quhich vnder vs beneth haue your duellyng
Ressauen diuersely your auenturis[2],
    Off quhich the cure and principall melling[3]
  Apperit is[4], withoutin repellyng[5],
Onely to hir that has the cuttis two
In hand[6], bothe of your wele and of your wo.

And how so be that sum clerkis trete,
  That all your chancë[7] causit is tofore
Heigh in the hevin, by quhois effectis grete
    Ye movit are to wrething[8], lesse or more,
  Thar[9] in the warld, thus calling that therefore
'Fortune,' and so that the diuersitee
Off thaire wirking[10] suld cause necessitee.

Bot othir clerkis halden that the man
  Has in him-self the chose[11] and libertee
To cause his awin fortune, how or quhan
    That him best lest, and no necessitee
  Was in the hevin at his natiuitee,
Bot yit the thingis happin in commune
Efter purpose[12], so cleping thame 'fortune.'

[1] heartily without sloth.

[2] Receive your courses of life variously.
[3] care and chief guidance (*lit.* meddling).
[4] Appertains.
[5] recall.
[6] *i.e.* Fortune.

[7] lot.

[8] action.

[9] MS. Quhare.

[10] working.

[11] choice.

[12] according to purpose.

¹ previous know-
ledge.

And quhare a persone has tofore knawing[3]
    Off it that is to fall purposely,
Lo, Fortune is bot wayke in suich a thing,

² note.

    Thou may wele wit[2], and here ensample quhy;

³ MS. it.

    To God, that[3] is the first cause onely
Off euery thing, there may no fortune fall :

⁴ is previously
aware.

And quhy? for he foreknawin is[4] of all.

And therefore thus I say to this sentence ;

⁵ is greatest and
strongest.

    Fortune is most and strangest[5] euermore
Quhare lest foreknawing or intelligence
    Is in the man ; and, sone, of wit or lore
    Sen thou are wayke and feble, lo, therefore,

⁶ communion.

The more thou art in dangere and commune[6]
With hir that clerkis clepen so Fortune.

Bot for the sake, and at the reuerence
    Off Venus clere, as I the said tofore,
I haue of thy distresse compacience ;

⁷ assuagement.

    And in confort and relesche[7] of thy sore,

⁸ advice.

    The schewit [haue] here myn avise[8] therefore ;
Pray Fortune help, for mich vnlikly thing
Full oft about sche sodeynly dooth bring.

Now go thy way, and haue gude mynde vpone

⁹ in the way of
teaching thee.

    Quhat I haue said in way of thy doctryne[9]."

¹⁰ MS. he.

    " I sall, madame," quod I[10]; and ryght anone
    I tuke my leve.   Als straught as ony lyne,
    With-in a beme that fro the contree dyvine

¹¹ *i.e.* in a beam
which she shot
forth as a path
from heaven.

Sche, percyng throw the firmament, extendit[11],
To ground ageyne my spirit is descendit.

Quhare, in a lusty[1] plane, tuke I my way,
   Endlang[2] a ryuer, plesant to behold,
Enbroudin[3] all with freschë flouris gay,
   Quhare, throu the grauel, bryght as ony gold,
   The cristall water ran so clere and cold,
That, in myn erë maid contynualy
A maner soune, mellit[4] with armony;

That full of lytill fischis by the brym,
   Now here, now there, with bakkis blewe as lede,
Lap and playit, and in a rout can swym
   So prattily, and dressit[5] thame to sprede
   Thaire curall[6] fynnis, as the ruby rede,
That in the sonnë on thaire scalis bryght
As gesserant[7] ay glitterit in my sight:

And by this ilkë ryuer-syde alawe[8]
   Ane hyë-way fand I like to bene[9],
On quhich, on euery syde, a long rawe
   Off treis saw I, full of leuis grene,
   That full of fruyte delitable were to sene[10],
And also, as it come vnto my mind,
Off bestis sawe I mony diuerse kynd:

The lyoun king, and his fere[11] lyonesse;
   The pantere, like vnto the smaragdyne[12];
The lytill squerell, full of besynesse;
   The slawë ase, the druggare beste of pyne[13];
   The nycë[14] ape; the werely[15] porpapyne;
The percyng lynx; the lufare vnicorne[16],
That voidis venym with his euour[17] horne.

---

[1] pleasant.
[2] Along.
[3] Embroidered, adorned.
[4] A kind of sound, mingled.
[5] addressed.
[6] coral.
[7] shining mail.
[8] down by this same river-side.
[9] like as it were.
[10] to be seen.
[11] companion.
[12] emerald.
[13] drudging beast of pain.
[14] foolish.
[15] warlike.
[16] the "lover unicorn" was to be taken, Samson-like, by maiden lures.
[17] ivory.

There sawe I dresse him new out of [his] haunt

1 active.
2 cruelty.

The fery[1] tigere, full of felonye[2];

3 standing.

The dromydare; the standar[3] oliphant;

The wyly fox, the wedowis inemye;

4 climbing goat.
5 elk strong
against missiles.

The clymbare gayte[4]; the elk for alblastrye[5];

6 heark'ning
boar.

The herknere bore[6]; the holsum grey for hortis[7];

7 badger good for
hurts.

The haire also, that oft gooth to the wortis[8].

8 plants.
9 ox.

The bugill[9], draware by his hornis grete;

10 marten.
11 beech-marten.

The martrik[10], sable, the foynyee[11], and mony mo;

The chalk-quhite ermyn, tippit as the iete;

12 skilful.

The riall hert, the conyng[12], and the ro;

13 MS. say.

The wolf, that of the murthir noght sayis[13] "Ho!"

14 skilful.
15 ravening bear.

The lesty[14] beuer, and the ravin bare[15];

16 camlet cloth.

For chamelot[16], the camel full of hare;

With mony ane-othir beste diuerse and strange,

That cummyth noght as now vnto my mynd.

Bot now to purpose,—straucht furth the range

I held a-way, oure-hailing in my mynd

From quhenes I come, and quhare that I suld fynd

17 in haste.

Fortune, the goddesse, vnto quhom in hye[17]

Gude-hope, my gyde, has led me sodeynly.

And at the last, behalding thus asyde,

A round place, wallit, haue I found;

18 soon after.
19 MS. spide.

In myddis quhare eftsone[18] I have aspide[19]

20 lodging. *Mod.
Scot.* houf, a
resort.

Fortune, the goddesse, hufing[20] on the ground:

And ryght before hir fete, of compas round,

21 clinging I saw.

A quhele, on quhich cleuering I sye[21]

A multitude of folk before myn eye.

And ane surcote sche werit[1] long that tyde,   1 wore.
   That semyt to me of diuerse hewis,
Quhilum thus, quhen sche wald [hir] turne asyde,
   Stude this goddesse of fortune and [of glewis[2]];   2 sports, freaks.
   A chapellet, with mony fresche anewis[3]   3 little rings.
                                      Fr. anneau.
Sche had vpon her hed; and with this hong
A mantill on hir schuldris, large and long,

That furrit was with ermyn full quhite,
   Degoutit with the self[4] in spottis blake :   4 self-spotted.
And quhilum in hir chiere[5] thus a lyte[6]   5 cheer,
                                          demeanour.
   Louring sche was; and thus sone it wold slake[7],   6 a little.
                                        7 slacken, cease.
   And sodeynly a maner[8] smylyng make,   8 manner of.
An[9] sche were glad; [for] at one contenance   9 If. MS. And.
Sche held noght, bot [was] ay in variance.

And vnderneth the quhelë sawe I there
   Ane vgly pit, depe as ony helle,
That to behald thereon I quoke for fere ;
   Bot o thing herd I, that quho there-in fell
   Come no more vp agane, tidingis to telle ;
Off quhich, astonait of that ferefull syght,
I ne wist quhat to done, so was I fricht[10].   10 affrighted.

Bot for to se the sudayn weltering
   Off that ilk quhele, that sloppare[11] was to hold,   11 slippery.
It semyt vnto my wit a strangë[12] thing,   12 MS. strong.
   So mony I sawe that than clymben wold,
   And failit foting, and to ground were rold ;
And othir eke, that sat aboue on hye,
Were ouerthrawe in twinklyng of ane eye.

And on the quhele was lytill void space,

    Wele nere oure-straught[1] fro lawë vnto[2] hye;

And they were ware[3] that long sat in place,

    So tolter quhilum did sche it to-wrye[4];

    There was bot clymbe and ryght dounward hye[5],

And sum were eke that fallyng had [so] sore,

There for to clymbe thaire corage was no more.

I sawe also that, quhere sum were slungin,

    Be quhirlyng of the quhele, vnto the ground,

Full sudaynly sche hath [thaim] vp ythrungin[6],

    And set thame on agane full sauf and sound:

    And euer I sawe a new swarme abound,

That [thought] to clymbe vpward vpon the quhele,

In stede of thame that myght no langer rele[7].

And at the last, in presence[8] of thame all

    That stude about, sche clepit[9] me be name;

And therewith apon kneis gan I fall

    Full sodaynly hailsing[10], abaist for schame;

    And, smylyng thus, sche said to me in game,

" Quhat dois thou here? Quho has the hider sent?

Say on anone, and tell me thyne entent.

I se wele, by thy chere and contenance,

    There is sum thing that lyis the on hert,

It stant[11] noght with the as thou wald, perchance?"

    " Madame," quod I, " for lufe is all the smert

    That euer I fele, endlang and ouerthwert[12].

Help, of your grace, me wofull wrechit wight,

Sen[13] me to cure ye powere haue and myght."

Side notes:

1 very nearly straight across.
2 MS. to.
3 wary.
4 So unsteadily at times she turned it awry.
5 hasten.
6 thrust them up.
7 go round.
8 MS. presene.
9 called.
10 saluting.
11 stands.
12 along and across. *Mod. colloq.* to tell the long and the short of it.
13 Since.

"Quhat help," quod sche, "wold thou that I ordeyne,
  To bring the vnto thy hertis desire?"
" Madame," quod I, "bot that your grace dedeyne[1], [1] deign.
  Off your grete myght, my wittis to enspire,
  To win the well that slokin may the fyre
In quhich I birn. A, goddesse fortunate!
Help now my game, that is in point to mate[2]." [2] on point of being checkmated.

" Off mate?" quod sche, "O! verray sely wrech[3], [3] truly helpless wretch.
  I se wele by thy dedely colourc pale,
Thou art to feble of thy-self to streche
  Vpon my quhele, to clymbe or to hale[4] [4] haul.
  Withoutin help; for thou has fundin stale[5] [5] found stall (prison).
This mony day, withoutin werdis wele[6], [6] happy fate.
And wantis now thy veray hertis hele[7]. [7] health.

Wele maistow be a wrechit man callit,
  That wantis the confort suld[8] thy hert glade; [8] MS. that suld.
And has all thing within thy hert stallit[9], [9] installed.
  That may thy youth oppressen or defade[10]. [10] dispirit.
  Though thy begynnyng hath bene retrograde,
Be froward opposyt quhare till aspert[11], [11] Opposed by froward men towards whom thou art exasperated.
Now sall thai turne, and luke on the dert[12]." [12] dirt.

And therewith-all vnto the quhele in hye[13] [13] in haste.
  Sche hath me led, and bad me lere[14] to clymbe, [14] learn.
Vpon the quhich I steppit sudaynly.
  " Now hald thy grippis," quod sche, "for thy tyme,
  Ane houre and more it rynnis ouer prime;
To count the hole, the half is nere away;
Spend wele, therefore, the remanant of the day.

1 these folk
before (thee).

Ensample," quod sche, " tak of this tofore[1],
That fro my quhele be rollit as a ball;
For the nature of it is euermore,

2 descend.

After ane hicht, to vale[2] and geue a fall,

3 to cause to fall.

Thus, quhen me likith, vp or doune to fall[3].
Fare-wele," quod sche, and by the ere me toke
So ernestly, that therewithall I woke.

4 restless spirit.

O besy goste[4]! ay flikering to and fro,
That neuer art in quiet nor in rest,
Till thou cum to that place that thou cam fro,
Quhich is thy first and verray proper nest:

5 art thou treated.

From day to day so sore here artow drest[5],

6 always while
waking.

That with thy flesche ay walking[6] art in trouble,

7 pain.

And sleping eke; of pyne[7] so has thou double.

8 MS. Couert.
9 have regard.

Towart[8] my-self all this mene I to loke[9].
Though that my spirit vexit was tofore

10 dreaming.
MS. sueuyng.

In sueuenyng[10], alssone as euer I woke

11 MS. xxty fold.

By twenty-fold[11] it was in trouble more,
Bethinking me with sighing hert and sore
That [I] nane othir thingis bot dremes had,

12 certainty.

Nor sekernes[12], my spirit with to glad.

13 addressed.

And therewith sone I dressit[13] me to ryse,

14 Filled full.

Fulfild[14] of thoght, pyne, and aduersitee;

15 MS. in.

And to my-self I said vpon[15] this wise;
" A! merci, Lord! quhat will ye do with me?
Quhat lyf is this? quhare hath my spirit be?
Is this of my forethoght impressioun,
Or is it from the hevin a visioun?

And gif ye goddis, of youre puruiance[1],
   Haue schewit this for my reconforting,
In relesche[2] of my furiouse pennance,
   I yow beseke full humily of this thing,
     That of youre grace I myght haue more takenyng[3],
Gif it sal be as in my slepe before
Ye shewit haue." And forth, withoutin more,

In hye vnto the wyndow gan I walk,
   Moving within my spirit of this sight,
Quhare sodeynly a turture[4], quhite as chalk[5],
   So evinly vpon my hand gan lyght,
     And vnto me sche turnyt hir full ryght;
Off quham the chere in hir birdis aport[6]
Gave me in hert kalendis of confort[7].

This fair bird ryght in hir bill gane hold
   Of red iorofflis[8] with thair stalkis grene
A fair branche, quhare writtin was with gold,
   On euery list[9], with branchis bryght and schene[10]
     In compas fair, full plesandly to sene[11],
A plane sentence, quhich, as I can deuise
And haue in mynd, said ryght on this wise:

"Awak! awake! I bring, lufar[12], I bring
   The newis glad, that blisfull bene and sure
Of thy confort; now lauch, and play, and syng,
   That art besid[13] so glad ane auenture;
     For in the hevyn decretit is the cure[14]."
And vnto me the flouris fair present[15]:
With wyngis spred, hir wayis furth sche went.

[1] providence.

[2] assuagement.

[3] token.

[4] turtle-dove.
[5] MS. calk.

[6] demeanour.

[7] beginnings of comfort.

[8] gillyflowers.

[9] edge.
[10] flourishes bright and beautiful.

[11] pleasant to see.

[12] lover.

[13] near to.

[14] cure is decreed thee.
[15] she presented.

Quhilk vp a-none I tuke, and as I gesse,
　　Ane hundreth tymes, or[1] I forthir went,
I haue it red, with hertfull glaidnese;
　　And, half with hope, and half with dred, it hent[2],
　　And at my beddis hed, with gud entent,
I haue it fair pynnit vp, and this
First takyn was of all my help and blisse.

The quhich treuly efter, day be day,
　　That all my wittis maistrit had tofore,
From hennesferth[3] the paynis did away.
　　And schortly, so wele Fortune has hir bore,
　　To quikin treuly day by day my lore,
To my larges that[4] I am cumin agayne,
To blisse with hir that is my souirane.

Bot for als moche as sum micht think or seyne,
　　Quhat nedis me, apoun so litill evyn[5],
To writt all this? I ansuere thus ageyne,—
　　Quho that from hell war croppin onys in hevin[6],
　　Wald efter o thank for ioy mak sex or sevyn[7]:
And euery wicht his awin suete[8] or sore
Has maist in mynde: I can say you no more.

Eke quho may in this lyfe haue more plesance
　　Than cum to largesse[9] from thraldom and peyne,
And by the mene[10] of Luffis ordinance,
　　That has so mony in his goldin cheyne?
　　Quhich thinkis[11] to wyn his hertis souereyne,
Quho suld me wite[12] to write thar-of, lat se!
Now sufficiante is my felicitee.

Side notes:

[1] ere.

[2] took.

[3] MS. Quhich hensferth.

[4] That to my freedom.

[5] upon so small a foundation. *Mod. Scot.* a supposition.

[6] had once crept into heaven.

[7] MS. vi or vii.

[8] sweet, happiness.

[9] liberty.

[10] means.

[11] MS. this.

[12] blame.

Beseching vnto fair Venus abufe,
    For all my brethir that bene in this place,
This is to seyne, that seruandis ar to Lufe,
    And of his lady can no thank purchase,
    His paine relesch[1], and sone to stand in grace,   1 relieve.
Boith to his worschip[2] and to his first ese;   2 honour.
So that it hir and resoune noght displese:

And eke for thame that ar noght entrit inne
    The dance of lufe, bot thidder-wart on way,
In gudë tyme and sely[3] to begynne   3 seasonable.
    Thair prentissehed, and forthir-more I pray
    For thame that passit ben the mony affray
In lufe, and cummyn[4] ar to full plesance,   4 MS. cunnyng.
To graunt thame all, lo! gude perseuerance:

And eke I pray for all the hertis dull,
    That lyven here in sleuth and ignorance,
And has no curage at the rose to pull,
    Thair lif to mend and thair saulis auance
    With thair suete lore, and bring thame to gude
        chance;
And quho that will noght for this prayer turne,
Quhen thai wald faynest speid, that thai may spurne[5].   5 *i.e.* I pray that they may trip.

To rekyn of euery-thing the circumstance,
    As hapnit me quhen lessen gan my sore,
Of my rancoure and [of my] wofull chance,
    It war to long, I lat it be tharefor.
    And thus this floure[6], I can seye no more,   6 *i.e.* flower of womanhood.
So hertly has vnto my help attendit,
That from the deth hir man sche has defendit.

1 working. And eke the goddis mercifull virking[1],
  For my long pane and trewe seruice in lufe,
That has me gevin halely myn asking,
  Quhich has my hert for euir sett abufe
  In perfyte ioy, that neuir may remufe,
2 praise. Bot onely deth: of quhom, in laud and prise[2],
With thankfull hert I say richt in this wise :—

3 may. " Blissit mot[3] be the goddis all,
  So fair that glitteren in the firmament!
And blissit be thare myght celestiall,
  That haue convoyit hale, with one assent,
  My lufe, and to [so] glade a consequent!
4 axle-tree. And thankit be Fortunys exiltree[4]
And quhele, that thus so wele has quhirlit me.

Thankit mot be, and fair and lufe befall
  The nychtingale, that, with so gud entent,
Sang thare of lufe the notis suete and small,
  Quhair my fair hertis lady was present,
5 ere.   Hir with to glad, or[5] that sche forthir went!
6 gillyflower. And thou gerafloure[6], mot i-thankit be
All othir flouris for the lufe of the!

And thankit be the fair castell wall,
  Quhare as I quhilom lukit furth and lent.
7 saints of March. Thankit mot be the sanctis marciall[7],
  That me first causit hath this accident.
  Thankit mot be the grenë bewis bent,
8 happened to me. Throu quhom, and vnder, first fortunyt me[8]
9 healing. My hertis hele[9], and my confort to be.

For to the presence suete and delitable,
　Rycht of this floure that full is of plesance,
By processe and by menys fauorable,
　First of the blisful goddis purueyance[1],
　And syne[2] throu long and trew contynuance
Of veray[3] faith in lufe and trew seruice,
I cum am, and [yit] forthir in this wise.

[1] providence.
[2] afterwards.
[3] true.

Vnworthy, lo, bot onely of hir grace,
　In lufis yok, that esy is and sure,
In guerdoune of all my lufis space[4]
　Sche hath me tak, hir humble creature.
　And thus befell my blisfull auenture,
In youth, of lufe, that now from day to day
Flourith ay newe, and yit forthir, I say.

[4] duration.

Go litill tretise, nakit of eloquence,
　Causing simplese and pouertee to wit[5];
And pray the reder to haue pacience
　Of thy defaute, and to supporten it[6],
　Of his gudnese thy brukilnese to knytt[7],
And his tong for to reule and to stere,
That thy defautis helit may bene here.

[5] simplicity and poverty to be known.
[6] to bear with it.
[7] thy brokenness to piece together.

Allace ! and gif thou cummyst in the presence,
　Quhare as[8] of blame faynest thou wald be quite,
To here thy rude and crukit eloquens,
　Quho sal be thare to pray for thy remyt[9]?
　No wicht, bot geve[10] hir merci will admytt
The for Gud-will, that is thy gyd and stere :
To quhame for me thou pitousely requere[11].

[8] Where that.
[9] excuse.
[10] No person, unless.
[11] do thou piteously entreat.

And thus endith the fatall[1] influence
    Causit from hevyn, quhare power is commytt
Of gouirnance, by the magnificence
    Of Him that hiest in the hevin sitt;

2 give thanks.
  MS. think.
To Quham we thank[2] that all oure [lif] hath writt,

3 Who could read
  it many a year
  ago.
Quho coutht it red, agone syne mony a yere[3],
Hich in the hevynnis figure circulere.

4 hymns.
  MS. inpnis.
Vnto [the] impnis[4] of my maisteris dere,
    Gowere and Chaucere, that on the steppis satt
Of rethorike quhill thai were lyvand here,
    Superlatiue as poetis laureate,
    In moralitee and eloquence ornate,
I recommend my buk in lynis sevin,
And eke thair saulis vn-to the blisse of hevin.   Amen.

**Quod explicit Jacobus Primus, Scotorum Rex
Illustrissimus.**

GOOD COUNSEL.

[From "The Gude and Godlie Ballates," 1578.]

SEN throw vertew incressis dignitie,
　And vertew is flour and rute of noblesse ay,
Of ony wit, or quhat estait thow be,
　His steppis follow, and dreid for none effray[1]:　　[1] fear no affright-
　Eject vice, and follow treuth alway:　　　　　　　　　ing.
Lufe maist thy God that first thy lufe began,
And for ilk[2] inche he will the quyte[3] ane span.　　[2] each.
　　　　　　　　　　　　　　　　　　　　　　　　　　　　　　[3] requite.

Be not ouir[4] proude in thy prosperitie,　　　　　　[4] over.
　For as it cummis, sa will it pas away;
The tyme to compt[5] is schort, thow may weill se,　[5] count, reckon.
　For of grene gress sone cummis wallowit[6] hay.　 [6] withered.
　Labour in treuth, quhilk suith is of thy fay[7];　[7] which is the
Traist maist in God, for he best gyde the can,　　　truth (substance)
And for ilk inche he will the quyte ane span.　　　 of thy faith.

Sen word is thrall, and thocht is only fre,
　Thou dant[8] thy toung, that power hes and may[9],　[8] Tame thou.
Thou steik[10] thy ene fra warldis vanitie:　　　　　 [9] is mighty.
　Refraine thy lust, and harkin quhat I say:　　　　 [10] Close thou.
　Graip or[11] thow slyde, and keip furth[12] the hie-way, [11] Grope ere.
Thow hald the fast upon thy God and man,　　　　　　　[12] forward.
And for ilk inche he will the quyte ane span.

Quod King James the First.

ROBERT HENRYSON.

ROBERT HENRYSON.

LINKING the latter days of the First James to the brilliant age of James the Fourth shines the name of Robert Henryson, writer of the earliest Scottish pastoral. First of the greater Scottish makars whose life and work bore no direct relation to the political history of the country, the Dunfermline poet struck on the national lyre certain sweet and quaint new keys which ring yet with an undiminished charm, and preserve for him a unique place among the master-singers of the north.

Little is known of the personal history of this "most exquisite of the Scottish Chaucerians." According to the tradition of last century he was the representative of the family of Henryson or Henderson of Fordell in Fife; and in Douglas's *Baronage of Scotland* he is stated to have been the father of James Henderson, King's Advocate and Lord Justice-Clerk in the reign of James IV., who redeemed the family lands and had them erected into a barony in 1510. Of these facts, however, though possible and even probable enough, there exists no absolute proof. In the Chartulary of Dunfermline there are three deeds dated March, 1477-8, and July, 1478, by Henry, Abbot of Dunferm-line, granting to George de Lothreisk and Patrick

Baron the lands of Spitalfield near Inverkeithing.
To each of these documents the name of *Magister
Robertus Henryson, notarius publicus*, is appended as
witness. From the title of notary public Dr. Irving,
in his *History of Scottish Poetry*, infers that Henryson
was probably an ecclesiastic, and could therefore have
no legitimate offspring. It has to be noted, however,
that Henryson is nowhere styled *clericus* or *presbyter*,
the usual titles of churchmen. By an Act of James
III., moreover, in 1469, laymen had been admitted
to act as notaries in matters civil. It is quite
possible, therefore, that the poet may have been
the father of the Lord Justice-Clerk who fell with
James IV. at Flodden. Whether this was the case,
however, and whether the lands of Fordell had formerly
belonged to the family of Henryson, and had been
wadsett or alienated by them previous to the acqui-
sition by the Justice-Clerk,* are questions hardly
likely to find conclusive settlement now.

In one of his works Henryson describes himself as
"ane man of age," and Sir Francis Kynaston, who
translated the *Testament of Cresseid* into Latin verse
in the time of Charles I., stated upon what seems
good authority that the poet " being very old, died of
a diarrhœa or flux." It is certain that he had passed
away before 1506, for Dunbar, in his well-known
" Lament for the Makaris," written about that year,
says of Death—

> In Dunfermelyne he hes done roun
> With gud Maister Robert Henrisoun.

* See Appendix to Laing's edition of Henryson, pp. 44-5.

Laing therefore conjectures that we cannot greatly err in supposing the poet to have been born not later than the year 1425. From the general tone, no less than the various classical allusions in his work, it might be gathered that he had received an education unusually liberal for laymen of that age. This is made certain by the fact that he is uniformly styled Master Robert Henryson, a title confined exclusively in those days to persons who had taken an academic degree. His name, nevertheless, does not appear on the registers of St. Andrews, at that time the only university in Scotland, and it must therefore be inferred that he pursued or completed his studies at some foreign university, such as Louvain or Paris. This was a custom from an early date in Scotland. In 1365 and 1368, as we know from existing permits, John Barbour, Archdeacon of Aberdeen, and others passed through England to France for purposes of scholarship; and fifty years after Henryson's time there was hardly a university in Europe which did not count among its members wandering Scottish scholars like George Buchanan and the Admirable Crichton. Glasgow University, the second in Scotland, was founded by a bull of Pope Nicholas V. in 1451, and among those incorporated as members appears on 10th September, 1462, "the venerable Master Robert Henryson, Licentiate in Arts and Bachelor in Decrees." Such a title would imply that the poet had qualified for the legal profession, and upon the strength of this Laing suggests that "although no such record is preserved, it is by no means improbable that he became a Fellow of Glasgow University for the purpose of reading lectures in law." But it seems as likely that his enrolment, with that of others, was for the purpose of giving weight and dignity to the new foundation.

Whatever may have been his functions as a notary public, Henryson, according to common tradition, followed the occupation of schoolmaster in Dunfermline. He is so designated first on the title of his Fables in 1570 and 1571, and again on the edition of his "Cresseid" in 1593. Various conjectures have been hazarded as to the exact professional position of the poet.* It is now, however, well known† that a "Sang Scule" existed at an early period in almost every one of the cathedral cities of Scotland, as well as in many of the smaller towns. The "Sang Scule" of Aberdeen, the most famous of these ancient institutions, is believed to have existed as early as 1370, and so popular did it become that it attracted teachers of even continental fame. The original purpose of these "scules" was the instruction of youths in the music and Latin necessary for proper performance of the church services. Gradually, however, other branches of instruction were added, until the institutions assumed the complete functions of grammar schools. Laing quotes from the Privy Council Register of 13th

* Lord Hailes' *Ancient Scottish Poems*, p. 273; Sibbald's *Chronicle of Scottish Poetry*, vol. i., p. 87; and Chalmers' Preface to "Robene and Makyne," &c., p. vii., note 2.
† See an interesting article on "Music in Early Scotland" by Mr. J. Cuthbert Hadden in the *Scottish Review* for October, 1888.

October, 1573, a complaint at the instance of
"John Henryson of the Grammar School within
the Abbey of Dunfermline," which states that "he
and his predecessors had continued Masters and
Teachers of the Youth, in letters and doctrine, to
their great commodity, within the said school, past
memory of man, admitted thereto by the Abbots of
Dunfermling for the time," &c. This, without doubt,
was the school of which the poet was in his time
chief master, and curiously enough it is the only
"sang scule" in Scotland of which traces still remain.
According to Mr. Cuthbert Hadden, "the precentor
of the parish church of Dunfermline still enjoys a
yearly salary of £8 6s. 8d. as teacher of music in
the Sang or Grammar School, which is a sinecure."

No further facts of Henryson's life are known,
though it may be possible to conjecture something
of the poet's character and experience from the
character and tone of his work. Twelve years of
age when the poet-king, James I., was slain at
Perth, the greater part of his life was comprised in
the reigns of James II. and James III., the darkest
and most stormy period of Stuart rule in Scotland,
and though it cannot be supposed that he had any
personal share in the troubles of the time, their
shadow can be distinctly seen resting here and there
upon his verse. A quiet, thoughtful man he appears
to have been, who, as the echoes of the changeful
strife without reached him in his still abbey walk,
came to ask himself what were the true ideals and
the meaning of human existence. The answer at

which he arrived is to be read everywhere between the lines of his poems.

Henryson's works have been preserved scattered amid the following collections:—The Asloan MS. in the Auchinleck Library, the Bannatyne MS. and Gray's MS. in the Advocates' Library, the Maitland MS. in the Pepysian Library at Cambridge, the Harleian MS. in the British Museum, and Makculloch's MS. which was in the possession of his editor, Laing. Of editions of the separate poems there may be mentioned "Orpheus and Eurydice," printed by Chepman & Millar in 1508, the "Moral Fables" by Lekprevik in 1570, and the "Testament of Cresseid" by Henry Charteris in 1593. From the Bannatyne MS., in which are included the greater number of Henryson's existing poems, the Bannatyne Club printed "Robene and Makyne" and "The Testament of Cresseid" in 1824; and in 1832 the Maitland Club reprinted the "Moral Fables" from an edition of 1621. The poet's works, however, did not exist in complete collected form until 1865, in which year an edition, "leaving nothing to be desired," was edited by David Laing and published at Edinburgh.

"The Testament of Cresseid" has generally been esteemed the greatest of Henryson's compositions, though it cannot be considered the most complete. It suffers from the fact that it forms the sequel to a poem by another writer. Upon reading Chaucer, whose works had but lately been printed, the Scottish poet appears to have been struck by the unjust ending of the tale of "Troilus and Creseide." In that tale, while the noble Troilus perishes on the battlefield, the false Creseide is left living with Diomed. To remedy this defect, and bring about a catastrophe more in accordance with poetic justice, Henryson wrote his episode. This formed part of the contents of the lost folios of the Asloan MS. (1515), and Laing conjectures that it was probably printed by Chepman & Millar with other works of Henryson in 1508; but so close a relation did it bear to Chaucer's poem, and so much did it enhance the interest of the narrative, that it was included, without its author's name, in all the early editions of the English poet after 1532. "It was even," says Laing, "enumerated in the list of Chaucer's works by Leland, Bale, and other early writers, who seem never to have heard of the name of Henryson." The true authorship of the "Testament" was first acknowledged in 1635 by Sir Francis Kynaston in the introduction to his Latin translation of "Troilus and Creseid." "For the author of this supplement," he says, "called the Testament of Creseid, which may pass for the sixth and last book of this story, I have very sufficiently been informed by Sir Thomas Erskine, late Earle of Kelly, and divers aged scholars of the Scottish nation, that it was made and written by one Mr. Robert Henderson, sometime chiefe Schoolemaster in Dunfermling, much about the time that Chaucer was first printed; and dedicated to King Henry VIII. by Mr. Thinne, which was neere the end of his raigne" (*i.e.,* in 1532).

The historian of Scottish poetry has remarked that

"for 'the tale of Troy divine' neither Chaucer nor
Henryson had recourse to the classical sources.
This, like some other subjects of ancient history, had
been invested with all the characteristics of modern
romance.   The personages are ancient, but the
institutions and manners are all modern."   At another
place, adverting to the poet's account of Mercury, the
same writer expresses the hope "that Henryson taught
one system of mythology to his scholars, and adopted
another for the embellishment of his poetry."   Such
freedom of treatment, however, was common to all
the writers as well as the painters of the time, and it
detracts little from the actual value and beauty of the
poem.   The chief objection to the "Testament of
Cresseid" has been that in afflicting the heroine with
so loathsome a disease as leprosy Henryson departed
from the delicacy of Chaucer's original work.   Godwin,
the biographer of Chaucer, observes :   " Henryson
perceived what there was defective in the close of the
story of Troilus and Creseide as Chaucer left it ; but
the Scottish poet was incapable of rising to the refine-
ment, or conceiving the delicacies of the English
poet ; though it must be admitted that in the single
instance of the state of mind, the half-recognition, half-
ignorance, attributed to Troilus in his last encounter
with Creseide, there is a felicity of conception
impossible to be surpassed.   In some respects the
younger poet has clearly the advantage over the more
ancient.   There is in his piece abundance of incident,
of imagery, and of painting, without tediousness, with
scarcely one of those lagging, impertinent, and un-

meaning lines, with which the production of Chaucer is so frequently degraded." With the latter part of this criticism Dr. Merry Ross* entirely agrees, saying of the lament of Cresseid in the spittal-house in particular, " The pathos throughout is so sweet and tender, the imagery so rich and various, the word-painting so felicitous, in spite of an excessive allitera-tion, that we venture to pronounce this part of the poem the highest achievement of Henryson's genius." Attention may be drawn to the opening of the poem as a passage of singular charm. Nothing could be happier than the introduction, wherein the poet, after regarding from his chamber the beauty of the frosty night outside, mends the fire, comforts his spirits with "ane drink," and, taking a book in hand, settles himself "to cut the winter nicht and mak it schort." And altogether, there can be no question that in the " Testament of Cresseid " the Scottish makar has, to quote his editor, "produced as a distinct episode a picture of touching pathos and beauty."

"Orpheus and Eurydice," a metrical version of the well known classical story, of equal length with the "Testament of Cresseid," has been attributed alter-nately to the early years and to the old age of the poet. Holding close to the incidents of the tale as narrated by Virgil and Ovid, it certainly exhibits little of the master-touch seen in its sister composition, and may be considered as chiefly of note for illustrating its author's familiarity with the classic learning of his time.

* *Scottish History and Literature*, p. 165.

Most bulky and perhaps best known of Henryson's works is his series of "Moral Fables." These claim to be Scottish metrical versions of thirteen of the fables of Æsop, each with a moral appended, and the whole introduced by two prologues. Of the Latin collection of fables attributed to the Phrygian Æsop, it is conjectured that the first printed edition was made at Rome, in the year 1473, and that proving extremely popular, the work was translated before long into most European languages. At anyrate, collections of such apologues, under the names of Æsop, Avianus, and other ancient writers, afforded popular amusement for all classes of people towards the end of the fifteenth century. Which of these collections Henryson used as a model is not known, but it is believed, from their allusions to the corruptions and disturbances of the time, that his own "Moral Fables" were written between the years 1470 and 1480, and he has the credit of being one of the first of the British poets to employ the apologue as a distinct class of literature. In telling these stories Henryson departs from the terse manner of his classic models, and his work bears little likeness to the short, neat fables of Gay and La Fontaine. His tales are full of descriptive imagery, pleasant dialogue, humorous incident, and allusions to the everyday life and manners of his time. He had the artistic instinct to perceive that such productions take their chief value from the human sentiment behind them. So much, indeed, has he raised the interest of the narratives by the reflection in them of human feeling and character

that he may be said to have by them added to
literature a novel and fascinating poetic form. From
the fable which has generally been considered his
best, "The Taill of the Uplandis Mous and the Burges
Mous," a good deal is to be gathered, as one critic has
pointed out, of the social institutions of Henryson's
age. Among other details the town mouse, a "gild-
brother" and "free burges," when she travels to visit
her upland sister, who lives "as outlawis dois," goes
barefoot and with pikestaff in her hand, "as pure
pilgrym." Some light is even cast upon the diet of
those days—wine, cheese, thraf-cakes, and "all the
coursis that cuikis culd defyne." But if manners have
altered, human nature has not changed. The modern
reader is tempted to smile in curious recognition of
the city madame who, when offered the plain fare of
her sister's shieling, "prompit furth in pryde." In
short, under the guise of apologue this and the other
twelve fables present us with pictures of real life whose
shrewd accuracy is all the more delightful that it is
veiled behind a playful name.

Henryson's shorter pieces are marked no less
strongly than his more ambitious works with the
individuality of their author. Among them "The
Bludy Serk" has been called one of the earliest
specimens of ballad writing. But it is in reality a
subtle allegory which might have afforded Bunyan a
suggestion for his episode of Giant Despair. A better
example of the poet's allegorical fancy is found in
"The Garmond of Gude Ladeis," a typical work of its
kind, containing a touch or two, as in the third verse,

which our modern tongue could hardly approach. The other short poems, like "The Abbay Walk" and "The Prais of Aige," with their gentle temper and pensive benignity, bring the reader nearest, perhaps, to the character of the poet himself.

It is by his single short pastoral, however, that Henryson, after all has been said, is likely to linger longest in the memory of the reader. "Robene and Makyne" is the earliest specimen of pastoral poetry in the language, but in no respect does it fall short of later efforts in the same field. Dr. Irving, indeed, considered it "superior in many respects to the similar attempts of Spenser and Browne," finding it "free from the glaring improprieties which sometimes appear in the pastorals of those distinguished writers," while Dr. Merry Ross declared it to be "one of the loveliest pastorals in all literature." Every point in the poem is true to nature, and every stanza strikes a chord in the common heart of humanity. Nothing could be more profoundly pathetic than the lines beginning "Robene that warld is all away," simple as the words appear ; and when the poem has been read throughout, the whole remains in the mind, clear and vivid, a picture to which no touch could add effect.

In this poem, within a brief compass, is perhaps to be discovered the main secret of Henryson's charm. Here the art and the heart of the master-singer are revealed together—the lines are still lightened by a quaint and kindly humour while his pen is touching the tender fountains of passion and regret.

ROBENE AND MAKYNE.

ROBENE sat on gud grene hill,
    Kepand a flok of fe[1];
    Mirry Makyne said him till[2],
      "Robene, thow rew on me[3];
I haif thé luvit lowd and still[4]
    Thir yeiris two or thre;
My dule in dern bot gif thow dill[5],
    Doutless but dreid I de[6]."

Robene answerit, " Be the Rude,
    Na-thing of lufe I knaw,
Bot keipis my scheip undir yone wude,
    Lo, quhair thay raik on raw[7]!
Quhat hes marrit thé in thy mude,
    Makyne, to me thow schaw?
Or quhat is lufe or to be lude[8]?
    Fane wald I leir[9] that law.

" At luvis lair[10] gife thow will leir,
    Tak thair ane A, B, C;
Be heynd[11], courtass, and fair of feir[12],
    Wyse, hardy, and fre:

[1] sheep.
[2] to.
[3] have pity on me.
[4] openly and secretly.
[5] My secret woe unless thou share.
[6] for lack of endurance I die
[7] range in row.
[8] loved.
[9] learn.
[10] lore.
[11] gentle.
[12] carriage.

So that no denger do thé deir[1],
    Quhat dule in dern thow dre[2];
Preiss[3] thee with pane at all poweir
    Be pacient, and previe."

Robene answerit hir agane,
    " I wait[4] nocht quhat is lufe ;
But I haif mervell incertaine,
    Quhat makis thé this wanrufe[5].
The weddir is fair, and I am fane[6],
    My scheip gois haill aboif[7],
And[8] we wald play us in this plane
    Thay wald us bayth reproif[9]."

" Robene, tak tent[10] unto my taill,
    And wirk all as I reid[11],
And thow sall haif my hairt all haill[12],
    Eik and[13] my maidenheid.
Sen God sendis bute for baill[14],
    And for murnyng remeid ;
In dern with thee bot giff I daill[15]
    Dowtles I am bot deid."

" Makyne, to-morne this ilka tyde[16]
    And ye will meet me heir
Peraventure my scheip may gang besyd
    Quhill we haif liggit[17] full neir ;
Bot mawgre haif I and I byd[18]
    Fra thay begin to steir[19].
Quhat lyis on hairt I will nocht hyd ;
    Makyne than mak gud cheir."

1 daunt thee.
2 Whatsoever woe in secret thou endure.
3 Exert.
4 wot.
5 thus uneasy.
6 glad.
7 healthy on the heights.
8 If.
9 bring reproof.
10 take heed.
11 advise.
12 whole.
13 And also.
14 salve for sorrow.
15 In secret with thee unless I deal.
16 this same time.
17 While we have lain.
18 ill-will have I if I tarry.
19 stir.

" Robene, thow reivis me roiff[1] and rest !
    I luve bot thé allane."
" Makyne, adew ! the sone gois west,
    The day is neir-hand gane."
" Robene, in dule I am so drest[2],
    That lufe wil be my bane."
" Ga lufe, Makyne, quhair-evir thow list,
    For lemman I luve nane."

" Robene, I stand in sic a style[3]
    I sicht[4], and that full sair."
" Makyne, I haif bene heir this quhyle,
    At hame God gif I wair[5]."
" My huny, Robene, talk ane quhyle,
    Gif thow will do na mair."
" Makyne, sum uthir man begyle,
    For hamewart I will fair."

Robene on his wayis went
    Als licht as leif of tre.
Mawkyn murnit in hir intent[6],
    And trowd him nevir to se.
Robene brayd atour the bent[7];
    Than Makyne cryit on hie,
" Now ma thow sing, for I am schent[8];
    Quhat alis lufe at me ?"

Mawkyne went hame withowttin faill
    Full wery eftir cowth weip[9].
Than Robene in a ful fair daill[10]
    Assemblit all his scheip.

[1] robbest me of quiet.

[2] beset.

[3] such a state.
[4] sigh.

[5] God grant I were.

[6] desire.

[7] " strode across the brake."

[8] lost.

[9] weary and like to weep.
[10] deal, number.

Be that sum parte of Mawkynis aill
  Out-throw his hairt cowd creip;
He fallowit hir fast thair till assaill
  And till hir tuke gude keep[1].

"Abyd, abyd, thow fair Makyne!
  A word for ony-thing!
For all my luve it sal be thyne,
  Withowttin departing[2].
All haill thy harte for till haif myne[3]
  Is all my cuvating.
My scheip to-morn, quhill[4] houris nyne,
  Will neid of no keping."

"Robene, thow hes hard soung and say
  In gestis[5] and storeis auld
'The man that will nocht quhen he may,
  Sall haif nocht quhen he wald.'
I pray to Jesu, every day
  Mot eik[6] thair cairis cauld,
That first preissis[7] with thé to play
  Be firth[8], forrest, or fauld[9]."

"Makyne, the nicht is soft and dry,
  The weddir is warme and fair,
And the grene woid rycht neir us by
  To walk atour all quhair[10]:
Thair ma na janglour[11] us espy
  That is to lufe contrair;
Thairin, Makyne, bath ye and I
  Unsene we ma repair."

1 to her took good heed.

2 Without dividing.
3 To have thy whole heart mine.
4 till.

5 romances.

6 May add to.
7 endeavour.
8 enclosed land.
9 open pastures.

10 To walk over everywhere.
11 tattler.

" Robene, that warld is all away,
  And quyt brocht till ane end;
And nevir agane thairto, perfay¹,
  Sall it be as thow wend².
For of my pane thow maid it play,
  And all in vane I spend;
As thow hes done, sa sall I say,
  Murne on, I think to mend."

" Makyne, the howp of all my heill³,
  My hairt on thé is sett,
And evir-mair to thé be leill⁴
  Quhill I may leif, but lett⁵;
Nevir to faill, as utheris feill⁶,
  Quhat grace that evir I gett."
" Robene, with thé I will nocht deill;
  Adew! for thus we mett."

Makyne went hame blyth anewche⁷
  Attour the holtis hair⁸.
Robene murnit, and Makyne lewche⁹;
  Scho sang, he sichit sair¹⁰:
And so left him bayth wo and wreuch¹¹,
  In dolour and in cair,
Kepand his hird under a huche¹²
  Amang the holtis hair.

¹ by my faith.

² weened, expected.

³ hope of all my health.

⁴ loyal.

⁵ without ceasing.
⁶ as others fail.

⁷ enough.

⁸ Over the grey hills.
⁹ laughed.

¹⁰ sighed sore.

¹¹ woeful and wretched.

¹² cliff.

THE GARMOND OF GUDE LADEIS.*

WALD my gud Lady lufe me best,
  And wirk eftir my will,
I suld ane garmond gudliest

  Gar mak hir body till[1].

Off he[2] honour suld be hir hud,
  Upoun hir heid to weir,
Garneist with governance so gud,

  Na demyng suld hir deir[3].

Hir sark suld be hir body nixt,
  Of chestetie so quhyt,
With schame and dreid togidder mixt,
  The same suld be perfyt.

Hir kirtill suld be of clene constance,
  Lasit with lesum lufe[4],
The mailyheis of continuance[5]
  For nevir to remufe.

* Lord Hailes considered this poem "a sort of paraphrase
of 1 Tim. ii., 9-11," and Laing remarks that "Pinkerton
(History, vol i., p. 434) refers to it as giving the best idea of the
dress of a lady of that period ; 'the complete attire consisting of
hood, shift, kirtle (or gown and petticoat) tied with laces and
adorned with mails or spangles ; an upper gown or robe, purfled
and furred, and adorned with ribbons ; a belt ; a mantle or cloak
in bad weather ; a hat, tippet, *patelet*, perhaps small ruff ; a
ribbon about the neck ; sleeves, gloves, shoes and hose.'"

Hir gown suld be of gudliness,
   Weill ribband with renowne,
Purfillit with plesour in ilk place[1],
   Furrit with fyne fassoun[2].

[1] each place.
[2] fashion.

Hir belt suld be of benignitie,
   About hir middill meit;
Hir mantill of humilitie,
   To tholl[3] bayth wind and weit.

[3] endure.

Hir hat suld be of fair having[4],
   And hir tepat of trewth,
Hir patelet of gude pansing[5],
   Hir hals-ribbane[6] of rewth[7].

[4] carriage.

[5] Her ruff of good thought.
[6] throat-ribbon.
[7] pity.

Hir slevis suld be of esperance,
   To keip hir fra dispair;
Hir gluvis of the gud govirnance,
   To hyd hir fyngearis fair.

Hir schone[8] suld be of fickernes[9],
   In syne that scho nocht slyd;
Hir hois of honestie, I ges,
   I suld for hir provyd.

[8] shoes.
[9] certainty.

Wald scho put on this garmond gay,
   I durst sweir by my seill[10],
That scho woir nevir grene nor gray
   That set hir half so weill.

[10] happiness, salvation.

THE ABBAY WALK.*

ALLONE as I went up and doun
   In ane Abbay was fair to se,
Thinkand quhat consolatioun
   Was best in-to adversitie;
   On caiss[1] I kest on syd myne é,
And saw this written upoun a wall,
   Of quhat estait, Man, that thow be,
Obey, and thank thy God of all.

Thy kindome and thy grit empyre,
   Thy ryaltie, nor riche array,
Sall nocht endeur at thy desyre,
   Bot, as the wind, will wend away;
   Thy gold, and all thy gudis gay,
Quhen fortoun list will fra thee fall:
   Sen thow sic fampillis seis ilk day[2],
Obey, and thank thy God of all.

[1] By chance.

[2] Since thou seest such examples each day.

* This title was given to the poem by Lord Hailes "from a like title given to a popular poem mentioned by Sir James Inglis" in *The Complaynt of Scotland.*

Job was maist riche, in Writ we find,
   Thobè maist full of cheritie ;
Job woux pure[1], and Thobè blynd,   1 waxed poor.
   Baith tempit with adversitie.
   Sen blindnes wes infirmitie,
And poverty wes naturall ;
   Thairfoir rycht patiently bath he and he
Obeyit, and thankit God of all.

Thocht[2] thow be blind, or haif ane halt,   2 Though.
   Or in thy face deformit ill,
Sa it cum nocht throw thy defalt,
   Na man suld thé repreif by skill[3].   3 reprove by
                                                reason (of it).
   Blame nocht thy Lord, sa is his will ;
Spurn nocht thy fute aganis the wall ;
   Bot with meik hairt and prayer still
Obey, and thank thy God of all.

God of his justice mon[4] correct   4 must.
   And of his mercie petie haif ;
He is ane Juge, to nane suspect[5],   5 by none to be
                                                suspected.
   To puneis synfull man and saif.
   Thocht thow be lord attour the laif[6],   6 over the rest.
And eftirwart maid bound and thrall,
   Ane pure begger, with skrip and staiff,
Obey, and thank thy God of all.

This changeing and grit variance
   Off erdly[7] staitis up and doun   7 earthly.
Is nocht bot[8] casualitie and chance,   8 only.
   Sa[9] sum men sayis, without ressoun,   9 As.

Bot be the grit provisioun
Of God aboif that rewel thé sall;
    Thairfoir evir thow mak thé boun[1]
To obey, and thank thy God of all.

1 ready.

In welth be meik, heich[2] not thy-self;
    Be glaid in wilfull povertie;
Thy power and thy waildis pelf
    Is nocht bot verry vanitie.
    Remembir him that deit on tre,
For thy saik taistit the bittir gall,
    Quha heis law hairtis, and lawis he[3];
Obey, and thank thy God of all.

2 exalt.

3 Who raises lowly hearts and puts down the high.

THE PRAIS OF AIGE.

In-tyl ane garth[1], under ane reid roseir[2],
   Ane auld man, and decrepit, hard I syng;
Gay wes the noit, sweit was the voce and cleyr;
   It wes grit joy to heir of sic ane thyng.
     "And to my doume[3]," he said, in his dytyng[4],
"For to be young I wald nocht, for my wyss[5],
   Of all this warld to mak me lord and king:
The moyr of aige the nerar hevynis bliss.

"Fals is this warld, and full of varyance,
   Oureset with syt and uther synnys mo[6];
Now trewth is tynt[7], gyle hes the governance,
   And wrachitness hes wrocht al weill to wo;
     Fredoume is tynt, and flemyt[8] the lordis fro,
And cuvattyce is all the cause of this:
   I am content that yowthheid is ago[9]:
The moyr of aige the nerar hevynis blis.

"The stait of yowth I repute[10] for na gude,
   For in that stait grit perrell now I se;
Can nane gane-stand the rageing of his blude
   Na yit be stabil quhill that he aigit be[11]:

[1] garden.
[2] a red rose-tree.

[3] As to my fate.
[4] tale, ditty.
[5] after what I know.

[6] Overcome with sorrow and other pities more.
[7] lost.
[8] driven away.

[9] gone.

[10] esteem.

[11] till he be aged.

Than of the thing that maist rejoysit he,
Na-thing remaynis for to be callit his;
  For quhy? it was bot verray vanite :
The moyr of aige the nerar hevynis blyss.

[1] trust.

"This wrechit warld may na man trow[1]; for quhy?
  Of erdly joy ay sorrow is the end;
The gloyr of it can na man certify,
  This day a king, the morne na-thing to spend!
  Quhat haif we heyr bot grace us to defend!
[2] to amend our fault.   The quhilk God grant us till amend our myss[2],
  That till his joy he may our saullis send;
The moyr of aige the nerar hevynis bliss."

THE TESTAMENT OF CRESSEID.

ANE doolie sessoun to ane cairfull dyte[1]
  Suld correspond, and be equivalent.
Richt sa it wes quhen I began to wryte
  This tragedie, the wedder richt fervent[2],
  Quhen Aries in middis of the Lent;
Schouris of haill can fra the north discend,
That scantlie fra the cauld I micht defend.

Yet nevertheles within myne oratur[3]
  I stude, quhen Titan had his bemis bricht
Withdrawin doun, and sylit under cure[4],
  And fair Venus, the bewtie of the nicht,
  Uprais, and set unto the west full richt
Hir golden face, in oppositioun
Of god Phebus, direct discending doun.

Throwout the glas hir bemis brast[5] sa fair,
  That I micht se on everie syde me by,
The northin wind had purifyit the air,
  And sched the mistie cloudis fra the sky;
  The froist freisit, the blastis bitterly
Fra Pole Artick come quhisling loud and schill[6],
And causit me remufe aganis my will.

[1] A doleful season to a tale full of woe.

[2] the weather right severe.

[3] oratory.

[4] concealed under care.

[5] burst.

[6] shrill.

For I traistit that Venus, luifis quene,
　To quhome sum-tyme I hecht[1] obedience,
My faidit hart of lufe scho wald mak grene;
And therupon, with humbill reverence,
I thocht to pray hir hie magnificence;
Bot for greit cauld as than I lattit was[2],
And in my chalmer to the fyre can pas.

Thocht lufe be hait[3], yit in ane man of age
　It kendillis nocht sa sone as in youtheid,
Of quhome the blude is flowing in ane rage,
And in the auld the curage doif and deid[4];
Of quhilk the fire outward is best remeid,
To help be phisike quhair that nature faillit
I am expert, for baith I have assailit[5].

I mend the fyre, and beikit[6] me about,
　Than tuik ane drink my spreitis to comfort,
And armit me weill fra the cauld thairout;
　To cut the winter nicht, and mak it schort,
I tuik ane quair[7], and left all uther sport,
Writtin be worthie Chaucer glorious,
Of fair Cresseid and worthie Troylus.

And thair I fand, efter that Diomeid
　Ressavit had that lady bricht of hew,
How Troilus neir out of wit abraid[8],
　And weipit soir, with visage paill of hew;
　For quhilk wanhope[9] his teiris can renew,
Quhill[10] Esperus rejoisit him agane :
Thus quhyle[11] in joy he levit, quhile in pane.

Side notes:
[1] promise.
[2] was prevented.
[3] Though love be hot.
[4] dull and dead.
[5] attempted.
[6] basked.
[7] quire, book.
[8] started aside.
[9] which despair.
[10] Till.
[11] by whiles.

Of hir behest he had greit comforting,
  Traisting to Troy that scho suld mak retour,
Quhilk he desyrit maist of eirdly thing;
  For why? scho was his only paramour:
  Bot quhen he saw passit baith day and hour
Of hir ganecome[1], than sorrow can oppres   [1] coming again.
His wofull hart, in cair and hevines.

Of his distres me neidis nocht reheirs,
  For worthie Chauceir, in the samin buik,
In gudelie termis and in joly veirs
  Compylit hes his cairis, quha will luik.
  To brek my sleip ane uther quair I tuik,
In quhilk I fand the fatall destenie
Of fair Cresseid, that endit wretchitlie.

Quha wait[2] gif all that Chauceir wrait was trew?   [2] Who knows.
  Nor I wait nocht gif this narratioun
Be authoreist, or fenyeit of the new[3]   [3] feigned anew.
  Be sum poeit, throw his inventioun
  Maid to report the lamentatioun
And wofull end of this lustie[4] Cresseid;   [4] pleasant.
And quhat distres scho thoillit[5], and quhat deid[6].   [5] suffered.
                                           [6] death.

Quhen Diomed had all his appetyte,
  And mair, fulfillit of this fair ladie,
Upon ane uther he set his haill delyte,
  And send to hir ane lybell of repudie;
  And hir excludit fra his companie.
Than desolait scho walkit up and doun,
And, sum men sayis, in-to the court commoun.

O, fair Cresseid! the floure and *A per se*
  Of Troy and Grece, how was thow fortunait!
To change in filth all thy feminitie,
    And be with fleschelie lust sa maculait[1],
    And go amang the Greikis air and lait,
Sa giglotlike, takand thy foull plesance!
I have pietie thow suld fall sic mischance.

[1] polluted.

Yit nevertheles, quhat-ever men deme[2] or say
  In scornefull langage of thy brukkilnes[3],
I sall excuse, als far furth as I may,
    Thy womanheid, thy wisdome, and fairnes;
    And quhilk Fortoun hes put to sic distres
As hir pleisit, and na-thing throw the gilt
Of thé, throw wickit langage to be spilt.

[2] censure.
[3] frailty.

This fair lady, in this wyse destitute
  Of all comfort and consolatioun,
Richt privelie, but[4] fellowschip, on fute
    Disagysit passit far out of the toun
    Ane myle or twa, unto ane mansioun,
Beildit full gay, quhair hir father Calchas
Quhilk than amang the Greikis dwelland was.

[4] without.

Quhen he hir saw, the caus he can inquyre
  Of hir cuming? Scho said, siching full soir,
"Fra Diomeid had gottin his desyre
  He wox werie, and wald of me no moir."
  Quod Calchas, "Douchter, weip thow not thairfoir,
Peraventure all cummis for the best,
Welcum to me, thow art full deir ane gest."

This auld Calchas, efter the law was tho[1],   1 then.
   Wes keeper of the tempill, as ane preist,
In quhilk Venus and hir sone Cupido
   War honourit, and his chalmer was thame neist[2],   2 next.
      To quhilk Cresseid, with baill aneuch[3] in breist,   3 woe enough.
Usit to pas, hir prayeris for to say;
Quhill at the last, upon ane solempne day,

As custome was, the pepill far and neir
   Befoir the none unto the tempill went
With sacrifice devoit in thair maneir:
   But still Cresseid, hevie in hir intent,
   In-to the kirk wald not hir-self present,
For givin of the pepill ony deming
Of hir expuls fra Diomeid the king;

Bot past into ane secreit orature,
   Quhair scho micht weip hir wofull desteny.
Behind hir bak scho cloisit fast the dure,
   And on hir kneis bair fell down in hy[4];   4 in haste.
   Upon Venus and Cupide angerly
Scho cryit out, and said on this same wyse,
" Allace that ever I maid yow sacrifice !

" Ye gave me anis ane devine responsaill,
   That I suld be the flour of luif in Troy,
Now am I maid an unworthie outwaill[5],   5 outcast.
   And all in cair translatit is my joy.
   Quha sall me gyde? quha sall me now convoy,
Sen[6] I fra Diomeid and nobill Troylus   6 Since.
Am clene excludit, as abject odious?

1 blame.

"O fals Cupide, is nane to wyte[1] bot thow,
   And thy mother, of lufe the blind goddess!
Ye causit me alwayis understand and trow
   The seid of lufe was sawin in my face,
   And ay grew grene throw your supplie and grace.
Bot now, allace! that seid with froist is slane,

2 neglected.

And I fra luifferis left, and all forlane[2]."

Quhen this was said, doun in ane extasie
   Ravischit in spreit, intill ane dreame scho fell,
And be apperance hard quhair scho did ly
   Cupide the king ringand ane silver bell,
   Quhilk men micht heir fra hevin unto hell;
At quhais sound befoir Cupide appeiris
The sevin Planetis discending fra thair spheiris,

Quhilk hes power of all thing generabill
   To reull and steir, be thair greit influence,
Wedder and wind and coursis variabill.
   And first of all Saturne gave his sentence,
   Quhilk gave to Cupide litill reverence,

3 fierce, bluster-
   ing.

Bot as ane busteous[3] churle on his maneir,
Come crabitlie with auster luik and cheir.

4 frosted.
5 skin.
6 shivered (?)

His face frosnit[4], his lyre[5] was lyke the leid,
   His teith chatterit, and cheverit[6] with the chin,

7 hollow.

His ene drowpit, how[7], sonkin in his heid,

8 end-drop.

   Out of his nois the meldrop[8] fast can rin,

9 livid.

   With lippis bla[9], and cheikis leine and thin,
The iceschoklis that fra his hair doun hang
Was wonder greit and as ane speir als lang.

Atouir[1] his belt his lyart[2] lokkis lay   [1] Over.
    Felterit[3] unfair, ovirfret[4] with froistis hoir,   [2] hoary.
His garmound and his gyis[5] full gay of gray,   [3] tangled.
    His widderit weid[6] fra him the wind out woir,   [4] overspread.
    Ane busteous bow within his hand he boir,   [5] guise, attire.
Under his girdill ane flasche of felloun flanis[7],   [6] withered dress.
Fedderit with ice and heidit with hailstanis.   [7] a sheaf of cruel arrows.

Than Juppiter richt fair and amiabill,
    God of the starnis in the firmament,
And nureis to all thing generabill,
    Fra his father Saturne far different,
    With burelie[8] face, and browis bricht and brent[9],   [8] pleasant.
Upon his heid ane garland wonder gay   [9] fair and smooth.
Of flouris fair, as it had bene in May.

His voice was cleir, as cristall wer his ene,
    As goldin wyre sa glitterand was his hair,
His garmound and his gyis full gay of grene,
    With golden listis[10] gilt on everie gair[11],   [10] edges.
    Ane burelie brand about his middill bair,   [11] strip.
In his right hand he had ane groundin[12] speir,   [12] sharpened.
Of his father the wraith fra us to weir[13].   [13] to ward off the apparition from us.

Nixt efter him come Mars, the god of ire,
    Of strife, debait, and all dissensioun,
To chide and fecht, als feirs as ony fyre,
    In hard harnes, hewmound and habirgeoun[14],   [14] helmet and coat of mail.
    And on his hanche ane roustie fell fachioun[15],   [15] falchion.
And in his hand he had ane roustie sword,
Wrything his face, with mony angrie word.

Schaikand his sword, befoir Cupide he come

1 angry-staring
  eyes.
    With reid visage and grislie glowrand ene[1],

2 mass.
And at his mouth ane bullar[2] stude of fome,

    Lyke to ane bair quhetting his tuskis kene,

3 brawler-like
  without t. in
  wrath.
    Richt tuilyeour lyke, but temperance in tene[3];

4 fierce defiance.
Ane horne he blew with mony bosteous brag[4],

5 war.
Quhilk all this warld with weir[5] hes maid to wag.

Than fair Phebus, lanterne and lamp of licht

    Of man and beist, baith frute and flourisching,

Tender nureis, and banischer of nicht,

    And of the warld causing, be his moving

    And influence, lyfe in all eirdlie thing,

Without comfort of quhome, of force to nocht

Must all ga die that in this warld is wrocht.

As king royall he raid upon his chair,

    The quhilk Phaeton gydit sum-tyme unricht,

The brichtness of his face, quhen it was bair,

    Nane micht behald for peirsing of his sicht;

    This goldin cart with fyrie bemes bricht

Four yokkit steidis, full different of hew,

6 Without pause. But bait[6] or tyring throw the spheiris drew.

The first was foyr, with mane als reid as rois,

7 Eōus (Ovid,
  Met. 77, 153).
    Callit Eoye[7] in-to the Orient;

8 called Æthon.
The secund steid to name hecht Ethios[8],

9 somewhat.
    Quhitlie and paill, and sum-deill[9] ascendent;

10 Pyrois.
    The thrid Peros[10], right hait and richt fervent;

11 Phlegon.
The feird was blak, callit Phlegonie[11],

Quhilk rollis Phebus down in-to the sey.

Venus was thair present, that goddess gay,
   Her sonnis querrel for to defend, and mak
Hir awin complaint, cled in ane nyce[1] array,   1 simple.
   The ane half grene, the uther half sabill blak,
   Quhyte hair as gold, kemmit and sched abak,
Bot in hir face semit greit variance,
Quhyles perfyte treuth, and quhyles inconstance.

Under smyling scho was dissimulait,
   Provocative with blenkis[2] amorous,   2 glances.
And suddanely changit and alterait,
   Angrie as ony serpent vennemous,
   Richt pungitive with wordis odious.
Thus variant scho was, quha list tak keip[3],   3 who chooses take heed.
With ane eye lauch, and with the uther weip.

In taikning[4] that all fleschelie paramour   4 token.
   Quhilk Venus hes in reull and governance,
Is sum-tyme sweit, sum-tyme bitter and sour,
   Richt unstabill, and full of variance,
   Mingit[5] with cairfull joy, and fals plesance,   5 Mingled.
Now hait, now cauld, now blyith, now full of wo,
Now grene as leif, now widderit and ago[6].   6 withered and gone.

With buik in hand than come Mercurius,
   Richt eloquent and full of rethorie,
With polite termis, and delicious,
   With pen and ink to report all reddie,
   Setting sangis[7], and singand merilie.   7 *i.e.* to music.
His hude was reid, heklit atouir his croun[8],   8 hooked over his head.
Lyke to ane poeit of the auld fassoun[9].   9 fashion.

Boxis he bair with fine electuairis,
  And sugerit syropis for digestioun,
Spycis belangand to the pothecairis,
  With mony hailsum sweit confectioun;
  Docteur in phisick, cled in skarlot goun,
And furrit weill, as sic ane aucht to be,
Honest and gude, and not ane word culd lie.*

Nixt efter him come Lady Cynthia,
  The last of all, and swiftest in hir spheir,
Of colour blak, buskit[1] with hornis twa,
  And in the nicht scho listis best appeir,
  Har as the leid, of colour na-thing cleir,
For all hir licht scho borrowis at hir brother
Titan, for of hir-self scho hes nane uther.

Hir gyse[2] was gray, and full of spottis blak,
  And on hir breist ane churle paintit full evin,
Beirand ane bunche of thornis on his bak,
  Quhilk for his thift micht clim na nar the hevin.
  Thus quhen thay gadderit war, thir Goddis sevin,
Mercurius they cheisit with ane assent
To be foir-speikar in the parliament.

Quha had bene thair, and lyking for to heir
  His facound[3] toung and termis exquisite,
Of rhetorick the prettick[4] he micht leir[5],
  In breif sermone ane pregnant sentence wryte[6].
  Befoir Cupide, veiling his cap alyte[7],
Speiris[8] [he] the caus of that vocation;
And he anone schew his intentioun.

* Mercury was "the god of thieves, pickpockets, and all dishonest persons."

1 decked.

2 attire.

3 graceful of utterance.
4 practice.
5 learn.
6 *i.e.* how to write.
7 a little.
8 Asks.

"Lo!" quod Cupide, "quha will blaspheme the name
  Of his awin god, outher in word or deid,
To all goddis he dois baith lak[1] and schame,   [1] reproach.
  And suld have bitter panis to his meid;
  I say this by yone wretchit Cresseid,
The quhilk throw me was sum-tyme flour of lufe,
Me and my mother starklie can reprufe;

"Saying of hir greit infelicitie
  I was the caus and my mother Venus;
Ane blind Goddes hir cald that micht not se,
  With sclander and defame injurious.
  Thus hir leving unclene and lecherous
Scho wald returne on me and my mother,
To quhome I schew my grace abone all uther.

"And sen[2] ye ar all sevin deificait,   [2] since.
  Participant of devyne sapience,
This greit injurie done to our hie estait,
  Me-think with pane we suld mak recompence;
  Was never to goddes done sic violence.
As weill for yow as for myself I say,
Thairfoir ga help to revenge, I yow pray."

Mercurius to Cupide gave answeir,
  And said, "Schir King, my counsall is that ye
Refer yow to the hiest planeit heir,
  And tak to him the lawest of degre,
  The pane of Cresseid for to modifie[3]:   [3] formulate.
As God Saturne, with him tak Cynthia."
"I am content," quod he, "to tak thay twa."

Than thus proceidit Saturne and the Mone,
  Quhen thay the mater rypelie had degest;
For the dispyte to Cupide scho had done,
  And to Venus oppin and manifest,
  In all hir lyfe with pane to be opprest,
And torment sair, with seiknes incurabill,
And to all lovers be abominabill.

This dulefull sentence Saturne tuik on hand,
  And passit doun quhair cairfull Cresseid lay,
And on hir heid he laid ane frostie wand,
  Than lawfullie on this wyse can he say;
  "Thy greit fairnes, and all thy bewtie gay,
Thy wantoun blude, and eik thy goldin hair,
Heir I exclude fra thé for evermair:

"I change thy mirth into melancholy,
  Quhilk is the mother of all pensivenes,
Thy moisture and thy heit in cald and dry,
  Thyne insolence, thy play and wantones
  To greit diseis, thy pomp and thy riches
In mortall neid and greit penuritie;
Thow suffer sall, and as ane beggar die."

O cruell Saturne! fraward and angrie.
  Hard is thy dome, and too malitious.
On fair Cresseid quhy hes thow na mercie,
  Quhilk was sa sweit, gentill, and amourous?
  Withdraw thy sentence, and be gracious,
As thow was never, so schawis thow thy deid,
Ane wraikfull[1] sentence gevin on fair Cresseid.

[1] revengeful.

Than Cynthia, quhen Saturne past away,
 Out of hir sait discendit down belyve¹,   1 quickly.
And red ane bill on Cresseid quhair scho lay,
 Contening this sentence diffinityve,
 "Fra heile² of bodie I thé now deprive,   2 health.
And to thy seiknes sal be na recure,
But in dolour thy dayis to indure.

"Thy cristall ene minglit with blude I mak,
 Thy voice sa cleir unplesand hoir and hace³,   3 aged (hoar) and
Thy lustie lyre⁴ ouirspred with spottis blak,   hoarse.
 And lumpis haw⁵ appeirand in thy face;   4 beauteous skin.
 Quhair thow cummis ilk man sall fle the place,   5 livid.
This sall thow go begging fra hous to hous,
With cop and clapper lyke ane lazarous."

This doolie dreame, this uglye visioun
 Brocht to ane end, Cresseid fra it awoik,
And all that court and convocatioun
 Vanischit away. Than rais scho up and tuik
 Ane poleist glas, and hir schaddow culd luik;
And quhen scho saw hir face sa deformait,
Gif scho in hart was wa aneuch, God wait⁶!   6 woeful enough,
                  God knows.

Weiping full sair, "Lo! quhat it is," quod sche,
 "With fraward langage for to mufe and steir
Our craibit goddis, and sa is sene on me!
 My blaspheming now have I bocht full deir,
 All eirdly joy and mirth I set areir⁷.   7 behind.
Allace this day! allace this wofull tyde!
Quhen I began with my goddis for to chyde!"

Be this was said ane chyld come fra the hall
  To warne Cresseid the supper was reddy;
First knokkit at the dure, and syne[1] culd call,
  "Madame, your father biddis you cum in hy[2],
He has mervell sa lang on grouf[3] ye ly;
And sayis, Your prayers bene too lang sum-deill[4],
The goddis wait all your intent full weill."

Quod scho, "Fair chylde, ga to my father deir,
  And pray him cum to speik with me anone."
And sa he did, and said, "Douchter, quhat cheir?"
  "Allace," quod scho, "father, my mirth is gone!"
  "How sa?" quod he; and scho can all expone,
As I have tauld, the vengeance and the wraik[5],
For hir trespas, Cupide on hir culd tak.

He luikit on hir uglye lipper face,
  The quhilk befor was quhite as lillie flour;
Wringand his handis oftymes, he said, Allace,
  That he had levit to se that wofull hour!
  For he knew weill that thair was na succour
To hir seiknes, and that dowblit his pane;
Thus was thair cair aneuch betuix thame twane.

Quhen thay togidder murnit had full lang,
  Quod Cresseid, "Father, I wald not be kend[6],
Thairfoir in secreit wyse ye let me gang[7],
  Unto yone hospitall at the tounis end;
  And thidder sum meit for cheritie me send
To leif upon; for all mirth in this eird[8]
Is fra me gane, sic is my wickit weird[9]."

---

[1] afterwards.

[2] in haste.

[3] grovelling, *lit.* on belly.

[4] somewhat.

[5] wreaking.

[6] known.

[7] go.

[8] earth.

[9] fate.

Than in ane mantill, and ane bavar hat,
  With cop and clapper, wonder prively
He opnit ane secreit yett[1], and out thairat   [1] gate.
  Convoyit hir, that na man suld espy,
  Unto ane village half ane myle thairby,
Delyverit hir in at the spittail hous,
And daylie sent hir part of his almous.*

Sum knew hir weill, and sum had na knawledge
  Of hir, becaus scho was sa deformait,
With bylis[2] blak ovirspred in hir visage,   [2] boils.
  And hir fair colour faidit and alterait;
  Yit thay presumit for hir hie regrait,
And still murning scho was of nobill kin,
With better will thairfoir they tuik hir in.

The day passit, and Phebus went to rest,
  The cloudis blak ovirquhelmit all the sky,
God wait gif Cresseid was ane sorrowfull gest,
  Seeing that uncouth fair and herbery[3];   [3] unaccustomed fare and lodging.
  But meit[4] or drink scho dressit hir to ly   [4] without.
In ane dark corner of the hous allone,
And on this wyse, weiping, scho maid hir mone.

* Sir Walter Scott in the notes to his edition of *Sir Tristrem*,
p. 362, says, in reference to a passage of that poem, "Want of
cleanliness, of linen, of vegetables, of fresh meat in winter, but,
above all, sloth and hardship, concurred to render the leprosy as
common in Europe during the middle ages as it is in some eastern
countries at this day. Nor were its ravages confined to the poor
and destitute. Robert de Bruce died of this disorder, as did
Constance, duchess of Bretagne, and Henry IV. of England.
Various hospitals were founded by the pious for the reception of
those miserable objects, whose disease, being infectious, required
their exclusion from society. For the same reason, while they
begged through the streets they usually carried the cup and
clapper mentioned in the text. The former served to receive
alms, and the noise of the latter warned the passenger to keep
aloof, even while bestowing his charity."

The Complaint of Cresseid.

"O sop of sorrow sonken into cair!

O, cative Cresseid! now and ever-mair

1 earth.   Gane is thy joy and all thy mirth in eird[1],

2 blackened bare. Of all blyithnes now art thow blaiknit bair[2].

Thair is na salve may saif thé of thy sair!

3 evil is thy fate. Fell is thy fortoun, wickit is thy weird[3],

4 thy woe putting   Thy blys is baneist, and thy baill on breird[4],
forth leaf.

Under the eirth God gif I gravin wer,

Quhair nane of Grece nor yit of Troy micht heird!

5 furnished.   "Quhair is thy chalmer wantounlie besene[5],

6 pleasant.   With burely[6] bed, and bankouris browderit bene[7],
7 abundant
embroidered
tapestries.   Spycis and wyne to thy collatioun,

8 beauty.   The cowpis all of gold and silver schene[8],

The sweit meitis servit in plaittis clene,

9 saffron(?) sauce.   With saipheron sals[9] of ane gude sessoun[10],
10 seasoning.

Thy gay garmentis with mony gudely goun,

11 pin.   Thy plesand lawn pinnit with goldin prene[11]?

12 behind.   All is areir[12], thy greit royall renoun!

"Quhair is thy garding with thir greissis gay,

And fresche flowris, quhilk the Quene Floray

13 piece.   Had paintit plesandly on everie pane[13],

Quhair thow was wont full merilye in May

To walk, and tak the dew be it was day,

14 thrush.   And heir the merle and mavis[14] mony ane,

15 go.   With ladyis fair in carrolling to gane[15],

16 persons.   And se the royal rinks[16] in thair array,

17 green.   In garmentis gay, garnischit on everie grane[17]?

" Thy greit triumphand fame and hie honour,
Quhair thow was callit of eirdlye wichtis flour,
  All is decayit; thy weird is welterit so[1],
Thy hie estait is turnit in darknes dour[2]!
This lipper ludge tak for thy burelie bour,
  And for thy bed tak now ane bunche of stro,
  For waillit[3] wyne and meitis thow had tho[4],
Tak mowlit[5] breid, peirrie[6], and ceder sour;
  Bot cop and clapper now is all ago.

" My cleir voice and courtlie carrolling,
Quhair I was wont with ladyis for to sing,
  Is rawk as ruik[7], full hiddeous hoir and hace;
My plesand port all utheris precelling,
Of lustines[8] I was hald maist conding[9],
  Now is deformit; the figour of my face
  To luik on it na leid[10] now lyking hes:
Sowpit in syte[11], I say with sair siching,
  Ludgeit amang the lipper leid, Allace !

" O ladyis fair of Troy and Grece attend
My miserie, quhilk nane may comprehend,
  My frivoll fortoun, my infelicitie,
My greit mischief, quhilk na man can amend.
Be-war in tyme, approchis neir the end,
  And in your mynd ane mirrour mak of me;
  As I am now, peradventure that ye,
For all your micht, may cum to that same end,
  Or ellis war[12], gif ony war may be.

" Nocht is your fairnes lot ane faiding flour,
Nocht is your famous laud and hie honour

1 thy fate is
  tossed so.
2 hard.

3 chosen.
4 then.
5 mouldy.
6 small ale?

7 hoarse as rook.

8 beauty.
9 agreeable.

10 man.

11 Drenched in
  grief.

12 worse.

Bot wind inflat in uther mennis eiris;
Your roising reid to rotting sall retour.
Exempill mak of me in your memour,
    Quhilk of sic thingis wofull witnes beiris.
    All welth in eird away as wind it weiris:
Be-war, thairfoir, approchis neir the hour;
    Fortoun is fikkill quhen scho beginnis and steiris[1]."

Thus chydand with her drerie destenye,
    Weiping, scho woik the nicht fra end to end.
Bot all in vane; hir dule, hir cairfull cry,
    Micht not remeid, nor yit hir murning mend.
    Ane lipper lady rais, and till hir wend[2],
And said, " Quhy spurnis thow aganis the wall,
To sla thyself, and mend na-thing at all?

[2] passed.

" Sen thy weiping dowbillis bot thy wo,
    I counsall thé mak vertew of ane neid;
To leir to clap thy clapper to and fro,
    And leir efter the law of lipper leid[3]."
    Thair was na buit[4], bot furth with thame scho yeid[5]
Fra place to place, quhill cauld and hounger sair
Compellit hir to be ane rank[6] beggair.

[3] leper folk.

[4] help.
[5] went.

[6] importunate.

That samin tyme of Troy the garnisoun,
    Quhilk had to chiftane worthie Troylus,
Throw jeopardie of weir had strikken down
    Knichtis of Grece in number mervellous.
    With greit tryumphe and laude victorious
Agane to Troy richt royallie they raid
The way quhair Cresseid with the lipper baid[7].

[7] abode.

Seing that companie thai come all with ane stevin[1],   [1] noise.
   Thay gaif ane cry, and schuik coppis gude speid.
Said, "Worthie lordis, for Goddis lufe of Hevin,
   To us lipper part of your almous deid."
   Than to thair cry nobill Troylus tuik heid;
Having pietie, neir by the place can pas
Quhair Cresseid sat, not witting what scho was.

Than upon him scho kest up baith her ene,
   And with ane blenk[2] it come in-to his thocht   [2] glance.
That he sum tyme hir face befoir had sene;
   Bot scho was in sic plye[3] he knew hir nocht.   [3] such plight.
   Yit than hir luik into his mynd it brocht
The sweit visage and amorous blenking
Of fair Cresseid, sumtyme his awin darling.

Na wonder was, suppois[4] in mynd that he   [4] although.
   Tuik hir figure sa sone, and lo, now, quhy:
The idole of ane thing in cace[5] may be   [5] chance.
   Sa deip imprentit in the fantasy
   That it deludis the wittis outwardly,
And sa appeiris in forme and lyke estait
Within the mynd, as it was figurait.

Ane spark of lufe than till his hart culd spring,
   And kendlit all his bodie in ane fyre
With hait fevir ane sweit and trimbilling
   Him tuik, quhill he was reddie to expyre;
   To beir his scheild his breist began to tyre;
Within ane quhyle he changit mony hew,
And nevertheless not ane ane-uther knew.

For knichtlie pietie and memoriall
  Of fair Cresseid ane gyrdill can he tak,
Ane purs of gold, and mony gay jowall,
  And in the skirt of Cresseid doun can swak[1]:
  Than raid away, and not ane word he spak,
Pensive in hart, quhill he come to the toun,
And for greit cair oft-syis[2] almaist fell doun.

The lipper folk to Cresseid than can draw,
  To se the equall distributioun
Of the almous, but quhan the gold they saw
  Ilk ane to uther prevelie can roun[3],
  And said, "Yone lord hes mair affectioun,
How-ever it be, unto yone lazarous,
Than to us all; we knaw be his almous."

"Quhat lord is yone," quod scho, "have ye na feill[4],
  Hes done to us so greit humanitie?"
"Yes," quod a lipper man, "I knaw him weill:
  Schir Troylus it is, gentill and fre[5]."
  Quhen Cresseid understude that it was he
Stiffer than steill thair stert ane bitter stound[6]
Throwout hir hart, and fell doun to the ground.

Quhen scho, ovircome with siching sair and sad,
  With mony cairfull cry and cald "Ochane!
Now is my breist with stormie stoundis stad[7],
  Wrappit in wo, ane wretch full will of wane[8]."
  Than swounit scho oft or scho culd refrane,
And ever in hir swouning cryit scho thus:—
"O, fals Cresseid, and trew knicht Troylus!

1 cast heavily.

2 ofttimes.

3 whisper.

4 knowledge.

5 noble.

6 stun of pain.

7 bested.

8 at loss for a dwelling.

"Thy lufe, thy lawtie[1], and thy gentilnes
   I countit small in my prosperitie;
Sa elevait I was in wantones,
   And clam upon the fickill quheill[2] sa hie;
   All faith and lufe I promissit to thé
Was in the self fickill and frivolous:
O, fals Cresseid, and trew knicht Troylus!

  [1] loyalty.

  [2] *i.e.* of Fortune. See *Kingis Quair.*

"For lufe of me thow keipt gude continance,
   Honest and chaist in conversatioun;
Of all wemen protectour and defence
   Thow was, and helpit thair opinioun.
   My mynd in fleschelie foull affectioun
Was inclynit to lustis lecherous.
Fy, fals Cresseid! O, trew knicht Troylus!

"Lovers be war, and tak gude heid about
   Quhome that ye lufe, for quhome ye suffer paine,
I lat yow wit, thair is richt few thairout
   Quhome ye may traist to have trew lufe againe:
   Preif[3] quhen ye will, your labour is in vaine.
Thairfoir I reid[4] ye tak thame as ye find,
For thay ar sad as widdercock[5] in wind.

  [3] Try.

  [4] counsel.

  [5] serious as weather-vane.

"Becaus I knaw the greit unstabilnes,
   Brukkil[6] as glas, into my-self I say,
Traisting in uther als greit unfaithfulnes,
   Als unconstant, and als untrew of fay.
   Thocht sum be trew, I wait richt few are thay.
Quha findis treuth, lat him his lady ruse[7];
Nane but myself, as now, I will accuse."

  [6] brittle.

  [7] extol.

Quhen this was said, with paper scho sat doun,
    And on this maneir maid hir testament:
"Heir I beteiche[1] my corps and carioun
    With wormis and with taidis[2] to be rent;
    My cop and clapper, and myne ornament,
And all my gold, the lipper folk sall have,
Quhen I am deid, to burie me in grave.

"This royall ring, set with this rubie reid,
    Quhilk Troylus in drowrie[3] to me send,
To him agane I leif it quhan I am deid,
    To mak my cairfull deid unto him kend[4]:
    Thus I conclude schortlie, and mak ane end.
My spreit I leif to Diane, quhair scho dwellis,
To walk with hir in waist woddis and wellis[5].

"O, Diomeid! thow hes baith broche and belt
    Quhilk Troylus gave me in takning
Of his trew lufe."—And with that word scho swelt[6].
    And sone ane lipper man tuik of the ring,
    Syne[7] buryit hir withouttin tarying.
To Troylus furthwith the ring he bair,
And of Cresseid the deith he can declair.

Quhen he had hard hir greit infirmitie,
    Hir legacie and lamentatioun,
And how scho endit in sic povertie,
    He swelt for wo, and fell doun in ane swoun,
    For greit sorrow his hart to birst was boun[8]:
Siching full sadlie, said, "I can no moir,
Scho was untrew, and wo is me thairfoir!"

[1] bequeath.
[2] toads.
[3] troth-token.
[4] known.
[5] marshes.
[6] expired.
[7] Afterwards.
[8] ready.

Sum said he maid ane tomb of merbell gray,
   And wrait hir name and superscriptioun,
And laid it on hir grave, quhair that scho lay,
   In goldin letteris conteining this ressoun:
"Lo, fair ladyis, Cresseid of Troyis toun,
Sumtyme countit the flour of womanheid,
Under this stane, late lipper, lyis deid!"

Now, worthie Wemen, in this ballet schort,
   Made for your worschip[1] and instructioun,
Of cheritie I monische and exhort
   Ming[2] not your lufe with fals deceptioun;
   Beir in your mynd this schort conclusioun
Of fair Cresseid, as I have said befoir.
Sen scho is deid I speik of hir no moir.

[1] honour.

[2] Mix.

PROLOGUE TO THE MORAL FABLES.

In middis of June, that joly sweit seasoun,
  Quhen that fair Phebus with his bemis bricht
Had dryit up the dew fra daill and doun,
  And all the land maid with his lemis[1] licht,
  In ane mornyng, betuix mid-day and nicht,
I rais and put all sleuth and sleip asyde,
And to ane wod I went alone, but gyde[2].

Sweit wes the smell of flouris quhyte and reid,
  The noyis of birdis richt delitious,
The bewis[3] braid blomit abone my heid,
  The ground growand with gersis gratious.
  Of all plesance that place wes plenteous,
With sweit odouris and birdis harmonie,
The morning myld, my mirth wes mair forthy[4].

The roisis reid arrayit on rone and ryce[5],
  The prymerois and the purpour viola;
To heir it wes ane poynt of Paradyce,
  Sic mirth the mavis and the merle couth ma[6].
  The blossummis blyith brak up on bank and bra[7],
The smell of herbis, and of foullis cry,
Contending quha suld haif the victorie.

[1] radiance.

[2] without guide.

[3] boughs.

[4] therefore.

[5] bushes and twigs.

[6] did make.

[7] hillside.

Me to conserve then fra the sonnis heit,
    Under the schadow of ane hawthorne grene
I lenit doun amang the flouris sweit,
    Syne[1] cled my heid and closit baith my ene.   [1] Presently.
    On sleip I fell amang thir bewis bene[2],   [2] abundant.
And, in my dreme, methocht come throw the schaw[3] [3] covert.
The fairest man that euer befoir I saw.

His gowne wes of ane claith als quhyte as milk,
    His chymeris[4] wes of chambelote[5] purpour broun; [4] loose light gown.
His hude of scarlet, bordourit weill with silk,   [5] camlet cloth.
    On hekillit wyis[6] untill his girdill doun;   [6] in manner of a cock's neck-feathers.
    His bonat round and of the auld fassoun;
His beird wes quhyte, his ene wes greit and gray,
With lokker[7] hair, quhilk ouer his schulderis lay.   [7] curling.

Ane roll of paper in his hand he bair,
    Ane swannis pen stikkand under his eir,
Ane inkhorne, with ane prettie gilt pennair[8],   [8] pen-case.
    Ane bag of silk, all at his belt can beir:
    Thus was he gudelie graithit[9] in his geir.   [9] clad.
Of stature large and with ane feirfull face
Evin quhair I lay he come ane sturdie pace;

And said, "God speid, my sone:" and I wes fane[10] [10] glad.
   Of that couth[11] word and of his cumpanie.   [11] familiar.
With reverence I salusit him agane,
    "Welcome, father:" and he sat doun me by.
    "Displeis you nocht, my gude maister, thocht I[12] [12] though I.
Demand your birth, your facultie, and name,
Quhy ye come heir, or quhair ye dwell at hame?"

"My sone," said he, "I am of gentill blude.
My native land is Rome, withouttin nay,

¹ went.

And in that towne first to the sculis I yude¹,
In civile law studyit full mony ane day,*

² dwelling.

And now my winning² is in hevin for ay.

³ am called.

Esope I hecht³; my wryting and my werk

⁴ known.

Is couth and kend⁴ to mony cunning clerk."

"O Maister Esope, poet laureate,
God wait⁵ ye ar full deir welcum to me.

⁵ knows.

Ar ye nocht he that all thir fabillis wrait

⁶ though they be feigned.

Quhilk in effect, suppois they fenyeit be⁶,
Ar full of prudence and moralitie?"
"Fair sone," said he, "I am the samin man."
God wait gif that my hert was merie than.

I said, "Esope, my maister venerabill,
I yow beseik hartlie, for cheritie,
Ye wald nocht disdayne to tell ane prettie fabill,
Concludand with ane gude moralitie."
Schaikand his heid, he said, "My sone, lat be;
For quhat is worth to tell ane fenyeit taill
Quhen haly preiching may no-thing availl?

"Now in this world me-think richt few or nane
To Goddis word that hes devotioun.
The eir is deif, the hart is hard as stane,
Now oppin sin without correctioun,
The ee inclynand to the eirth ay doun.
Sa roustie is the warld with canker blak
That now my taillis may lytill succour mak."

* Laing suggests that Henryson may in this passage be describing his own experience.

"Yit, gentill Schir," said I, "for my requeist,
   Nocht to displeis your fatherheid, I pray,
Under the figure of ane brutale beist
   Ane morall fabill ye wald denyie[1] to say.   [1] deign.
   Quha wait nor I may leir[2] and beir away   [2] learn.
Sum-thing thairby heirefter may availl?"
"I grant," quod he, and thus begouth ane taill.

THE TAILL OF THE UPLANDIS MOUS AND THE BURGES MOUS.

ESOPE, myne author, makis mentioun
Of twa myis, and thay wer sisteris deir,
Of quham the eldest dwelt in ane borrowis toun[1],
The uther wynnit uponland weill neir[2],
Richt solitar, quhyles under busk and breir,
Quhylis in the corne, and uther mennis skaith[3],
As outlawis dois, and levis on thair waith[4].

This rurall Mous in-to the wynter-tyde
Had hunger, cauld, and tholit[5] greit distress;
The uther Mous that in the burgh can byde
Wes gild-brother and maid ane free burgess,
Toll-fre als, but custum[6] mair or less,
And fredome had to ga quhair-ever scho list,
Amang the cheis in ark and meill in kist[7].

Ane tyme quhen scho wes full and unfute-sair
Scho tuke in mynde hir sister uponland,
And langit for to heir of hir weilfair,
To se quhat lyfe scho had under the wand[8];
Bairfute, allone, with pykestalf in hir hand,
As pure pilgryme scho passit out of toun
To seik hir sister baith over daill and doun.

[1] a royal borough.
[2] dwelt in the country conveniently near.
[3] damage.
[4] chance gettings.
[5] suffered.
[6] without taxes.
[7] chest.
[8] in state of subjection.

Furth mony wilsum[1] wayis can scho walk,   [1] lonely.
  Throw mosse and muir, throw bankis, busk, and breir
Scho ranne cryand, quhill scho cam to ane balk[2],   [2] ridge of lea land.
  "Cum furth to me my awin sister deir!
  Cry peip anis[3]!" With that the Mous culd heir, [3] once.
And knew her voce, as kinnisman will do,
Be verray kynd[4], and furth scho come hir to.   [4] By very kinship.

The hartlie[5] joy, Lord God! gif ye had sene,   [5] cordial.
  Was kithit[6] quhen that thir twa sisteris met,   [6] shown.
And greit kyndenes was schawin thame betuene;
  For quhylis thay leuch, and quhylis for joy they gret[7], [7] wept.
  Quhylis kissit sweit, and quhylis in armis plet[8];   [8] folded.
And thus thay fure quhill[9] soberit wes thair mude, [9] fared till.
Syne fute for fute unto the chalmer yude[10].   [10] went.

As I hard say, it was ane sober wane[11]   [11] dwelling.
  Of fog[12] and fairn full febillie wes maid,   [12] moss.
Ane sillie scheill[13] under ane steidfast stane,   [13] A frail sheiling, shelter.
  Of quhilk the entres wes nocht hie nor braid;
  And in the samyn thay went but mair abaid[14], [14] without more delay.
Withoutin fyre or candill birnand bricht,
For commounlie sic pykeris[15] luffis not licht.   [15] such pilferers.

Quhen thay wer lugit thus, thir selie[16] myse,   [16] these poor.
  The youngest sister unto hir butterie yeid,
And brocht furth nuttis and peis in-stead of spyce.
  Gif this wes gude fair I do it on thame besyde.
  The burges Mous prompit furth in pryde,
And said, "Sister, is this your daylie fude?"
"Quhy not," quod scho, "is nocht this meit rycht
    gude?"

"Na, be my saull, I think it bot ane scorne."
   "Madame," quod scho, "ye be the mair to blame.
My mother said, sister, quhen we were borne,
   That ye and I lay baith within ane wame:
   I keip the rate and custume of my dame,
And of my leving in-to povertie,
For landis haif we nane in propertie."

"My fair sister," quod scho, "haif me excusit.
   This rude dyet and I can nocht accord.
Till tender meit my stomok is ay usit,
   For quhylis I fair als weill as ony lord.
   Thir widderit[1] peis and nuttis, or[2] thay be bord,
Will brek my teith and mak my wame full sklender[3],
Quhilk wes befoir usit to meittis tender."

"Weill, weill, sister," quod the rurall Mous,
   "Gif it pleis yow, sic thingis as ye se heir,
Baith meit and drink, harberie[4] and hous,
   Sal be your awin, will ye remane all yeir;
   Ye sall it haif with blyith and merie cheir,
And that suld mak the maissis[5] that ar rude,
Amang freindis richt tender and wonder gude.

"Quhat plesure is in feistis delicate,
   The quhilkis ar gevin with ane glowmand brow?
Ane gentill hart is better recreat
   With blyith curage than seith[6] till him ane kow:
   Ane modicum is mair for till allow,
Swa that gude-will be kerver at the dais,
Than thrawin vult[7] and mony spycit mais."

[1] These withered.
[2] ere.
[3] lank.
[4] lodging.
[5] messes, provisions.
[6] give possession of.
[7] ill-humoured look.

For all hir merie exhortatioun,
   This burges Mous had lytill will to sing,
Bot hevilie scho kest hir browis doun,
   For all the daynteis that scho culd hir bring.
     Yit at the last scho said, half in hething[1],   1 scorn.
"Sister, this victuall and your royall feist
May weill suffice unto ane rurall beist.

"Lat be this hole, and cum in-to my place,
   I sall to yow schaw be experience
My Gude-Fryday is better nor your Pace[2].   2 Easter-feast.
   My dische-weschingis is worth your haill[3] expence; 3 whole.
     I haif housis anew[4] of greit defence;   4 enough.
Of cat nor fall-trap I haif na dreid."
"I grant," quod scho; and on togidder thay yeid[5]. 5 went.

In stubbill array, throw rankest gers and corne,
   And under buskis[6], prevelie couth they creip.   6 bushes.
The eldest wes the gyde and went beforne,
   The younger to hir wayis tuke gude keip[7].   7 heed.
     On nicht thay ran, and on the day can sleip,
Quhill in the morning or the laverock sang[8]   8 ere lark sang.
Thay fand the toun, and in blythlie couth gang[9]. 9 did go.

Nocht fer fra thyne[10] unto ane worthie wane   10 thence.
   This burges brocht thame sone quhar thai suld be.
Without God speid thair herberie wes tane
   In-to ane spence[11] with vittell greit plentie,   11 larder.
     Baith cheis and butter upone thair skelfis hie[12], 12 shelves high.
And flesche and fische aneuch, baith fresche and salt,
And sekkis full of meill and eik of malt.

Efter, quhen thay disposit wer to dyne,
[1] washed.   Withouttin grace thay wesche[1] and went to meit,
With all the coursis that cuikis culd defyne,
[2] cut off in great slices.   Muttoun and beif strikin in tailyeis greit[2];
And lordis fair thus couth thay counterfeit,
Except ane thing—thay drank the watter cleir
Instead of wyne ; bot yit thay maid gude cheir.

[3] raillery.   With blyith upcast[3] and merie countenance
[4] asked her guest.   The eldest sister sperit at hir gaist[4],
Gif that scho be ressone fand difference
[5] sorry.   Betuix that chalmer and hir sarie[5] nest?
"Yea dame," quod scho, "How lang will this lest?"
[6] wot.   "For evermair, I wait[6], and langer to."
"Gif it be swa ye ar at eis," quod scho.

[7] To add to.
[8] second course.   Til eik[7] thair cheir ane subcharge[8] furth scho brocht,
[9] oats with husks removed.   Ane plait of grottis[9] and ane dische full of meill,
[10] wheaten cakes.   Thraf-caikkis[10] als I trow scho spairit nocht
Aboundantlie about hir for to deill,
[11] a rich bread.
[12] jelly.   And mane[11] fyne scho brocht in-steid of geill[12],
[13] stolen.   And ane quhyte candill out of ane coffer stall[13]
In-steid of spyce to gust thair mouth withall.

[14] till.   Thus maid thay merie quhill[14] thay micht na mair,
And, Haill, Yule, haill ! cryit upon hie.
Yit efter joy oftymes cummis cair,
And troubill efter greit prosperitie,
Thus, as thay sat in all thair jolitie,
[15] butler.   The Spenser[15] come with keyis in his hand,
Opinit the dure, and thame at denner fand.

Thay taryit nocht to wesche as I suppose,
   But on to ga quha that micht formest win[1].   1 attain.
The burges had ane hoill, and in scho gois,
   Hir sister had na hoill to hyde hir in;
   To se that selie Mous it wes greit syn,
So desolate and will of ane gude reid[2],   2 at a loss for
                            good counsel.
For veray dreid scho fell in swoun neir deid.

Bot, as God wald, it fell ane happy cace[3]   3 chance.
   The Spenser had na laser for to byde,
Nouther to seik nor serche, to skar nor chace,
   Bot on he went, and left the dure up wyde.
   The bald burges his passing weill hes spyde;
Out of hir hoill scho come, and cryit on hie,
"How fair ye sister? Cry peip quhair-ever ye be?"

This rural Mous lay flatling on the ground,
   And for the deith scho wes full sair dredand,
For till hir hart straik mony wofull stound[4];   4 pain-shocks.
   As in ane fever scho trimbillit fute and hand,
   And quhan hir sister in sic ply[5] hir fand,   5 such plight.
For verray pietie scho began to greit[6],   6 weep.
Syne confort hir with wordis hunny sweit.

"Quhy ly ye thus? Ryse up my sister deir!
   Cum to your meit, this perrell is overpast."
The uther answerit hir, with hevie cheir,
   "I may nocht eit, sa sair I am agast.
   I had levir[7] thir fourtie dayis fast,   7 liefer, rather.
With watter-caill[8], and to gnaw benis or peis,   8 broth made
                            without meat.
Than all your feist, in this dreid and diseis."

With fair tretie yit scho gart[1] hir upryse,
  And to the burde thay went and togidder sat,
And scantlie had thay drunkin anis or twyse
  Quhen in come Gib-Hunter, our jolie cat,
  And bad God-speid.   The burges up with that,
And till the hoill scho went as fyre of flint.

2 Grimalkin.
3 seized.
Bawdronis[2] the uther be the bak hes hint[3].

Fra fute to fute he kest hir to and fra,

4 playful.
  Quhylis up, quhylis doun, als cant[4] as ony kid.

5 Sometimes.
Quhylis[5] wald he lat hir run under the stra,

6 hide-and-seek.
  Quhylis wald he wink, and play with her buk-hid[6]
  Thus to the selie Mous greit pane he did,
Quhill at the last, throw fortune and gude hap,
Betuix ane burde and the wall scho crap.

7 partition.
And up in haist behind ane parpalling[7]
  Scho clam so hie that Gilbert micht not get hir,

8 claw.
Syne be the cluke[8] thair craftelie can hing
  Till he wes gane, hir cheir wes all the bettir;

9 prevent.
  Syne doun scho lap quhen thair wes nane to let[9]
    hir,
And to the burges Mous loud can scho cry,
"Fairweill, sister, thy feist heir I defy!"

10 Thy feast is
  mingled.
"Thy mangerie is myngit[10] all with cair,

11 sauce.
  Thy guse is gude, thy gansell[11] sour as gall;
The subcharge of thy service is bot sair,
  So sall thow find heir-efterwart may fall.

12 partition wall.
  I thank yone courtyne and yone perpall wall[12]
Of my defence now fra ane crewell beist.
Almychty God keip me fra sic ane feist!

"Wer I in-to the kith[1] that I come fra,   [1] familiar place.
   For weill nor wo, suld never cum agane."
With that scho tuke hir leif and furth can ga,
   Quhylis throw the corne and quhylis throw the
      plane.
   Quhen scho wes furth and fre scho wes ful fane[2],   [2] glad.
And merilie merkit[3] unto the mure.   [3] hastened, *lit.* rode.
I can nocht tell how efterwart scho fure[4],   [4] fared.

Bot I hard say scho passit to hir den,
   Als warme als woll, suppose[5] it wes nocht greit,   [5] although.
Full benely stuffit, baith but and ben[6],   [6] abundantly furnished, both outer and inner room.
   Of beinis and nuttis, peis, ry, and quheit;
   Quhen-ever scho list scho had aneuch to eit
In quyet and eis, withoutin ony dreid;
Bot to hir sisteris feist na mair scho yeid.

MORALITAS.

Friendis, ye may fynd, and[7] ye will tak heid,   [7] if.
   In-to this fabill ane gude moralitie.
As fitchis myngit ar with nobill feid,
   Swa intermynglit is adversitie
   With eirthlie joy, swa that na estait is fre,
And als troubill and sum vexatioun;
   And namelie[8] thay quhilk climmis up maist hie,   [8] notoriously.
That ar nocht content with small possessioun.

Blissit be sempill lyfe withoutin dreid!
   Blissit be sober feist in quyetie!
Quha hes aneuch, of na mair hes he neid,
   Thocht it be lytill in-to quantitie.

Greit abondance and blind prosperitie
Oftymes makis ane evill conclusioun.
    The sweitest lyfe thairfor in this cuntrie

Is sickernes[1], with small possessioun.

O wantoun man, that usis for to feid
    Thy wambe, and makis it ane god to be,
Luik to thy-self! I warne thee wele, but dreid[2]:
    The cat cummis and to the mous hes ee.
    Quhat vaillis than thy feist and rialtie,
With dreidfull hart and tribulacioun?
    Thairfoir best thing in eird, I say, for me,
Is blyithnes in hart, with small possessioun.

Thy awin fyre, my friend, sa it be bot ane gleid[3],
    It warmis weill, and is worth gold to thee;
And Solomon sayis, gif that thow will reid,
    " Under the hevin it can nocht better be
    Than ay be blyith and leif in honestie."
Quhairfoir I may conclude be this ressoun,
    Of eirthly joy it beiris maist degrie,
Blyithnes in hart, with small possessioun.

WILLIAM DUNBAR.

WILLIAM DUNBAR.

A LIKENESS in some respects has already been remarked between the temper and condition of Rome in the time of Augustus and of Scotland in the time of James IV. The resemblance may even be traced in the personality of the poets of the two epochs. Gavin Douglas, the courtly poet-churchman of James the Fourth's time, may in some degree be likened to the grave and stately Virgil, whose work he translated; and still more closely may a likeness be remarked, in character and fortunes, between the Roman Horace and the most brilliant poet of the middle ages in Scotland, William Dunbar. Both of these latter were courtiers by compulsion, longing continually to escape to the quiet of easy ways. Both were keen men of the world and epicureans by nature, loving pleasure, and without any burning desire to inflame the world with new ideals; both had a twinkle of the eye for the peccadilloes of themselves or their friends, and a curl of the lip that could give a bitter turn to satire upon their enemies; while both used supreme poetic gifts, prodigal of form and colour, largely for the purpose of securing material favours, and as a resource for the expression of private and personal feeling. If in anything they differed it was that while the Roman poet apparently with calm wisdom took what fortune brought him, and made the most of it, there was in the heart of the Scottish makar* a hunger, wistful, eager, that was to ask to the end unsatisfied. Behind all the glory of those days the reign of James IV. was a time of failing faith in Scotland. The ancient religion of the country was crumbling in corruption to ruin, and men, Dunbar among them, were seeking, in the absence of a larger vision, to live for the immediate pleasures of the hour. Of the dweller in such a time, the heart self-centred in its own desires, the ancient saying remains perennially true, "He that seeketh his life shall lose it."

Born, it is supposed, about the year 1460, Dunbar, from allusions in his famous "Flyting with Kennedy," appears to have been a native of Lothian and a member of Cospatrick's clan. Laing was inclined to consider him a grandson of Sir Patrick Dunbar of Beill in East Lothian, a younger son of the tenth Earl of March. In 1475 he was sent to the University of St. Andrews, where he received the degree of B.A. in 1477, and of M.A. in 1479. His life for the following twenty years is but vaguely known. It is possible that he pursued his studies at Oxford, one of his poems bearing the colophon "Quod Dunbar

---

* Dr. Irving quotes from Sir Philip Sidney's *Apologie for Poetry* a remark upon the similarity between the European word "poet," from the Greek ποιειν, to make, and the native northern term "makar," or maker ; "which name, how high and incomparable a title it is, I had rather were knowne by marking the scope of other sciences, then by my partiall allegation."

at Oxinfurde." But there is an Oxenford Castle near Edinburgh whence the poem may have been dated, or Dunbar may have written it when casually visiting the English university town. From his poem "How Dunbar wes desyrd to be ane Freir" it is to be gathered that, entering the Order of St. Francis, the Gray Friars, he spent several years of novitiate as a wandering preacher, making good cheer in every pleasant town between Berwick and Calais, mounting the pulpit at Dernton and Canterbury, even crossing the Straits of Dover, and exercising his profession through Picardy. In these wanderings he pleads guilty to "mony wrink and wyle, quhilk mycht be flemit with na haly watter;" from which confession it may be understood that he was neither much better nor much worse than the other preaching friars of his time.

A little later, from allusions in his poems, he appears to have entered the service of James IV., and to have been employed on several of that monarch's numerous embassies to foreign courts. It is known, at any-rate, that in 1491 he was residing at Paris, probably in connection with the embassy there. In 1500 he received from his royal master a pension of £10 as a foretaste of favours to come. In the following year he went to England with the ambassadors sent to conclude negotiations for the marriage of James to the Princess Margaret. There during the state festivities he was styled "the Rhymer of Scotland," and upon at least one occasion he is recorded as having given evidence of his powers. "In the Cristmas week," says the chronicler,

"the Mair had to dyner the ambassadors of Scotland,
whom accompanyed my Lord Chaunceler and other
Lords of the realm; where, sittying at dyner, ane of
the said Scottis givying attendance upon a Bishop
Ambassador, the which was reputed to be a Proto-
notary of Scotland and servant of the Ld. Bishop,
made this balade." The "balade," which is given
at length, is that beginning, "London thou art of
townes *A per se.*"*

During the embassy Dunbar is known to have
received from Henry VII. two separate gifts of £6
13s. 4d., and on his return to Edinburgh the
Treasurer's accounts show him to have received £5
in addition to his salary. Apart from the joyous
occasion, it is probable that these gifts mark the
special approbation of the poet's services by the
English and Scottish monarchs. It was at this period
(1503) that, besides several poems describing the
attractions of the young princess, he composed his
magnificent allegory, "The Thrissil and the Rois,"
upon the marriage of James and Margaret. This
work may be taken to have crowned his services as
laureate. At anyrate it is certain that from the time
of its composition he lived much at court, apparently
on familiar terms with the king and queen. In one
poem he describes "A Dance in the Quenis Chalmer"
in which he himself takes part.

> Than cam in Dunbar the mackar;
> On all the flure there was nane frackar.

* The incident is quoted from MS. Cott. Vitell. A.xvi., by
Dr. Æneas Mackay (*Introduction to Dunbar*), who notes that
though the reference is to Dunbar, it was Foreman who was the
Protonotary.

To another composition, "The Petition of the Gray Horse, Auld Dunbar," in which the poet begs to be housed and stalled, there are appended, under the heading "Responsio Regis," eight lines of direction to the royal treasurer, which, there is fair reason to suppose, may have been added by the king's own hand.

But with whatever familiarity James was willing to treat Dunbar at court, and however far he may have seen fit to assist him in other ways, he refrained from putting the coping-stone upon his benefits, and died without granting the chief object of the poet's ambition, a church benefice. There is no reason for doubting the kindliness of the king's regard for his courtier. In 1504 Dunbar performed mass before James for the first time, and on that occasion was munificently rewarded. In 1507 his pension was increased to £20, and in 1510 to £80, to be paid until he should be promoted to a benefice of £100 or more. And in 1511 he appears to have been in the queen's train when she visited the north of Scotland, to judge from the circumstantial description of her welcome in his poem "Blyth Aberdein." Nevertheless, for reasons which can now only be conjectured, the long-hoped-for benefice was never conferred. It has been suggested that for this omission Dunbar's own imprudence may have been to blame. By his own confession his career as a friar had not been of the most circumspect sort, and many of his poems are, it must be confessed, both indecent and irreverent, one of them, "We that are here in Hevin's

Glory," being a deliberate profane parody of the
litanies, while another, " To the Quene," contains
language which might offend a modern courtezan.
Conspicuous piety, however, was by no means neces-
sary to the candidate for church preferment in those
days, and only the most open and gross profligacy could
have stood in the way of the promotion of an
ecclesiastic.   A more probable cause of Dunbar's
prayers for a benefice remaining unanswered, Laing
has suggested, might be the desire of James to keep
the poet about his court.   It is well known to have
been part of the policy of that gallant and enlightened
sovereign to retain about him a court of such
learning and brilliance as should both impress the
ambassadors of foreign powers and render illustrious
the country's annals of the time.   Whatever the
reason, though Dunbar never ceased, by petition,
innuendo, and satire, to beg for what he desired,
James with a smile, as little embarrassed as might be,
appears to have put the petition aside, making up for the
main refusal by sundry gifts, pensions, and perquisites.
The last of these, a payment of the small sum of forty-
two shillings, appears in the treasurer's accounts for
1st April, 1513.   Five months afterwards the fortunes
of Dunbar were to fall with the pride of Scotland, the
gallant James himself, on the field of Flodden.

The cloud which then settled on the country
obscures the remainder of the poet's life.   It is pos-
sible that his pension continued to be paid, the
treasurer's accounts from 1513 to 1515, and from 1518
to 1522 having been lost.   And it is just possible that

before marching to the field James conferred upon
Dunbar his long-craved-for desire, a benefice. But
the probability is that with the death of the king,
and the unpopularity of the queen, the lamp of
the poet's hopes went out, leaving the rest of his life
in the darkness of disappointment. From several of
his poems it is to be gathered that he lived to an
advanced age. He was alive in 1517, as one of his
compositions celebrates the passing of the Regent
Albany into France in that year. The year 1520 is
generally assigned as the date of the poet's death,
and it is at least certain that he was dead ten years
later, since the fact is alluded to in the prologue to
" The Complaynt of the Papingo " written by Sir
David Lindsay about 1530.

Before he died a change seems to have come upon
the spirit of Dunbar. The levity of his earlier years
appears to have been forsaken, and several of his
poems are composed in a moral and religious strain.
It would seem as if at last "the false world's wavering,"
the bitterness of final disappointment, had broken his
gay and ambitious heart, and filled him with a pro-
found sadness. It was a fit if sorrowful end for a
career so full of contradictions. At war throughout
with destiny, denied the worldly prize he craved,
debarred by his vows from the solace of woman's
love, Dunbar's life was typical of the *genus irritabile.*
A parallel cannot fail to be seen between his fate and
the fate of his great successor Robert Burns. Both,
with hearts too keenly alive and eager for the joy of
life, were doomed to meet only "the slings and arrows

of outrageous fortune," and in both their real achievement, the blaze of poetry which has been their magnificent legacy to Scotland, was struck, as if by accident, out of too sharp contact with the flinty ways of life. But between the two there was a vital difference. While the sorrows of the Ayrshire poet opened his heart to the pathos of existence and gave to his verse its high tragic quality, its profound pity and tenderness, disappointment only filled the heart of Dunbar with bitterness and drove the iron into his soul.

The first volume issued from the Scottish press, the book printed by Chepman & Myllar in 1508, contained several of Dunbar's poems, including "The Thrissil and the Rois," "The Goldyn Targe," and "The Lament for the Makaris." Only one copy of this volume, that in the Advocates' Library, is known to exist, but from this copy the book was reprinted in 1827 with the title of *The Knightly Tale of Gologras and Gawane, and other Ancient Poems.* The majority of the poet's existing works have been preserved in manuscripts, the Bannatyne MS., 1568, the Asloan MS., 1575, the Maitland MS. in the Pepysian Library, and the Reidpeth MS., 1623, in the University Library, Cambridge, each containing several. From these sources detached poems were printed in the collections of Allan Ramsay, John Pinkerton, Lord Hailes, and James Sibbald. But it remained to Mr. David Laing in 1834 to issue the first collected edition of the works of Dunbar, as "the best monument that could be erected to his genius." A supplement to this was issued in 1875 ; in 1873 appeared in Edinburgh " The Works of William Dunbar, including his Life," by James Paterson ; and in 1883 a new edition of the poet's works was prepared for the Scottish Text Society by Mr. John Small, M.A., with, in 1888, a copious introduction by Dr. Æneas Mackay. Dunbar has also received attention on the Continent, Dr. Mackay declaring Prof. Schipper's edition (Berlin, 1884), to be the best book on the poet.

Apart from the works which must inevitably have been lost, no fewer than a hundred and one poems remain to the present day accredited to the genius of Dunbar. Of eleven of these, including the scarcely doubtful " Freiris of Berwik," the authenticity is not absolutely proved, but the remaining ninety include the work upon which his chief fame rests. No early poet has attempted so great a variety, either in subject, in style, or in form of verse, as Dunbar. In varying temper and on varying occasion he has essayed nearly every rôle of poetry, and to each he has given the supreme touch of the master-hand. Allegory, satire, and moral musing, invective, comic narrative, and natural description, personal pleading, courtly compliment, and the wild riot of Rabelaisian farce, all are here, treading each inimitably its appropriate measure. Smock and gay doublet, blackthorn cudgel and friar's hood, flashing rapier and dazzling pageant dress, each is assumed as occasion asks, and none is laid down till its part has been played to perfection.

In the stateliest efforts of his muse Dunbar followed the poetic fashion of his time. " The Goldyn Targe "

and "The Thrissil and the Rois" are allegories in the
strain introduced to Scotland by the great poem of
James the First.   Of these two "The Thrissil and the
Rois" shares the advantage of "The Kingis Quair" in
having for its subject a historic fact.   An interest beyond
that of most allegories is added to Dunbar's poem by
the knowledge that it celebrates the union between
James IV. and the Princess Margaret, daughter of
Henry VII., which was to have such momentous issue
three generations later in the union of the English and
Scottish crowns.   The event is celebrated with a rich-
ness of colour, imagery, and music, and a wealth and
splendour of description which are hardly to be rivalled
in the same field.   In this poem, describing the
young queen, Dunbar rises to his noblest vision of
womanhood, and it may well be believed that such
an epithalamium set the seal to a lasting friendship
between the royal pair and the poet.   By Langhorne
in his *Genius and Valour* it was named as the chief
work of its author.

> In nervous strains Dunbar's bold music flows
> And Time still spares the Thistle and the Rose.

"The Goldyn Targe," nevertheless, has by some been
considered Dunbar's masterpiece in that style of poetry.
"All the beauties of 'The Thistle and the Rose,'"
says Dr. Merry Ross, "are here seen in rarer and
more sparkling perfection.   The scenes and figures
are painted in brighter colours, and the music of the
verse has a more voluptuous swell."   The intention
of the poem is to set forth that the golden targe, or
shield of reason, proves an untrustworthy defence

against the assaults of love. From its gorgeous opening the pageant of the poet's fantasy moves on, glowing and glittering, fair, and alive with swaying, sensuous imagery, without a lapse, to the end, a picture appropriate to, and worthy of, the vital truth which it illustrates.

Another brief allegory by Dunbar on a like subject, beginning "Sen that I am a Presoneir," has a charm of its own in its lighter but still perfect setting.

To Chaucer must be attributed the suggestion of the two considerable poems, "The Tua Mariit Wemen and the Wedo" and "The Freiris of Berwik." The latter is a comic tale, modelled exactly on Chaucer's style, but related with a sustained vigour and interest which characterises only the best of that poet's work. It is to be regretted that the authorship of the poem is not absolutely attested. "If," says a competent critic, "'The Freiris of Berwik' is not the work of Dunbar, then Scotland has a nameless poet of the same age, who, in comic humour, richness of invention, knowledge of human nature, skill in the arrangement of detail, and a charming vivacity of narrative, rivals the author of the *Canterbury Tales*." "The Freiris of Berwik" furnished Allan Ramsay with something more than the suggestion of his tale of "The Monk and the Miller's Wife." "The Tua Mariit Wemen and the Wedo" treats of a subject somewhat similar to that of Chaucer's "Wife of Bath's Tale," but the methods and morals of the two poems are widely different. Dunbar's poem "presents us with the only specimen of blank verse which the ancient

Scottish language affords." The rhythm is of the kind
employed by the early Anglo-Saxon poets, and bor-
rowed from them by the author of " Piers Plowman."
Alliteration supplies the place of rhyme. In each
double line there should be three words beginning
with the same letter, and by the rule two of these
should occur in the first and the other should begin
the second part of the line. Neither Dunbar nor the
author of "Piers Plowman," however, followed the rule
exactly. The Scottish poem has been justly praised
for its richness of description, though its language,
owing to the necessities of the versification, may
sometimes appear obscure. The opening passage, as
perhaps the finest, may be quoted :

Apon the Midsumer ewin, mirriest of nichtis,
I muvit furth allane, neir as midnicht wes past,
Besyd ane gudlie grein garth, full of gay flouris,
Hegeit of ane huge hicht with hawthorne treis,
Quhairon ane bird on ane bransche so birst out hir notis
That neuer ane blythfullar bird was on the beuche harde.
Quhat throw the sugarat sound of hir sang glaid
And throw the sauar sanatiue of the sueit flouris,
I drew in derne to the dyk to dirkin efter myrthis ;
The dew donkit the daill and dynnit the foulis.
     I hard, vnder ane holyn hewinlie grein hewit,
Ane hie speiche, at my hand, with hautand wourdis ;
With that in haist to the hege so hard I inthrang
That I was heildit with hawthorn and with heynd leveis.
Throw pykis of the plet thorne I presandlie luikit
Gif ony persoun wald approche within that plesand garding.
     I saw thre gay ladeis sit in ane grein arbeir,
All grathit in-to garlandis of fresche gudelie flouris.
So glitterit as the gold wer thair glorius gilt tressis,
Quhill all the gressis did gleme of the glaid hewis.
Kemmit was thair cleir hair, and curiouslie sched

Attour thair schulderis doun schyre, schyning full bricht,
With curches, cassin thame abone, of kirsp cleir and thin.
Thair mantillis grein war as the gress that grew in May sessoun,
Fetrit with thair quhyt fingaris about thair fair sydis.
Of ferlifull fyne favour war thair faceis meik,
All of flurist fairheid, as flouris in June,
Quhyt, seimlie, and soft, as the sweit lillies,
New vpspred vpon spray, as new spynist rose.
    Arrayit ryallie about with mony rich wardour,
That Nature full nobillie annamalit fine with flouris
Off alkin hewis under hewin that ony heynd knew,
Fragrant, all full of fresche odour fynest of smell,
Ane marbre tabile coverit wes befoir thai thre ladeis
With ryale cowpis apon rawis, full of ryche wynis.
And of thir fair wlonkes, with tua [that] weddit war with lordis,
Ane wes ane wedow I wist, wantoun of laitis.
And as thai talkit at the tabill of mony taill funde
Thay wauchtit at the wicht wyne, and warit out wourdis,
And syne thai spak more spedelie, and sparit no materis.

The "materis" treated of in this long conversation
are the opinions of the three ladies upon the obliga-
tions of marriage. The sentiments uttered are of the
most profligate sort, one of the wives expressing her
wishes thus :

Chenyeis ay ar to eschew, and changeis ar sueit.
Sic cursit chance till eschew had I my chois anis
Out of the chenyeis of ane churle I chaip suld for euir.
God gif matrimony were made to mell for ane yeir !
It war bot monstrous to be mair bot gif our myndis pleisit.

Dunbar's idea of womanhood touches its nadir in
this poem, and the effect is the more unwholesome from
the fact that the most licentious and sensual imaginings
are put into the mouths, not of degraded women, but
of the most lovely and modest-seeming of the sex.
    But it is when he leaves the initiative of others

behind and enters a realm of his own that Dunbar's
powers are seen in their full strength and exuberance.
"The Dance of the Sevin Deidly Synnis" is the most
powerful of all his works.   No such daring grotesquerie
ever was painted, before or since, for a carnival riot
on the eve of Lent.   In "Tam o' Shanter" there
is a familiar touch which softens the horrible, and
Goethe's "Walpurgis Night" has a mournful human
under-strain; but here the picture is unrelieved; an
iron curtain seems pushed aside, and a moment's
bewildering glimpse is caught of the actual lurid
turmoil of hell.   The poem is realistic and fearfully
vivid in its details, and in the days when it was
written must have appeared to its readers as horrible
as it is startling.

In the same lower region the poet set the scene of
another grotesque production, "The Turnament,"
a contest between a tailor and souter, or shoemaker.
This and the long and somewhat obscure "Flyting of
Dunbar and Kennedy" furnish specimens of such
extravagant scurrility and dirt, without containing
anything morally impure, as it would be difficult to
match out of Rabelais.   It is curious to think that
the "Flyting," with all its villanous abuse, was
probably nothing more than a friendly tilting match
between two famous free-lances.   Irving notes the
fact that a similar abusive contest was carried on
in the time of Lorenzo de Medici by Luigi Pulci
and Matteo Franco, who were nevertheless close
friends, and that in our country the example of
Dunbar and Kennedy was followed by James V.

and Sir David Lindsay, and by Montgomery and Hume. Formal rules, indeed, for such encounters were laid down by James VI. in his *Art of Poesie.* The elaborate "Flyting," nevertheless, it is to be feared, is apt to prove somewhat wearisome reading now-a-days. The "Turnament," on the other hand, with its wild, if coarse, fun, would appear to have excited the ire of members of the crafts burlesqued, and under the guise of an apology to the offended guildsmen the poet wrote an "Amendis," which is one of the most salt of his satires.

It was personal feeling, however, which gave their bitterest tang to many of the satires of Dunbar. Two of these concern a certain Italian impostor, one John Damian from Lombardy, who, on the strength of a professed ability to convert the baser metals into gold, effected a footing as physician and alchemist at the court of James IV., and in 1504 was made Abbot of Tungland in Galloway. Three years later, according to Bishop Lesley,* having failed to produce the promised gold, Damian, to maintain his reputation, gave out that he would fly from the walls of Stirling Castle to France. This he actually attempted, and on the appointed day, furnished with a huge pair of wings, he plunged from the castle rampart ; but instead of flying through the heavens he fell to the ground beneath and broke his thigh-bone. Such a subject was not to be missed by the satirist, affording, as it did, a contrast between the high preferment bestowed on quackery and the neglect to which modest merit was

* The historian of James the Fourth's reign.

relegated. In "The Fenyeit Freir of Tungland" the poet has made the most of the episode. It is "a rare specimen of burlesque spiced with gay malice."

In many poems Dunbar did not hesitate to set forth his grievance in plain words to the king, coming in several cases as near to the accent of reproach as was politic in addressing a sovereign. Sometimes these appeals for promotion are almost pathetic in their expression of the sickness that comes of hope deferred; sometimes, though less frequently, they are couched in a humorous form, as in "The Petition of the Gray Horse." They give here and there a pitiful revelation of the poet in his need, improvident while his means last, watching with a sigh the constant preferment of duller souls, while age creeps fast upon him, and the hunger of his heart remains unsatisfied.

In one considerable class of his poems, as has been said, a moral and philosophical vein is touched, and it is supposed that these were chiefly written in his latter days. Some of them, such as "Best to be Blyth" and "Meditatioun in Wynter," take a cheerful turn, but, like the personal petitions addressed to the king, most are tinged with the shade of melancholy. All, however, show a deep appreciation of the peculiarities of human nature, and an accurate gauging of the secret springs of human motives, foibles, and passions. "The Lament for the Makaris" is the best known of these moral poems, and is, besides, a specimen of the sort of macaronic verse, the fantastic mixture of tongues, which was then a poetic fashion. The reflections of the poem are simple, and its tone uniformly sad. Youth and loveliness, bravery and wit, all come to an end, and even the poets, for all their sweet service, cannot escape the hand of death. As a historical document, a record of the names of early Scottish singers, this composition has been of the greatest value; but it is something more than this; it is a noble elegy on the illustrious dead, sung by lips that have thirsted and found life bitter.

Of Dunbar's work and character as a whole numerous estimates have been made. Merry Ross appears inclined to consider as his highest quality " a certain unique intensity of feeling," the expression of that " passionate or indomitable force, even tending to extravagance and one-sided zeal, which distinguishes and differentiates the people of the north from their southern neighbours, and is particularly conspicuous in all their foremost men."* Scott did not hesitate to set Dunbar in several respects upon a level with Chaucer. " In brilliancy of fancy," he declares, " in force of description, in the power of conveying moral precepts with terseness, and marking lessons of life with conciseness and energy, in quickness of satire and in poignancy of humour, the Northern Makar may boldly aspire to rival the Bard of Woodstock."† On the makar's vital shortcoming, on the other hand, the critics seem agreed. Brilliant beyond any of the poet company he sang, Dunbar still lacked one thing to set him in the ranks of the greatest of the immortals. That place is reserved for those

---

* *Scottish History and Literature*, p. 215.
† *Memoirs of George Bannatyne*, 1829, p. 14.

alone who, supreme in other gifts, possess also the key to the fountain of tears. Humour the wildest, wit the keenest, imagination the richest and most glowing, illumine his page; but nowhere, except lightly in "The Lament for the Makaris," and in one little love poem perhaps, does he stir the deeper currents of the heart. No storm of tragic passion or tenderness sweeps through his verse, the joys and sorrows, the hopes and fears, the toils and hardships of common life were nothing to him. The gentler part of existence was shut from him, with the pure ministry of womanhood, by his priestly vows, and while lord alike of beauty and terror, of bewitching fantasies and mocking laughter, he leaves one side of life, and that the truest, entirely untouched. His work reflects the ideals and life of Scotland at a time when the old world with its faith was passing away. Nothing of the warm breath and promise of a spring-time is to be found in his pages. His gorgeous colour and splendid imaginings are like the glories of the autumn forest, the fires in the withering leaf.

In the spirit of his time is to be found at once the keynote and the shortcoming of Dunbar's life and poetry. In an atmosphere of nobler aspiration his genius might have burned with a purer flame. As it is, he holds a great place, second only to that of Robert Burns, in the gallery of Scottish poets.

THE GOLDYN TARGE.

YGHT as the stern of day begouth to schyne,
    Quhen gone to bed war Vesper and Lucyne,
        I raise and by a rosere[1] did me rest;   [1] rose-tree.
Wp sprang the goldyn candill matutyne
With clere depurit bemes cristallyne,
    Glading the mirry foulis in thair nest;
    Or[2] Phebus was in purpur kaip revest   [2] ere.
Wp sprang the lark, the hevinis menstrale fyne,
    In May, in-till a morow[3] myrthfullest.   [3] morning.

Full angellike thir birdis sang thair houris[4]   [4] morning prayers.
Within thair courtyns[5] grene in-to thair bouris,   [5] gardens.
    Apparalit quhyte and red, wyth blumys suete;
Anamalit was the felde wyth all colouris,
The perly droppis schuke in silvir schouris,
    Quhill all in balme did branch and levis flete[6];   [6] float.
    Depairt fra Phebus, did Aurora grete[7],   [7] weep.
Hir cristall teris I saw hyng on the flouris,
    Quhilk he for lufe all drank vp with his hete.

For mirth of May, wyth skippis and wyth hoppis,
The birdis sang vpon the tender croppis[8]   [8] tree tops.
    With courius note, as Venus chapell clerkis:
The rosis reid, now spreding of thair knoppis[9],   [9] knobs, tufts.

War powderit brycht with hevinly beriall[1] droppis,
Throu bemes rede birnyng as ruby sperkis;
The skyes rang for schoutyng of the larkis,
The purpur hevyn our-scailit[2] in silvir sloppis,
Our-gilt the treis, branchis, leivis and barkis.

Doun thrwch ryss[3] ane ryuir ran wyth stremys,
So lustily[4] agayn thai lykand lemys[5]
That all the lake as lamp did leme of licht,
Quhilk schadovit all about wyth twynkling glemis,
That bewis[6] bathit war in secund bemys
Throu the reflex of Phebus visage brycht.
On every syde the hegeis raise on hicht[7],
The bank was grene, the bruke vas full of bremys,
The stanneris[8] clere as stern in frosty nycht.

The cristall air, the sapher firmament,
The ruby skyes of the orient,
Kest beriall bemes on emerant bewis grene;
The rosy garth[9], depaynt and redolent
With purpur, azure, gold, and goulis gent[10],
Arayed was by dame Fflora the quene
So nobily that ioy was for to sene[11]:
The roch[12] agayn the rywir resplendent
As low[13] enlumynit all the leues schene[14].

Quhat throu the mery foulys armony,
And throu the ryueris sounn that ran me by,
On Fflorais mantill I slepit quhair I lay,
Quhare sone in-to my dremes fantasy

[1] beryl.

[2] over-spilled.

[3] brushwood.
[4] pleasantly.
[5] likened flames.

[6] branches.

[7] on high.

[8] gravel.

[9] garden.
[10] rose-red, delicate.

[11] to see.

[12] rock.

[13] shining.

I saw approch agayn the orient sky
    Ane saill als quhite as blossum vpon spray,
    Wyth mast of gold, brycht as the stern of day,
Quhilk tendit to the land full lustily,
    As falcoun swift desyrouse of hir pray.

And hard on burd[1] vnto the blomyt medis,   [1] ground.
Amangis the grene rispis[2] and the redis,   [2] coarse grasses.
    Arrivit scho ; quhar-fro anone thare landis
Ane hundreth ladyes, lusty in-till wedis,
Als fresch as flouris that in the May vp spredis,
    In kirtillis grene, withoutyn kell[3] or bandis[4];   [3] caul, cap.   [4] neckerchiefs.
    Thair brycht hairis hang gletering on the strandis
In tressis clere, wyppit[5] wyth goldyn thredis,   [5] bound round.
    With pappis quhite, and middillis small as wandis.

Discriue I wald, bot quho cowth wele endyte
How all the feldis wyth thai lilies quhite
    Depaynt war brycht, quhilk to the hevin did glete[6]?   [6] gleam.
Noucht thou, Homer, als fair as thou cowth wryte,
For all thi ornate stylë so perfyte,
    Nor yit thou, Tullius, quhois lippis suete
    Off rethorike did in-to termis flete[7]:   [7] float.
Your aureate tongis both bene all to lyte[8]   [8] too little.
    For to compile that paradise complete.

Thare saw I Nature, and [dame] Venus quene,
The fresch Aurora, and lady Flora schene[9],   [9] beautiful.
    Iuno, [Latona,] and Proserpyna,
Dyane, the goddesse chaste of woddis grene,

¹ help of poets is. My lady Cleo that help of makaris bene[1],
                    Thetes, Pallas, and prudent Minerua,
² feigned.   Fair feynit[2] Fortune, and lemand[3] Lucina
³ shining.   Thir mychti quenis in crounis mycht be sene,
                    Wyth bemys blith, bricht as Lucifera.

                    There saw I May, of myrthfull monethis quene,
                    Betuix Aprile and June, her sisteris schene,
                      Within the gairdene walking vp and doun,
⁴ rejoice sud-   Quham of the foulis gladdith al bedene[4];
  denly.   Scho was full tender in-till hir yeris grene.
                      Thare saw I Nature present hir a goune
                      Rich to behald and nobil of renoune,
                    Off ewiry hew that vnder the hevin hes bene
                      Depaynt, and braid be gude proporcioun.

⁵ company.   Full lustily thir ladyes all in fere[5]
                    Enterit within this park of most plesere,
⁶ covered with   Quhare that I lay helit wyth leuis ronk[6];
  rank leaves.   The mery foulis, blisfullest of chere,
⁷ Saluted.   Salust[7] Nature, me-thocht, in thair manere,
                      And ewiry blome on branch and eke on bonk
                      Opnyt and spred thair balmy leuis donk,
                    Full low enclynyng to thair Quene full clere,
                      Quham of thair nobill nvrissing thay thonk.

⁸ Afterwards. Syne[8] to dame Flora on the samyn wyse
⁹ times.   Thay saluse and thay thank a thousand syse[9],
                      And to dame Wenus, lufis mychti quene,
¹⁰ guise, fashion. Thay sang ballattis in lufe, as was the gyse[10],

With amourouse notis most lusty to devise,
   As thay that had lufe in thair hertis grene;
   Thair hony throtis, opnyt fro the splene[1],
With warbillis suete did perse the hevinly skyes,
   Quhill loud resownyt the firmament serene.

[1] from the heart.

Ane-othir court thare saw I subsequent;
Cupide the king, wyth bow in hand ay bent
   And dredefull arowis grundyn scharp and square;
Thare saw I Mars, the god armypotent,
Aufull and sterne, strong and corpolent;
   Thare saw I crabbit Saturn ald and haire[2],
   His luke was lyke for to perturb the aire;
Thare was Marcourius, wise and eloquent,
   Of rhethorike that fand[3] the flouris faire.

[2] hoar.

[3] found.

Thare was the god of gardynis, Priapus;
Thare was the god of wildernes, Phanus;
   And Ianus, god of entres[4] delytable;
Thare was the god of fludis, Neptunus;
Thare was the god of windis, Eolus,
   With variand luke, rycht lyke a lord vnstable;
   Thare was Bachus, the gladder of the table;
Thare was Pluto, the elrich[5] incubus,
   In cloke of grene, his court usit no sable.

[4] entries.

[5] uncanny, elvish.

And ewiry one of thir[6], in grene arayit,
On harp or lute full merily thai playit,
   And sang ballettis with michty notis clere.
Ladyes to dance full sobirly assayit,

[6] these.

Endlang[1] the lusty rywir so thai mayit;
Thair obseruance rycht hevynly was to here.
Than crap I throu the leuis and drew nere,
Quhare that I was richt sudaynly affrayit
All throu a luke quhilk I haue coft[2] full dere.

And schortly for to speke, of lufis quene
I was aspyit. Scho bad hir archearis kene
Go me arrest; and thay no time delayit.
Than ladyes fair lete fall thair mantillis grene,
With bowis big in tressit hairis schene.
All sudaynly thay had a felde arayit;
And yit rycht gretly was I noucht affrayit,
The party was so plesand for to sene[3].
A wonder lusty bikar[4] me assayit.

And first of all, with bow in hand ay bent,
Come dame Bewty rycht as scho wald me schent[5];
Syne folowit all hir dammosallis in feir[6],
With mony diuerse aufull instrument,
Wnto the pres; Fair Having wyth hir went,
Fyne Portrature, Plesance, and lusty Chere.
Than come Resoun, with schelde of gold so clere.
In plate and maille, as Mars armypotent,
Defendit me that nobil cheuallere.

Syne tender Youth come wyth hir virgenis ying
Grene Innocence, and schamefull Abaising,
And quaking Drede, wyth humyll Obedience.
The Goldyn Targe harmyt thay no-thing;

Curage in thame was noucht begonne to spring;
    Full sore thay dred to done a violence.
    Suete Womanhede I saw cum in presence;
Of artilye[1] a warld sche did in bring,   [1] artillery.
    Seruit wyth ladyes full of reuerence.

Scho led with hir Nurture and Lawlyness,
Continwance[2], Pacience, Gude Fame, and Stedfastnes, [2] Continence.
    Discretioun, Gentrise[3], and Considerance,   [3] Gentlehood.
Lefull[4] Company and Honest Besynes   [4] Lawful.
Benigne Luke, Mylde Chere, and Sobirnes.
    All thir bure ganyeis[5] to do me greuance,   [5] darts.
    But Resoun bure the Targe wyth sik[6] constance   [6] such.
Thair scharp assayes mycht do no dures
    To me for all thair aufull ordynance.

Wnto the pres persewit Hie Degre;
Hir folowit ay Estate and Dignitee,
    Comparisoun, Honour, and Noble Array,
Will, Wantonness, Renoun, and Libertee,
Richesse, Fredome, and eke Nobilitee.
    Wit ye thay did thair baner hye display;
    A cloud of arowis as hayle-schour lousit thay
And schot, quhill[7] wastit was thair artilye,   [7] till.
    Syne went abak rebutit[8] of thair pray.   [8] repulsed.

Quhen Venus had persauit this rebute,
Dissymilance scho bad go mak persute,
    At all powere to perse the Goldyn Targe;
And scho that was of doubilnes the rute

¹ means of achievement. Askit hir choise of archeris in refute¹.

² choose. Wenus the best bad hir to wale² at large ;

³ pledge. Scho tuke Presence plicht³ anker of the barge,

⁴ an arrow. And Fair Callyng that wele a flayn⁴ coud schute,

And Cherising for to complete hir charge.

Dame Hamelynes scho tuke in company,

⁵ skilful. That hardy was, and hende⁵ in archery,

And brocht dame Bewty to the felde agayn.

With all the choise of Venus cheualry

⁶ made assault. Thay come, and bikkerit⁶ vnabaisitly.

The schour of arowis rappit on as rayn ;

⁷ "syouris," scions, shoots. Perrellus Presence, that mony syre⁷ has slayne,

⁸ took place on the beach. The bataill broucht on bordour⁸ hard me by ;

⁹ sorer, truth to say. The salt was all the sarar, suth to sayn⁹.

Thik was the schote of grundyn dartis kene ;

Bot Resoun with the Scheld of Gold so schene

¹⁰ In warlike fashion. Weirly¹⁰ defendit, quho-so-ewir assayit.

¹¹ storm. The aufull stoure¹¹ he manly did sustene,

Quhill Presence kest a pulder in his ene,

¹² went astray. And than as drunkyn man he all forvayit¹².

Quhen he was blynd the fule wyth hym thay playit,

And banyst hym amang the bewis grene.

That sair sicht me sudaynly affrayit.

Than was I woundit till the deth wele nere

And yoldyn as a wofull prisonnere

To lady Bewty in a moment space.

Me-thocht scho semyt lustiar of chere

Efter that Resoun had tynt[1] his eyne clere   1 lost.
  Than of before, and lufliare of face.
  Quhy was thou blyndit, Resoun? quhi, allace!
And gert[2] ane hell my paradise appere,   2 caused.
  And mercy seme, quhare that I fand no grace.

Dissymulance was besy me to sile[3]   3 blindfold.
And Fair Calling did oft vpoun me smyle
  And Cherising me fed wyth wordis fair;
New Acquyntance enbracit me a quhile,
And fauouryt me quhill men mycht ga ane myle,
  Syne tuk hir leif; I saw hir nevir mare.
  Than saw I Dangere toward me repair;
I couth eschew hir presence be no wyle;
  On syde scho lukit wyth ane fremyt fare[4].   4 foreign (unfriendly) bearing.

And at the last Departing cowth hir dresse[5],   5 Separation began her treatment.
And me delyuerit vnto Hevynesse
  For to remayne, and scho in cure[6] me tuke.   6 care.
Be this the Lord of Wyndis, wyth wodenes[7],   7 fury, madness.
God Eolus, his bugill blew I gesse,
  That with the blast the leuis all to schuke,
  And sudaynly, in the space of ane luke,
All was hyne[8] went, thare was bot wildernes,   8 hence.
  Thare was no more bot birdis, bank, and bruke.

In twynkling of ane e to schip thai went,
And swyth[9] vp saile vnto the top thai stent[10],   9 swiftly. 10 stretched.
  And with swift course atour[11] the flude thay frak[12].   11 over. 12 sped.
Thay fyrit gunnis wyth polder violent,

¹ smoke.   Till that the reke[1] raise to the firmament;

² crash.   The rockes all resoundit wyth the rak[2];

³ noise.   For reird[3] it semyt that the raynbow brak.

⁴ sprang.   Wyth spreit affrayit apon my fete I sprent[4],

⁵ cliffs, ravines. Amang the clewis[5] so carefull was the crak.

⁶ awake from my
   dreaming. And as I did awalk of my sueving[6]

           The ioyfull birdis merily did syng

             For myrth of Phebus tendir bemes schene;

⁷ morning.   Suete war the vapouris, soft the morowing[7],

           Halesum the vale, depaynt wyth flouris ying;

             The air attemperit, sobir, and amene;

⁸ furnished
   forth.   In quhite and rede was all the felde besene[8],

           Throu Naturis nobil fresche anamalyng,

             In mirthfull May of ewiry moneth quene.

           O reuerend Chaucere, rose of rhethoris all,

           As in our tong ane flour imperiall,

             That raise in Britane ewir, quho redis rycht,

           Thou beris of makaris the tryumph riall;

⁹ celestial. Thy fresch anamalit termes celicall[9]

             This mater coud illumynit haue full brycht.

             Was thou noucht of oure Inglis all the lycht,

           Surmounting **ewiry** tong terrestriall,

             Alls fer as Mayes morow dois mydnycht?

           O morall Gower, and Ludgate laureate,

           Your sugurit lippis and toungis aureate

             Bene to oure eris cause of grete delyte.

           Your angelik mouthis most mellifluate

Our rude langage has clere illumynate,
 And faire our-gilt oure speche, that imperfyte
  Stude or¹ your goldyn pennis schupe² to wryte.   ¹ ere.
   ² prepared.
This Ile before was bare and desolate
 Of rethorike, or lusty fresch endyte.

Thou lytill Quair, be ewir obedient,
Humble, subiect, and symple of entent
 Before the face of ewiry connyng³ wicht,   ³ skilful.
I knaw quhat thou of rethorike hes spent.
Off all hir lusty rosis redolent
 Is none in-to thy gerland sett on hicht⁴,   ⁴ on high.
 Eschame thairfoir, and draw thé out of sicht,
Rude is thy wede, destitute, bare, and rent,
 Wele aucht thou be affeirit⁵ of the licht.   ⁵ afraid.

THE THRISSIL AND THE ROIS.

QUHEN Merche wes with variand windis past,
   And Appryll had, with hir siluer schouris,
Tane leif at Nature with ane orient blast,
   And lusty[1] May, that mvddir is of flouris,
   Had maid the birdis to begyn thair houris[2]
Amang the tendir odouris reid and quhyt,
Quhois armony to heir it wes delyt;

In bed at morrow, sleiping as I lay,
   Me-thocht Aurora with hir cristall ene
In at the window lukit by the day,
   And halsit[3] me, with visage paill and grene;
   On quhois hand a lark sang fro the splene[4],
"Awalk, luvaris, out of your slomering!
Se how the lusty morrow dois vp spring."

Me-thocht fresche May befoir my bed vpstude,
   In weid depaynt of mony diuerss hew,
Sobir, benyng, and full of mansuetude[5],
   In brycht atteir of flouris forgit new,
   Hevinly of color, quhyt, reid, broun, and blew,
Balmit in dew, and gilt with Phebus bemys,
Quhill all the house illumynit of hir lemys[6].

[1] pleasant.
[2] morning prayers.
[3] greeted.
[4] from the heart.
[5] meekness.
[6] glowing.

" Slugird," scho said, " awalk[1] annone for schame,   1 awake.
   And in my honour sum-thing thou go wryt ;
The lark hes done the mirry day proclame,
   To raise vp luvaris with confort and delyt ;
   Yit nocht incressis thy curage to indyt,
Quhois hairt sum-tyme hes glaid and blisfull bene,
Sangis to mak vndir the levis grene."

" Quhairto," quod I, " sall I vpryse at morrow,
   For in this May few birdis herd I sing?
Thai haif moir cause to weip and plane thair sorrow ;
   Thy air it is nocht holsum nor benyng ;
   Lord Eolus dois in thy sessone ring[2] ;   2 reigns in thy season.
So busteous[3] ar the blastis of his horne,   3 rude, powerful.
Amang thy bewis[4] to walk I haif forborne."   4 boughs.

With that this lady sobirly did smyle,
   And said, " Vpryse, and do thy observance ;
Thow did promyt, in Mayis lusty quhyle,
   For to discryve[5] the Rois of most plesance.   5 describe.
   Go se the birdis how thay sing and dance,
Illumynit our[6] with orient skyis brycht,   6 over.
Annamyllit richely with new asur lycht."

Quhen this wes said, depairtit scho, this quene,
   And enterit in a lusty gairding gent[7] ;   7 neat (genteel).
And than, me-thocht, full hestely besene[8],   8 fitted out.
   In serk and mantill [eftir hir] I went
   In-to this garth[9], most dulce and redolent   9 inclosure.
Off herb and flour and tendir plantis sueit,
And grene levis doing of dew doun fleit[10].   10 causing dew to float down.

¹ The purple sun. The purpour sone¹, with tendir bemys reid,
In orient bricht as angell did appeir.
Throw goldin skyis putting vp his heid,
  Quhois gilt tressis schone so wondir cleir,
  That all the world tuke confort, fer and neir,
To luke vpone his fresche and blisfull face,
Doing all sable fro the hevynnis chace.

² the blissful sound of the angel choir. And as the blisfull sonne of cherarchy²
  The fowlis song throw confort of the licht;
The birdis did with oppin vocis cry,
  "O, luvaris fo, away thou dully Nycht!
  And welcum, Day, that confortis every wicht!
³ shining, beautiful. Haill May, haill Flora, haill Aurora schene³,
Haill princes Natur, haill Venus, luvis quene!"

Dame Nature gaif ane inhibitioun thair
  To ferss Neptunus and Eolus the bawld,
Nocht to perturb the wattir nor the air,
  And that no schouris [snell] nor blastis cawld
⁴ earth. Effray suld flouris nor fowlis on the fold⁴.
⁵ also. Scho bad eik⁵ Juno, goddis of the sky,
That scho the hevin suld keip amene and dry.

Scho ordand eik that every bird and beist
  Befoir hir hienes suld annone compeir,
And every flour of vertew, most and leist,
  And every herb be feild fer and neir,
  As thay had wont in May fro yeir to yeir,
To hir thair makar to mak obediens,
Full law inclynnand with all dew reuerens.

With that annone scho send the swyft Ro
   To bring in beistis of all conditioun;
The restles Suallow commandit scho also
   To feche all fowll of small and greit renown;
   And to gar[1] flouris compeir of all fassoun   [1] cause.
Full craftely conjurit scho the Yarrow,
Quhilk did furth swirk[2] als swift as ony arrow.   [2] dart.

All present wer in twynkling of ane e,
   Baith beist and bird and flour, befoir the quene.
And first the Lyone, gretast of degre,
   Was callit thair; and he, most fair to sene[3],   [3] to see.
   With a full hardy contenance and kene,
Befoir dame Natur come, and did inclyne,
With visage bawld and curage leonyne.

This awfull beist full terrible wes of cheir,
   Persing of luke, and stout of countenance,
Rycht strong of corpis, of fassoun fair, but feir[4],   [4] without com-
                                          panion.
   Lusty of schaip, lycht of deliuerance[5];   [5] movement.
   Reid of his cullour, as is the ruby glance,
On feild of gold he stude full mychtely,
With flour-de-lycis sirculit lustely.*

This Lady liftit vp his cluvis[6] cleir,   [6] claws
   And leit him listly[7] lene vpone hir kne,   [7] willingly.
And crownit him with dyademe full deir,
   Off radyous stonis, most ryall for to se,
   Saying, "The King of Beistis mak I thé,
And the cheif protector in woddis and schawis[8];   coverts.
Onto thi leigis go furth and keip the lawis.

      * A description of the royal arms of Scotland.

"Exerce justice with mercy and conscience,

1 hurt nor con-tumely.   And lat no small beist suffir skaith na skornis[1]

Of greit beistis that bene of moir piscence;

2 Make law alike.   Do law elyk[2] to aipis and vnicornis,

And lat no bowgle with his busteous hornis

The meik pluch-ox oppress, for all his pryd,

Bot in the yok go peciable him besyd."

Quhen this was said, with noyis and soun of joy,

All kynd of beistis in-to thair degre,

At onis cryit lawd, "Viue le Roy!"

And till his feit fell with humilite,

3 fealty.   And all thay maid him homege and fewte[3];

4 gestures.   And he did thame ressaif with princely laitis[4],

5 perhaps "does spare the prostrate."   Quhois noble yre is proceir prostratis[5].

Syne crownit scho the Egle King of Fowlis,

6 quills.   And as steill dertis scherpit scho his pennis[6],

And bawd him be als just to awppis and owlis,

7 parrots.   As vnto pacokkis, papingais[7], or crennis,

8 mighty.   And mak a law for wycht[8] fowlis and for wrennis;

9 do affrighting.   And lat no fowll of ravyne do efferay[9],

Nor devoir birdis bot his awin pray.

Than callit scho all flouris that grew on feild,

10 qualities.   Discirnyng all thair fassionis and effeiris[10].

Vpone the awfull Thrissill scho beheld,

And saw him kepit with a busche of speiris;

Concedring him so able for the weiris,

A radius croun of rubeis scho him gaif,

11 protect the rest.   And said, "In feild go furth, and fend the laif[11];

"And, sen[1] thow art a king, thou be discreit;   [1] since.
  Herb without vertew thou hald nocht of sic[2] pryce [2] such.
As herb of vertew and of odor sueit;
  And lat no nettill vyle and full of vyce,
  Hir fallow[3] to the gudly flour-de-lyce;   [3] fellow herself.
Nor latt no wyld weid, full of churlicheness,
Compair hir till the lilleis nobilness.

"Nor hald non vdir flour in sic denty[4]   [4] in such regard.
  As the fresche Rois, of cullour reid and quhyt;*
For gife thow dois, hurt is thyne honesty,
  Conciddering that no flour is so perfyt,
  So full of vertew, plesans, and delyt,
So full of blisfull angeilik bewty,
Imperiall birth, honour, and dignite."

Than to the Rois scho turnyt hir visage,
  And said, "O lusty dochtir most benyng,
Aboif the lilly illustare of lynnage,†
  Fro the stok ryell rysing fresche and ying,
  But ony spot or macull doing spring[5];   [5] Springing with-
Cum, blowme of joy, with jemis to be cround,   out spot or stain.
For our the laif[6] thy bewty is renownd."   [6] over the rest.

A coistly croun, with clarefeid stonis brycht,
  This cumly quene did on hir heid inclois,
Quhill all the land illumynit of the licht;
  Quhairfoir me-thocht all flouris did reiois,
  Crying attonis[7], "Haill be thou, richest Rois!   [7] at once.
Haill, hairbis empryce! haill freschest quene of flouris!
To thé be glory and honour at all houris!"

* An allusion, as Laing pointed out, to the union of the Houses
of York and Lancaster, the Red and White Roses, in the persons
of Henry VII. and his queen.
  † An allusion to the earlier effort to unite James IV. to a
daughter of the House of Valois.

Thane all the birdis song with voce on hicht,
   Quhois mirthfull soun wes mervelus to heir.
The mavyis[1] song, "Haill, Rois most riche and richt,
   That dois vp flureiss vndir Phebus speir!
Haill, plant of yowth, haill, princes dochtir deir,
Haill, blosome, breking out of the blud royall,
Quhois pretius vertew is imperiall!"

The merle scho sang, "Haill, Rois of most delyt,
   Haill, of all flouris quene and souerane!"
The lark scho song, "Haill, Rois, both reid and
      quhyt,
   Most plesand flour, of michty cullouris twane!"
   The nychtingaill song, "Haill, Naturis suffragane,
In bewty, nurtour, and every nobilness,
In riche array, renown and gentilness!"

The commoun voce vp raise of birdis small,
   Apone this wyis, "O blissit be the hour
That thow wes chosin to be our principall!
   Welcome to be our princes of honour,
   Our perle, our plesans, and our paramour,
Our peax[2], our play, our plane felicite,
Chryst thé conserf frome all aduersite!"

Than all the birdis song with sic a schout,
   That I annone awoilk quhair that I lay,
And with a braid[3] I turnyt me about
   To se this court; bot all were went away.
   Than vp I lenyt, halflingis in affrey[4],
And thus I wret, as ye haiff hard to-forrow[5],
Off lusty May vpone the nynt morrow.

[1] thrush.

[2] peace.

[3] cry.

[4] partly in affright.
[5] before.

BEWTY AND THE PRESONEIR.*

Sen that I am a presoneir
  Till hir that fairest is and best,
I me commend, fra yeir till yeir,
  In-till hir bandoun[1] for to rest.   [1] service.
  I govit[2] on that gudliest,   [2] gazed eagerly.
So lang to luk I tuk laseir,
  Quhill I wes tane withouttin test[3],   [3] contest.
And led furth as a presoneir.

Hir sweit having and fresche bewtie
  Hes wondit me but[4] swerd or lance,   [4] without.
With hir to go commandit me
  Ontill the castell of Pennance.
  I said "Is this your gouirnance,
To tak men for thair luking heir?"
  Fresche Bewty said "Ya, schir, perchance,
Ye be my ladeis presoneir."

Thai had me bundin to the yet[5]   [5] They conveyed
  Quhair Strangenes had bene portar ay,   me to the gate.
And in deliuerit me thairat,
  And in thir[6] termis can thai say,   [6] these.

* Laing suggests that in this poem Dunbar may have done
little more than delineate one of the pageants or masques of the
period which he had witnessed while in England.

1 Give attention.

"Do wait[1], and lat him nocht away."
Quo Strangnes vnto the porteir
    "Ontill my lady, I dar lay,
Ye be to pure a presoneir."

Thai kest me in a deip dungeoun,
    And fetterit me but lok or cheyne.

2 named.

3 disdain.
4 Though I was
   woful I dared
   not complain.
5 qualities
   (senses).
6 did I say.

The capitane hecht[2] Comparesone,
    To luke on me he thocht greit deyne[3].
    Thocht I wes wo I durst nocht pleyne[4],
For he had fetterit mony affeir[5];
    With petouss voce thus cuth I sene[6]
"Wo is a wofull presoneir!"

7 watch.

8 jester.
9 bauble.

Langour wes weche[7] vpoun the wall,
    That nevir sleipit, bot evir wouke;
Scorne wes bourdour[8] in the hall;
    And oft on me his babill[9] schuke,
    Lukand with mony a dengerous luke;

10 comes within
   bounds.
11 clownish (?)

"Quhat is he yone, that methis[10] ws neir?
    Ye be to townage[11], be this buke,
To be my ladeis presoneir."

12 whispered.

13 write.

Gud Houp rownit[12] in my eir,
    And bad me baldlie breve[13] a bill;
With Lawlines he suld it beir,
    With Fair Scherwice send it hir till.
    I wouk and wret hir all my will;

14 sped without
   companion.
15 secret words.

Fair Scherwice fur withouttin feir[14],
    Sayand till hir with wirdis still[15],
"Haif pety of your presoneir!"

Than Lawlines to Petie went,
    And said till hir in termis schort,
"Lat we yone presoneir be schent[1],   [1] undone.
    Will no man do to ws support;
    Gar[2] lay ane sege vnto yone fort."   [2] Cause.
Than Petie said, "I sall appeir;"
    Thocht sayis, "I hecht, com I ourthort[3],   [3] I promise, if I come over.
I houp to lowss the presoneir."

Than to battell thai war arreyit all,
    And ay the wawart[4] kepit Thocht;   [4] vanguard.
Lust bur the benner to the wall,
    And Bissines the grit gyn brocht[5].   [5] brought the great engine of war.
    Skorne cryis out, sayis, "Wald ye ocht?"
Lust sayis, "We wald haif entre heir;"
    Comparisone sayis, "That is for nocht;
Ye will nocht wyn the presoneir."

Thai thairin schup[6] for to defend,   [6] prepared.
    And thai thairfurth sailyeit[7] ane hour;   [7] assailed.
Than Bissiness the grit gyn bend,
    Straik doun the top of the foir tour.
    Comparisone began to lour[8],   [8] look gloomy.
And cryit furth, "I yow requeir,
    Soft and fair and do fawour,
And tak to yow the presoneir."

Thai fyrit the yettis deliuerly[9]   [9] gates speedily.
    With faggottis wer grit and huge;
And Strangenes, quhair that he did ly
    Wes brint in-to the porter luge.

Lustely thay lakit bot a juge,
Sic straikis and stychling wes on steir[1],
The semeliest wes maid assege
To quhome that he wes presoneir.

Thrucht Skornes noss[2] thai put a prik,
    This he wes banist and gat a blek[3];
Comparisone wes erdit quik[4],
    And Langour lap and brak his nek.
    Thai sailyeit fast, all the fek[5];
Lust chasit my ladeis chalmirleir[6];
    Gud Fame wes drownit in a sek.
Thus ransonit thai the presoneir.

Fra Sklandir hard[7] Lust had vndone
    His enemeis, him aganis
Assemblit[8] ane semely sort full sone,
    And raiss and rowttit all the planis.
    His cusing[9] in the court remanis,
Bot jalouss folkis and geangleiris[10]
    And fals Invy that no-thing lanis[11]
Blew out on Luvis presoneir.

Syne Matremony, that nobill king,
    Was grevit, and gadderit ane grit ost,
And all enermit, without lesing[12],
    Chest Sklander to the west se cost.
    Than wes he and his linege lost,
And Matremony, withouttin weir[13],
    The band of freindschip hes indost
Betuix Bewty and the presoneir.

Be that of eild[1] wes Gud Famiss air,
 And cumyne to continwatioun,
And to the court maid his repair,
 Quhair Matremony than woir the crowne.
 He gat ane confirmatioun
All that his modir aucht but weir[2],
 And baid[3] still, as it wes resone,
With Bewty and the presoneir.

[1] By that time Good Fame's heir was of age.

[2] owned assuredly.
[3] abode.

LONDON.*

LONDON, thou art of townes A per se!
　Soveraign of cities, semeliest in sight,
Of high renoun, riches, and royaltie;
　Of lordis, barons, and many goodly knight;
　Of most delectable lusty ladies bright;
Of famous prelatis in habitis clericall;
　Of merchauntis full of substaunce and myght:
London, thou art the flour of cities all!

1 Be glad.
2 pleasant.
3 named.

Gladdith[1] anon thou lusty[2] Troynovaunt,
　City that some-tyme cleped[3] was New Troy;
In all the erth, imperiall as thou stant,
　Pryncesse of townes, of pleasure, and of joy,
　A richer restith under no Christen roy;
For manly power, with craftis naturall,

4 Is formed.
5 since.

　Fourmeth[4] none fairer sith[5] the flode of Noy.
London, thou art the flour of cities all!

* The spelling of this poem, it will be noticed, follows the English model of the time in several respects, a fact owed perhaps to the courtesy of the poet, perhaps to the habit of the transcriber in the Cotton MS.

Gemme of all joy, jasper of jocunditie,
  Most myghty carbuncle of vertue and valour,
Strong Troy in vigour and in strenuytie[1],   [1] fortitude.
  Of royall cities rose and geraflour[2],   [2] gillyflower.
  Empresse of townes, exalt in honour,
In beawtie beryng the crone imperiall,
  Swete paradise precelling in pleasure,
London, thow art the floure of cities all!

Aboue all ryuers thy Ryuer hath renowne,
  Whose beryall[3] stremys, pleasaunt and preclare[4],   [3] beryl.
                                                          [4] most famous.
Under the lusty wallis renneth down,
  Where many a swanne doth swymme with wyngis
      fare,
  Where many a barge doth saile and row with are[5], [5] oar.
Where many a ship doth rest with toppe-royall.
  O towne of townes, patrone and not compare,
London, thou art the floure of cities all!

Upon thy lusty Brigge[6] of pylers white   [6] fair bridge.
  Been merchauntis full royall to behold:
Upon thy stretis goeth many a semely knyght
  [All clad] in velvet gownes and cheynes of gold.
  By Julyus Cesar thy Tour founded of old
May be the hous of Mars victoryall,
  Whos artillary with tonge may not be told.
London, thou art the flour of cities all!

Strong be thy wallis that about thee standis;
  Wise be the people that within thee dwellis;
Fresh is thy ryver with his lusty strandis;

Blith be thy churches, wele sownyng be thy bellis;
Riche be thy merchauntis in substaunce that
    excellis;
Fair be their wives, right lovesom, white, and small;
[1] Clere[1] be thy virgyns, lusty under kellis[2].
London, thow art the flour of cities all!

Thy famous Maire* by pryncely governaunce
    With swerd of justice thé rulith prudently.
No lord of Parys, Venyce, or Floraunce
    In dignytie or honoure goeth to hym nye.
He is examplar, loode-ster, and guye[3],
Principall patrone and roose[4] orygynalle,
    Above all maires as maister moost worthy;
London, thou art the flour of cities all!

[1] lovely.
[2] cauls, caps.
[3] guide.
[4] commendation.

* " Sir John Shaw, who was knighted on the field by Henry
VII."—*Gregory Smith.*

BE YE ANE LUVAR.

Be ye ane luvar, think ye nocht ye suld
   Be weill adwysit in your gouerning?
Be ye nocht sa it will on yow be tauld;
   Bewar thairwith for dreid of misdemyng[1].   1 evil report.
   Be nocht a wreche, nor skerche[2] in your spending, 2 a niggard, or sparing.
Be layth[3] alway to do amiss or schame,   3 loath.
   Be rewlit rycht and keip this doctring,
Be secreit, trew, incressing of your name.

Be ye ane lear[4], that is werst of all;   4 liar.
   Be ye ane tratlar[5], that I hald als ewill;   5 tattler.
Be ye ane janglar[6] and ye fra vertew fall;   6 wrangler.
   Be nevir-mair on-to thir vicis thrall.
   Be now and ay the maistir of your will;
Be nevir he that lesing[7] sall proclame;   7 falsehood.
   Be nocht of langage quhair ye suld be still;
Be secreit, trew, incressing of your name.

Be nocht abasit for no wicket tung,
   Be nocht sa set as I haif said yow heir:
Be nocht sa lerge vnto thir sawis sung[8],   8 Be not so heedless to these sayings sung.
   Be nocht our[9] prowd, thinkand ye haif no peir. 9 Be not over.
   Be ye so wyiss that vderis at yow leir[10],   10 learn.
Be nevir he to sklander nor defame;
   Be of your lufe no prechour as a freir;
Be secreit, trew, incressing of your name.

TO A LADYE.

SWEIT roiss of vertew and of gentilnes,
Delytsum lyllie of everie lustynes¹,
   Richest in bontie, and in bewtie cleir,
   And everie vertew that is [held most] deir,
Except onlie that ye ar mercyles.

² garden.
³ attend.

In-to your garthe² this day I did persew³,
Thair saw I flowris that fresche wer of hew;
   ⁴ see.   Baith quhyte and reid moist lusty wer to seyne⁴,
   ⁵ wholesome. And halsum⁵ herbis vpone stalkis grene;
Yit leif nor flour fynd could I nane of rew.

I dout that Merche with his cauld blastis keyne
Hes slane this gentill herbe that I of mene;
   ⁶ such pain. Quhois petewous deithe dois to my hart sic pane⁶
   That I wald mak to plant his rute agane,
So comfortand his levis vnto me bene.

LAMENT FOR THE MAKARIS

QUHEN HE WES SEIK.

I THAT in heill[1] wes and glaidnes   [1] health.
Am trublit now with gret seiknes
And feblit with infirmitie;
    Timor Mortis conturbat me.*

Our plesance heir is all vane glory,
This fals warld is bot transitory,
The flesche is brukle[2], the Feynd is sle[3];   [2] brittle, frail.
    Timor Mortis conturbat me.   [3] sly.

The stait of man dois change and vary,
Now sound, now seik, now blyth, now sary[4],   [4] sorry.
Now dansand mirry, now like to dee;
    Timor Mortis conturbat me.

No stait in erd[5] heir standis sickir[6];   [5] earth.
As with the wynd wavis the wickir[7]   [6] secure.
So wavis this warldis vanite;   [7] osier twig.
    Timor Mortis conturbat me.

* The burden of this poem, "The fear of death troubles me,"
Laing points out, is borrowed from a poem by Lydgate, which
begins "So as I lay the other night."

Onto the ded¹ gois all estatis,
Princis, prelotis, and potestatis,
Baith riche and pur of all degre;
    Timor Mortis conturbat me.

He takis the knychtis in-to feild,
² armed.
Anarmit² vnder helme and scheild;
³ in all contest.
Wictour he is at all melle³;
    Timor Mortis conturbat me.

That strang vnmercifull tyrand
⁴ sucking.
Takis on the moderis breist sowkand⁴
The bab full of benignite;
    Timor Mortis conturbat me.

⁵ the champion
in the storm
(dust) of battle.
He takis the campion in the stour⁵,
The capitane closit in the tour,
The lady in bour full of bewte;
    Timor Mortis conturbat me.

⁶ power.
He spairis no lord for his piscence⁶,
Na clerk for his intelligence;
His awfull strak may no man fle;
    Timor Mortis conturbat me.

Art magicianis, and astrologgis,
Rethoris, logicians, and theologgis,
Thame helpis no conclusionis sle;
    Timor Mortis conturbat me.

In medecyne the most practicianis,
Lechis, surrigianis, and phisicianis,
Thame-self fra ded may not supple[1];   [1] succour, defend.
    Timor Mortis conturbat me.

I see that makaris[2] amang the laif[3]   [2] poets.
                                                    [3] rest.
Playis heir ther padyanis[4], syne gois to graif[5];   [4] pageants. grave.
Sparit is nocht ther faculte[6];   [6] their guild.
    Timor Mortis conturbat me.

He hes done petuously devour
The noble Chaucer, of makaris flouir,
The monk of Bery[7] and Gower all thre;   [7] *i.e.* Lydgate.
    Timor Mortis conturbat me.

The gude Syr Hew of Eglintoun,
Ettrik, Heryot, et Wyntoun
He hes tane out of this cuntre;
    Timor Mortis conturbat me.

That scorpioun fell hes done infek[8]   [8] has inhibited (?)
Maister Iohne Clerk and James Afflek
Fra balat making and trigidë;
    Timor Mortis conturbat me.

Holland and Barbour he has berevit;
Allace, that he nought with ws lewit
Schir Mungo Lokert of the Le!
    Timor Mortis conturbat me.

Clerk of Tranent eik he has tane,
That maid the anteris[1] of Gawane;
Schir Gilbert Hay endit has he;
     Timor Mortis conturbat me.

He has Blind Hary et Sandy[2] Traill
Slaine with his schot of mortall haill,
Quhilk Patrik Johnistoun mycht nought fle;
     Timor Mortis conturbat me.

He hes reft Merseir his endite[3],
That did in luf so lifly[4] write,
So schort, so quyk, of sentence hie[5];
     Timor Mortis conturbat me.

He hes tane Roull of Aberdene,
And gentill Roull of Corstorphin;
Two bettir fallowis did no man se;
     Timor Mortis conturbat me.

In Dunfermelyne he has done rovne[6]
With gud Maister Robert Henrisoun;
Schir Iohne the Ros enbrast[7] hes he;
     Timor Mortis conturbat me.

And he has now tane, last of aw[8],
Gud gentill Stobo and Quintyne Schaw,
Of quham all wichtis hes pete;
     Timor Mortis conturbat me.

[1] adventures.
[2] Alexander.
[3] writing.
[4] lively.
[5] high.
[6] whispered.
[7] embraced.
[8] all.

Gud Maister Walter Kennedy
In poynt of dede lyis veraly;
Gret reuth it wer that so suld be;
    Timor Mortis conturbat me.

Sen he has all my brether tane
He will naught lat me lif alane;
On forse I man[1] his nyxt pray be;   1 perforce I must.
    Timor Mortis conturbat me.

Sen for the deid[2] remeid is non,   2 since for death.
Best is that we for deid dispone[3],   3 dispose.
Eftir our deid that lif may we;
    Timor Mortis conturbat me.*

* It has been noted as curious that Dunbar in this Lament makes no mention of such well-known poets as Gavin Douglas, James I., and Thomas the Rhymer, unless indeed the last named be recognised under the cognomen of " Ettrik."

THE DANCE OF THE SEVIN DEIDLY SYNNIS.

Off Februar the fyiftene nycht
Full lang befoir the dayis lycht,
    I lay in-till a trance;
And then I saw baith Hevin and Hell:
Me-thocht amangis the feyndis fell

    Mahoun[1] gart cry ane dance
Off schrewis[2] that wer nevir schrevin[3],
Aganis the feist of Fasternis evin[4]
    To mak thair observance.
He bad gallandis ga graith a gyiss[5]
And kast vp gamountis[6] in the skyiss,
    As varlotis does in France.

Heilie[7] harlottis on hawtane[8] wyiss
Come in with mony sindrie gyiss,
    Bot yit luche[9] nevir Mahoun;
Quhill[10] preistis come in with bair schevin nekkis,
Than all the feyndis lewche and maid gekkis[11],
    Blak-Belly and Bawsy-Brown.*

* " Popular names of certain spirits. *Bawsy-Brown* seems to be the English Robin Goodfellow, known in Scotland by the name of Brownie."—Hailes. These six lines in the MSS. are made to follow the next stanza, but Laing must be considered right in assigning them an earlier place as above.

" Lat se," quod he, " Now quha begynnis?"
With that the fowll Sevin Deidly Synnis
    Begowth to leip at anis[1].   1 at once.
And first of all in dance wes Pryd,
With hair wyld bak and bonet on syd,
    Lyk to mak vaistie wanis[2]:   2 empty dwelling.
And round abowt him, as a quheill,
Hang all in rumpillis[3] to the heill   3 disordered folds.
    His kethat[4] for the nanis[5].   4 cassock.
                                   5 nonce.
Mony prowd trumpour[6] with him trippit, 6 deceiver.
Throw skaldand fyre ay as thay skippit
    Thay gyrnd[7] with hiddouss granis.   7 grinned.

Than Yre come in with sturt[8] and stryfe; 8 disturbance.
His hand wes ay vpoun his knyfe,
    He brandeist lyk a beir:
Bostaris, braggaris, and barganeris[9]   9 quarrellers.
Eftir him passit, in-to pairis,
    All bodin in feir of weir[10],   10 arrayed in feature of war.
In iakkis[11] and stryppis and bonettis of steill, 11 jackets of mail.
Thair leggis wer chenyeit[12] to the heill, 12 covered with chain-mail.
    Ffrawart wes thair affeir[13]:   13 Rude was their bearing.
Sum vpoun vdir with brandis beft[14],   14 buffeted.
Sum jaggit[15] vthiris to the heft   15 pricked.
    With knyvis that scherp cowd scheir.

Nixt in the dance followit Invy,
Fild full of feid and fellony[16],   16 feud and fierceness.
    Hid malyce and dispyte:
Ffor pryvie hatrent that tratour trymlit.
Him followit mony freik[17] dissymlit,   17 petulant folk.
    With fenyeit wirdis[18] quhyte;   18 feigned words.

And flattereris in-to menis facis,
And bakbyttaris in secreit placis
　　　To ley[1] that had delyte ;
And rownaris of fals lesingis[2] :
Allace, that courtis of noble kingis
　　　Of thame can nevir be quyte!

Nixt him in dans come Cuvatyce,
Rute of all evill and grund of vyce,
　　　That nevir cowd be content.
Catyvis, wrechis, and okkeraris[3],
Hud-pykis, hurdaris, and gadderaris[4]
　　　All with that warlo[5] went.
Out of thair throttis thay schot on vdder
Hett moltin gold, me-thocht, a fudder[6],
　　　As fyreflawcht[7] maist fervent :
Ay as thay tomit[8] thame of schot
Ffeyndis fild thame new vp to the thrott
　　　With gold of allkin prent[9].

Syne Sweirnes, at the secound bidding,
Come lyk a sow out of a midding,
　　　Full slepy wes his grunyie[10].
Mony sweir bumbard-belly huddroun[11],
Mony slute daw[12] and slepy duddroun[13],
　　　Him serwit ay with sounyie[14].
He drew thame furth in-till a chenyie,
And Belliall with a brydill renyie
　　　Evir lascht thame on the lunyie[15].
In dance thay war so slaw of feit
Thay gaif thame in the fyre a heit
　　　And maid thame quicker of counyie[16].

[1] lie.
[2] whisperers of false lies.
[3] usurers.
[4] Misers, hoarders, and gatherers.
[5] wizard.
[6] great quantity (properly 128 lb. weight).
[7] wildfire.
[8] emptied.
[9] all kinds of coinage.
[10] grunting mouth.
[11] Many lazy tun-bellied gluttons.
[12] slothful idler.
[13] drab.
[14] solicitude.
[15] loins.
[16] apprehension.

Than Lichery, that lathly corss,
Come berand[1] lyk ane bagit[2] horss
   And Ydilness did him leid.
Thair wes with him ane vgly sort,
Full mony stynkand fowll tramort[3],
   That had in syn bene deid.
Quhen they wer entrit in the dance
Thay wer full strenge of countenance
   Lyk turkass[4] birnand reid.
All led thay vthir by the tersis,
Suppoiss thay fyleit[5] with thair ersis,
   It mycht be na remeid.

Than the fowll monstir Glutteny
Off wame[6] vnsasiable and gredy
   To dance he did him dress[7].
Him followit mony fowll drunckart
With can and collep[8], cop and quart,
   In surffett and excess.
Full mony a waistless wallydrag[9],
With wamiss vnweildable, did furth wag
   In creische[10] that did incress.
" Drynk !" ay thay cryit, with mony a gaip ;
The feyndis gaif thame hait leid to laip ;
   Thair leweray[11] wes na less.

Na menstrallis playit to thame but dowt[12],
Ffor gle-men[13] thair wer haldin owt,
   Be day and eik by nycht,
Except a menstrall that slew a man,
Swa till his heretage he wan,
   Entering be brief of richt.

---

[1] snorting.
[2] *baguette.*
[3] dead bodies.
[4] torture-pincers.
[5] Although they defiled.
[6] belly.
[7] address.
[8] a drinking vessel.
[9] *lit.* the weakest bird in a nest.
[10] grease.
[11] desire, reward.
[12] without doubt.
[13] musicians.

Than cryd Mahoun for a Heleand padyane[1];
Syne ran a feynd to feche Makfadyane
Ffar northwart in a nuke.
Be he the correnoch had done schout[2]
Erschemen so gadderit him abowt
In Hell grit rowme thay tuke.
Thae tarmegantis[3] with tag and tatter
Ffull lowde in Ersche begowth to clatter,
And rowp lyk revin and ruke[4].
The Devill sa devit[5] wes with thair yell
That in the depest pot of Hell
He smorit[6] thame with smvke.*

[1] pageant.

[2] By the time that he had cried the dirge.

[3] heathenish crew; a play here on the word Ptarmigan.

[4] croak like raven and rook.

[5] deafened.

[6] smothered.

* A curious light is thrown by this satiric stanza upon the ancient antipathy of the Lowland Scots for the Highlanders. The antipathy appears to have been mutual.

AMENDIS TO THE TELYOURIS
AND SOWTARIS.

BETUIX twell houris and ellevin
I dremed ane angell came fra Hevin,
With plesand stevin[1] sayand on hie
"Telyouris and Sowtaris[2], blist be ye!

"In Hevin hie ordand is your place
Aboif all sanctis in grit solace
Nixt God, grittest in dignitie :
Tailyouris and Sowtaris, blist be ye!

"The causs to yow is nocht vnkend[3],
That God mismakkis ye do amend
Be craft and grit agilitie :
Tailyouris and Sowtaris, blist be ye!

"Sowtaris with schone weill-maid and meit
Ye mend the faltis of ill-maid feit ;
Quhairfoir to Hevin your saulis will fle :
Telyouris and Sowtaris, blist be ye!

"Is nocht in all this fair a flyrok[4]
That hes vpoun his feit a wyrok[5],
Knowll tais, nor mowlis in no degrie[6],
Bot ye can hyd thame : blist be ye!

[1] sound, voice.

[2] Tailors and shoemakers.

[3] unknown.

[4] deformed person.

[5] a corn or bony excrescence.

[6] Toes swollen at the joints, or chilblains to any extent.

1 clothes.

" And ye tailyouris with weil-maid clais[1]
Can mend the werst-maid man that gais,
And mak him semely for to se :
Telyouris and Sowtaris, blist be ye !

2 misfashioned.

" Thocht God mak ane misfassonit[2] man,
Ye can him all schaip new agane

3 than three such.

And fassoun him bettir be sic thre[3].
Telyouris and Sowtaris, blist be ye !

" Thocht a man haif a brokin bak

4 what matter.

Haif he a gude crafty tailyour, quhatt rak[4]?

5 cunning.

That can it cuver with craftis slie[5] :
Telyouris and Sowtaris, blist be ye !

" Off God grit kyndness may ye clame,

6 crookedness and lameness.

That helpis his peple fra cruke and lame[6],

7 help.

Supportand faltis with your supple[7] :
Tailyouris and Sowtaris, blist be ye !

8 In earth ye show such.

" In erd ye kyth sic[8] mirakillis heir,
In Hevin ye sal be sanctis full cleir,

9 Though.

Thocht[9] ye be knavis in this cuntre :
Telyouris and Sowtaris, blist be ye !"

THE FENYEIT FREIR OF TUNGLAND.

As yung Awrora with cristall haile
In Orient schew hir visage paile
A sweuyng swyth did me assaile[1]
    Off sonis of Sathanis seid ;
Me-thocht a Turk of Tartary
Come throw the boundis of Barbary
And lay forloppin[2] in Lumbardy
    Ffull lang in waithman weid[3].

Ffra baptasing for to eschew[4]
Thair a religious man he slew,
And cled him in his habit new ;
    Ffor he cowth wryte and reid.
Quhen kend[5] was his dissimvlance
And all his cursit govirnance[6]
Ffor feir he fled and come in France,
    With littill of Lumbard leid[7].

To be a leiche he fenyt[8] him thair,
Quhilk mony a man micht rew evir-mair,
For he left nowthir seik nor sair
    Vnslane or he hyne yeid[9].

[1] A vision suddenly came upon me.
[2] fugitive.
[3] in wanderer's dress.
[4] To avoid baptism.
[5] known.
[6] conduct.
[7] language, lore.
[8] To be a physician he feigned.
[9] ere he thence went.

Vane organis he full clenely carvit[1],
Quhen of his straik[2] so mony starvit[3],
Dreid he had gottin that he desarvit
    He fled away gud speid.

In Scotland than, the narrest way,
He come his cunnyng till assay;
To sum man than it was no play
    The preving[4] of his sciens.
In pottingry he wrocht grit pyne[5],
He murdreist mony in medecyne:
The jow[6] was of a grit engyne[7],
    And generit was of gyans[8].

In leichecraft he was homecyd;
He wald haif, for a nicht to byd[9],
A haiknay and the hurt manis hyd,
    So meikle he was of myance[10].
His yrnis[11] was rude as ony rawchtir[12],
Quhair he leit blude it was no lawchtir;
Full mony instrument for slawchtir
    Was in his gardevyance[13].

He cowth gif cure for laxatyve
To gar a wicht horss want[14] his lyve;
Quha-evir assay wald, man or wyve,
    Thair hippis yeid[15] hiddy-giddy.
His practikis nevir war put to preif
But suddane deid or grit mischief;
He had purgatioun to mak a theif
    To dee withowt a widdy[16].

Vnto no mess pressit this prelat
For sound of sacring[1] bell nor skellat[2];
As blak-smith bruikit was his pallat[3]
    Ffor battering at the study[4].
Thocht he come hame a new-maid channoun
He had dispensit with matynnis channoun;
On him come nowthir stole nor fannoun[5]
    For smowking of the smydy.

Me-thocht seir fassonis he assailyeit[6]
To mak the quintessance, and failyeit;
And, quhen he saw that nocht availyeit,
    A fedrem[7] on he tuke,
And schupe[8] in Turky for to fle.
And quhen that he did mont on he
All fowlis ferleit[9] quhat he sowld be
    That evir did on him luke.

Sum held he had bene Dedalus,
Sum the Mynataur mervalus,
Sum the Martis smyth Wlcanus,
    And sum Saturnus kuke.
And evir the cuschettis[10] at him tuggit,
The rukis him rent, the ravynis him druggit[11],
The hudit crawis his hair furth raggit[12],
    The hevin he micht not bruke[13].

The myttane[14] and Sanct Martynis fowle[15]
Wend[16] he had bene the hornit howle;
Thay set avpone him with a yowle[17],
    And gaif him dynt for dynt.

---

1 holy.
2 small bell or crier's rattle.
3 begrimed was his poll.
4 anvil.

5 scarf on left arm of a priest at mass.

6 many methods he tried.

7 feathering.
8 prepared.

9 marvelled.

10 wood pigeons.
11 dragged.
12 tore.
13 enjoy.

14 a hawk.
15 the marten.
16 Deemed.
17 scream.

1 Cuckoo, cormo-
rant, and hawk.
The golk, the gormaw, and the gled[1]
Beft him with buffettis quhill he bled;
The spar-halk to the spring him sped,
       Als fers as fyre of flynt.

2 a hawk.
The tarsall[2] gaif him tug for tug,
3 in each ear.
A stanchell hang in ilka lug[3],
4 magpie.
5 tear.
The pyot[4] furth his pennis did rug[5],
6 without stop.
       Thi stork straik ay but stynt[6].
The bissart, bissy but rebuik,
7 claws.
Scho was so cleverus of hir clvik[7]
8 possess.
His bawis he micht not langer bruik[8]
9 in a grasp.
       Scho held thame at ane hint[9].

10 jackdaws.
11 two kinds of
     hawk.
12 mews.
13 made attack.
Thik was the clud of kayis[10] and crawis,
Of marleyonis, mittanis[11], and of mawis[12],
That bikkrit[13] at his berd with blawis
       In battell him abowt.
14 pecked.
Thay nybillit[14] him with noyis and cry,
15 uproar.
The rerd[15] of thame raiss to the sky,
And evir he cryit on Fortoun, Fy!
       His lyfe was in-to dowt.

16 mocked with a
    screech.
17 at its pleasure.
The ja him skrippit with a skryke[16],
And skornit him as it was lyk[17];
The egill strong at him did stryke,
18 reached.
19 blow.
20 unwittingly
    he betrayed
    himself.
21 drenched.
22 oxen all
    streaked.
       And rawcht[18] him mony a rowt[19].
Ffor feir vncunnandly he cawkit[20],
Quhill all his pennis war drownd and drawkit[21];
He maid a hundreth nolt all hawkit[22]
       Beneth him with a spowt.

He schewre[1] his feddreme that was schene[2],
And slippit owt of it full clene,
And in a myre vp to the ene
    Amang the glar[3] did glyd.
The fowlis all at the fedrem dang[4]
As at a monster thame amang,
Quhill all the pennis of it owtsprang
    In-till the air full wyde.

[1] sheared, cut.
[2] beautiful.
[3] mud.
[4] struck.

And he lay at the plunge evir-mair
Sa lang as any ravin did rair[5];
The crawis him socht with cryis of cair
    In every schaw[6] besyde.
Had he reveild bene to the rwikis[7]
Thay had him revin all with thair clwikis[8],
Thre dayis in dub amang the dukis[9]
    He did with dirt him hyde.

[5] make noise.
[6] covert.
[7] rooks.
[8] claws.
[9] in gutter among the ducks.

The air was dirkit[10] with the fowlis
That come with yawmeris[11] and with yowlis[12],
With skryking[13], skrimming[14], and with scowlis,
    To tak him in the tyde,
I walknit[15] with the noyis and schowte,
So hiddowis beir[16] was me abowte.
Sen-syne[17] I curss that cankerit[18] rowte
    Quhair-evir I go or ryde.

[10] darkened.
[11] clamourings.
[12] screams.
[13] screeching.
[14] shrieking.
[15] wakened.
[16] noise of flight.
[17] Since then.
[18] ill-tempered.

THE LADYIS SOLISTARIS.[1]

[1] Solicitors.

THIR[2] ladyis fair that makis repair
 And in the court ar kend[3],
Thre dayis thair thay will do mair
 Ane mater for till end
Than thair gud men will do in ten
 For ony craft thay can ;
So weill thay ken quhat tyme and quhen
 Thair menes thay sowld mak than.

[2] These.
[3] known.

With littill noy[4] thay can convoy
 Ane mater fynaly,
Richt myld and moy[5], and keip it coy
 On evyns quyetly.
Thay do no miss, bot gif thay kiss
 And keipis collatioun[6],
Quhat rek[7] of this ? Thair mater is
 Brocht to conclusioun.

[4] trouble.
[5] gentle.
[6] keep feast.
[7] concern.

Ye may wit[8] weill, thay haif grit feill[9]
 Ane mater to solist[10];
Traist as the steill, syne nevir a deill[11]
 Quhen thay cum hame is mist.

[8] know.
[9] knowledge.
[10] solicit.
[11] whit.

Thir lairdis ar, methink, richt far
    Sic ladeis behaldin to,
That sa weill dar go to the bar
    Quhen thair is ocht ado[1].   1 aught astir.

Thairfoir I reid[2], gif ye haif pleid[3]   2 counsel.
    Or mater in-to pley[4],   3 pleading.
To mak remeid[5] send in your steid   4 in plea.
    Your ladeis grathit[6] vp gay.   5 remedy.
Thay can defend, evin to the end,   6 clad.
    Ane mater furth express;
Suppois[7] thay spend, it is vnkend,   7 Although.
    Thair geir[8] is nocht the les.   8 substance.

In quyet place, and thay haif space,
    Within less nor twa houris
Thay can, percaice[9], purchess sum grace   9 perchance.
    At the compositouris.
Thair compositioun, without suspitioun,
    Thair fynaly is endit;
With expeditioun and full remissioun
    And seilis thairto appendit.

Alhaill[10] almoist thay mak the coist   10 All whole.
    With sobir recompens
Richt littill loist, thay get indoist[11]   11 indorsed.
    Alhaill thair evidens.
Sic ladyis wyiss, thay ar to pryis[12],   12 praise.
    To say the veretie;
Swa can devyiss[13], and nane suppryiss   13 That can so
    Thame nor thair honestie.   contrive.

DISCRETIOUN IN ASKING.

OFF every asking followis nocht
Rewaird, but gif sum caus be wrocht,
   And quhair causs is men weill ma sie,
And quhair nane is it wil be thocht
   In asking sowld discretioun be.

Ane fule, thocht[1] he haif causs or nane
Cryis ay "Gif me," in-to a drene[2];
   And he that drones ay as ane bee
Sowld haif ane heirar dull as stane :
   In asking sowld discretioun be.

Sum askis mair than he deservis ;
Sum askis far les than he servis[3] ;
   Sum schames to ask and breidis of me[4],
And all withowt reward he stervis[5] :
   In asking sowld discretioun be.

To ask but[6] seruice hurtis gud fame ;
To ask for seruice is not to blame ;
   To serve and leif in beggartie
To man and maistir is baith schame :
   In asking sowld discretioun be.

[1] though.
[2] constant repetition, drone.
[3] serves for.
[4] is of my sort.
[5] dies.
[6] without.

He that dois all his best servyiss
May spill it all with crakkis[1] and cryis
   Be fowll inoportunitie,
Few wordis may suffice to the wyis:
   In asking sowld discretioun be.

[1] boastings.

Nocht neidfull is men sowld be dum;
Na-thing is gottin but wordis sum.
   Nocht sped but diligence we se;
For na-thing it allane will cum:
   In asking sowld discretioun be.

Asking wald haif convenient place,
Convenient tyme, lasar, and space,
   But haist or preiss of grit menyie[2],
But hairt abasit, but toung rekless:
   In asking sowld discretioun be.

[2] effect of great force.

Sum micht haif Ye, with littill cure[3],
That hes oft Nay, with grit labour;
   All for his tyme nocht byd[4] can he
He tynis[5] baith eirand and honour:
   In asking sowld discretioun be.

[3] Yea, with little care.

[4] abide, wait.

[5] loses.

Suppois the servand be lang vnquit[6]
The lord sumtyme rewaird will it.
   Gife he dois not, quhat remedy?
To flyte[7] with fortoun is no wit:
   In asking sowld discretioun be.

[6] unrequited.

[7] scold

THE PETITION OF THE GRAY HORSE, AULD DUNBAR.

1 Now when lovers come with gifts openly.
2 fillies will be decked and clothed.
3 commonality.

Now lufferis cummis with largess lowd[1]
Quhy sould not palfrayis thane be prowd,
Quhen gillettis wil be schomd and schroud[2]
That ridden ar baith with lord and lawd[3]?
    Schir, lett it nevir in toun be tald

4 Yule jade.

    That I sould be ane Yuillis yald[4]!

5 condition.
6 gambols.
7 outside.

Quhen I was young and into ply[5],
And wald cast gammaldis[6] to the sky,
I had beine bocht in realmes by[7],
Had I consentit to be sauld.
    Schir, lett it nevir in toun be tald
    That I sould be ane Yuillis yald!

8 crop grass.
9 To coal-heavers then must.
10 are scabbed, crooked, and rheumous.

With gentill horss quhen I wald knyp[8]
Thane is thair laid on me ane quhip;
To colleveris than man[9] I skip
That scabbit ar, hes cruik and cald[10].
    Schir, lett it nevir in toun be tald
    That I sould be ane Yuillis yald!

11 Though.
12 placed.
13 housing.
14 covered.

Thocht[11] in the stall I be nocht clappit[12]
As cursouris that in silk beine trappit,
With ane new houss[13] I wald be happit[14]

Aganis this Crysthinmes for the cald.
    Schir, lett it nevir in town be tald
    That I sould be ane Yuillis yald!

Suppois[1] I war ane ald yaid aver[2],
Schott furth our clewch[3] to pull the claver[4],
And had the strenth of all Stranaver,
I wald at Youll be housit and stald.
    Schir, latt it nevir in toun be tald
    That I suld be ane Yuillis yald!

I am ane auld horss, as ye knaw,
That evir in duill dois drug[5] and draw;
Great court horss puttis me fra the staw[6]
To fang the fog be firthe and fald[7].
    Schir, latt it nevir in toun be tald
    That I sould be ane Yuillis yald!

I haif run lang furth in the feild
On pastouris that ar plane and peild[8];
I mycht be now tein in for eild[9];
My beikis ar spruning he[10] and bauld.
    Schir, latt it nevir in toun be tald
    That I sould be ane Yuillis yald!

My mane is turned in-to quhyt,
And thairof ye haff all the wyt[11];
Quhen uther horss had bran to byt
I gat bot griss cnype[12] gif I wald.
    Schir, latt it nevir in toun be tald
    That I sould be ane Yuillis yald.

[1] Although.
[2] old spent horse.
[3] ravine, rough ground.
[4] clover.
[5] in sorrow does drag.
[6] from the stall.
[7] To bite the moss by outfield and infield.
[8] stripped.
[9] taken in for age.
[10] My corner teeth are projecting high.
[11] blame.
[12] but grass to crop.

¹ doted on.

I was nevir dautit¹ into stabell;
My lyf hes bene so miserable
My hyd to offer I am [bot] abill

² For ill-shorn straw that I would tear.

For evill schom strae that I reive wald².
    Schir, latt it nevir in toun be tald
    That I sould be ane Yuillis yald!

³ savings, goods.
⁴ possession.
⁵ shoemakers.
⁶ gnawed by ugly gums.

And yitt, suppois my thrift³ be thyne,
Gif that I die your aucht⁴ within
Latt nevir the soutteris⁵ have my skin
With uglie gumes to be gnawin⁶.
    Schir, latt it nevir in toun be tald
    That I sould be ane Yuillis yald!

⁷ over-ridden mule.
⁸ trappings.
⁹ joint, *lit.* shoulder-blade.

The court hes done my curage cuill,
And maid me ane forriddin muill⁷;
Yett, to weir trappouris⁸ at this Yuill,
I wald be spurrit at everie spald⁹.
    Schir, latt it nevir in toun be tald
    That I sould be ane Yuillis yald!

RESPONSIO REGIS.

¹⁰ treasurer.

Eftir our wrettingis, thesaurer¹⁰,
Tak in this gray horss, Auld Dunbar,

¹¹ Which.
¹² grey.

Quhilk¹¹ in my aucht with schervice trew
In lyart¹² changeit is in hew.
Gar howss him now aganis this Yuill,

¹³ deck.

And busk¹³ him lyk ane beschopis muill;
For with my hand I have indost
To pay quhat-euir his trappouris cost.

BEST TO BE BLYTH.

Full oft I muse and hes in thocht
How this fals warld is ay on flocht[1],
   Quhair no-thing ferme is nor degest[2];
And quhen I haif my mynd all socht,
   For to be blyth me-think it best.

This warld evir dois flicht and wary[3];
Ffortoun sa fast hir quheill dois cary,
   Na tyme in turning can it tak rest:
For quhois fals change suld none be sary[4];
   Ffor to be blyth me-think it best.

Wald men considdir in mynd richt weill,
Or[5] Fortoun on him turn hir quheill,
   That erdly honour may nocht lest,
His fall less panefull he suld feill:
   For to be blyth me-think it best.

Quha with this warld dois warsill and stryfe[6],
And dois his dayis in dolour dryfe,
   Thocht[7] he in lordschip be possest,
He levis bot ane wretchit lyfe:
   For to be blyth me-think it best.

1 on wing.

2 composed.

3 flit and vary.

4 sorry.

5 Ere.

6 wrestle and strive.

7 Though.

Off warldis gud and grit richess
Quhat fruct[1] hes man but miriness?
 Thocht he this warld had eist and west
All wer pouertie but[2] glaidness;
 For to be blyth me-think it best.

Quho suld for tynsall[3] drowp or de
For thyng that is bot vanitie,
 Sen[4] to the lyfe that evir dois lest
Heir is bot twynklyng of ane ee;
 For to be blyth me-think it best.

Had I for warldis vnkyndness
In hairt tane ony haviness,
 Or fro my plesans bene opprest,
I had bene deid langsyne[5], dowtless :
 For to be blyth me-think it best.

How-evir this warld do change and vary
Lat ws in hairt nevir-moir be sary,
 Bot evir be reddy and addrest
To pass out of this frawdfull fary[6];
 For to be blyth me-think it best.

[1] fruit.

[2] without.

[3] loss.

[4] Since.

[5] long ago.

[6] tumult.

MEDITATIOUN IN WYNTIR.

In-to thir dirk and drublie dayis[1]
Quhone[2] sabill all the hewin arrayis
  With mystie vapouris, cluddis, and skyis,
  Nature all curage me denyis
Of sangis, ballattis, and of playis.

Quhen that the nycht dois lenthin houris,
With wind, with haill, and havy schouris,
  My dule[3] spreit dois lurk forschoir[4],
  My hairt for languor dois forloir[5]
For laik of symmer with his flouris.

I walk[6], I turne, sleip can I nocht,
I vexit am with havy thocht;
  This warld all ouir I cast about,
  And euer the mair I am in dout,
The mair that I remeid have socht.

I am assayit on everie syde
Dispair sayis ay, " In tyme prowyde,
  And get sum-thing quhairon to leif,
  Or with grit trouble and mischeif
Thou sall in-to this court abyde."

Than Patience sayis, " Be nocht agast;
Hald Hoip and Treuthe within thé fast,
  And lat Fortoun wirk furthe hir rage,
  Quhen that no rasoun may assuage,
Quhill that hir glas be run and past."

[1] these dark and troubled days.
[2] When.
[3] doleful.
[4] dejected.
[5] become useless.
[6] wake.

And Prudence in my eir sayis ay,
"Quhy wald thou hald that will away[1]?
  Or craif that thou may have no space[2],
  Thow tending to ane-uther place,
A journay going everie day?"

And than sayis Age, "My freind, cum neir,
And be nocht strange, I thé requeir!
  Cum, brodir, by the hand me tak,
  Remember thou hes compt to mak
Off all thi tyme thow spendit heir."

Syne[3] Deid castis up his yettis[4] wyd,
Saying, "Thir oppin sall ye abyd[5].
  Albeid that thow were never sa stout,
  Vndir this lyntall sall thow lowt[6];
Thair is nane vther way besyd."

For feir of this all day I drowp:
No gold in kist[7], nor wyne in cowp,
  No ladeis bewtie, nor luiffis blys
  May lat[8] me to remember this,
How glaid that ever I dyne or sowp.

Yit, quhone the nycht begynnis to schort[9]
It dois my spreit sum part confort
  Off thocht oppressit with the schouris.
  Cum, lustie symmer! with thy flouris,
That I may leif in sum disport.

[1] that which will away.
[2] that which thou mayest in no wise have.
[3] Presently.
[4] gates.
[5] These open await you, *lit.* shall you endure.
[6] stoop.
[7] chest.
[8] prevent.
[9] shorten.

GAVIN   DOUGLAS.

GAVIN DOUGLAS.

On the eve of the great battle of Flodden, in which the flower of Scottish chivalry was fated to fall, when James IV., notwithstanding the urgent entreaty of his council and the obvious melting of his troops, had declared his resolve to fight, the last noble to urge prudence upon the king was the aged Earl of Angus. His years and his great services, apart from the wisdom of his words, entitled him to be heard; but James, as headstrong as he was gallant, merely turned upon him with a word of scorn: "Angus, if you are afraid, you may go home." Full of sorrow and foreboding, it will be remembered, the earl rode from the camp that night, but, loyal to the crown despite the insult he had received, he left his two eldest sons behind, and in the dire disaster which ensued, both of these, George, Master of Angus, and Sir William Douglas of Glenbervie, perished, along with two hundred others of the Douglas name.

This earl, fifth in succession from the first Earl Douglas of Angus and the youngest daughter of King Robert III., was Archibald, surnamed "Bell the Cat" from a famous historic incident of the

days of James III., but generally styled the Great Earl
of Angus. His wife was Elizabeth, daughter of Robert,
Lord Boyd, Lord High Chamberlain of Scotland, and
by her he had four sons, the third of whom was Gavin
Douglas, Bishop of Dunkeld.

These antecedents, together with some knowledge
of the feudal clan spirit of the times, throw a necessary
light upon the character and career of a man who,
while possessing the noble temper and ardent genius
of a poet, had to sustain the difficult part of a high
ecclesiastic of those days, and the obligations of the
scion of a great ruling house.

Tantallon castle, whose ruins frown yet out upon
the Bass ; Douglas castle, the cradle of his race, among
the Lanark hills; Dudhope near Dundee, or Abernethy
in Strathearn—any of these may have been the birth-
place of the poet, for all of them were residences
of the Earls of Angus. The date of his birth, from
his own words before the Lords of Council in 1515,
was at the end of 1474 or beginning of 1475. From
1489 to 1494 he studied at St. Andrews, his name
appearing upon the registers among the Licentiati
or Master of Arts in the latter year; and it is
probable that he afterwards spent some time at
seats of learning abroad, though the statement* that
"there is undoubted proof that his education was
finished at the University of Paris" still lacks corro-
boration.

His later career affords a striking contrast to that
of his contemporary Dunbar. It is as if the fortunes

* Warton's *History of English Poetry*, vol. iii., p. 3.

of the rival houses of March and Douglas had been
fated to find illustration in the lives of their respective
poet-descendants. Hardly had Douglas reached his
majority in 1496 when the king conferred upon him
the teinds of Monymusk in Aberdeenshire. This was
followed two years later by a presentation to the
parsonage of Glenquhorn when it should become
vacant by the resignation of Sir Alexander Symson.
He was also, probably through the interest of his
mother's family, made parson of Linton and rector of
Hauch, now Prestonkirk, near Dunbar. It was while
engaged in his pastoral duties there that he composed
his first allegorical poem, "The Palice of Honour,"
and Mr. Laing has suggested with much probability
that this production, dedicated as it was to James IV.,
induced the king to confer upon Douglas his next and
more important step in church preferment. At any-
rate, about 1501, the year in which "The Palice of
Honour" was finished, the poet, while allowed to
retain his former benefice, was appointed Dean or
Provost of the Collegiate Church of St. Giles in
Edinburgh. "This church, which was on a more
extensive scale than any other of the kind in the
country, except the Chapel-Royal at Stirling, supported
a provost, a curate, sixteen prebendaries, and seven
other offices, on the original foundation, to which was
superadded a vast number of altars and chaplainries,
some of them richly endowed."* Douglas's position
as head of this foundation was one not only of
ample emolument but of considerable consequence.

* *Works of Gavin Douglas*, ed. John Small, M.A., p. 7.

He is known from existing documents to have been conscientious in celebration of the religious services of the cathedral; his presence is recorded at meetings of the Lords of Council; in September, 1512, he was one of the great assize which passed an act anent "the resset of Rebellis, and Personis being at our souerane Lordis horne;" and he is supposed to have even visited Rome for the furtherance of certain interests at the papal court. Of more importance at the present day, however, was another of his occupations. Sometime during the early years of his Provostship of St. Giles, Douglas, it is believed, composed his allegory "King Hart," and made his translation of Ovid's "Art of Love." The latter performance has unfortunately been lost, but there can be no doubt that the effort prepared the way for the production of his greatest work. In January, 1512, he began his translation of Virgil, an arduous but apparently congenial task, and the speed at which he wrote may be judged from the fact that he finished it in July of the following year, two months before the national disaster which was to be the crisis of his own fortunes, the red field of Flodden.

It has already been mentioned that the two eldest brothers of the poet fell with their king on that fatal field. Upon hearing this dark news, the old earl, their father, retired to St. Mains, a religious house in Galloway, where he died of grief in the beginning of 1514.

This treble loss in his family, following the great

disaster to the country, was pregnant of stirring con-
sequences to Gavin Douglas.   At one blow it put
an end to his poetical efforts, and cast him into the
whirl of political affairs.   In the queen's first great
personal distress at the loss of her husband the Provost
of St. Giles had been appointed, with one or two other
Lords of Council, to wait daily upon her for purposes
of consolation and advice ; and on the 30th of
September, his father being then Provost of Edinburgh,
Douglas was made a free burgess of the city "communi
bono ville."

It has been concluded that this latter honour may
have been conferred out of compliment to the Earl of
Angus, or on account of the poet's own literary fame.
But in the circumstances of the time it seems more
probable that the freedom was conferred as stated "for
the town's common good "—as a further means of
attaching the personal and family interest of Douglas
to the city.   From this it would appear that already
the Provost of St Giles was recognized as exerting an
influence worth propitiating in matters of state.   An
impending event, however, was to place Douglas's
influence above all question.

Upon the death of the old lord, the earldom of
Angus was inherited by Archibald, the son of the
poet's eldest brother, a young nobleman as remarkable
for his personal comeliness as for his ambition and
feudal power.   The new earl speedily attracted the
attention of the youthful queen, who encouraged his
addresses, and finally, only eleven months after
Flodden, on the pretext that the support of the power-

ful Douglas clan was needed by the throne, gave him her hand in the church of Kinnoull.*

It is to be expected that, for feudal reasons, if from no more personal motives, the poet did all in his power to further his nephew's marriage, and this fact may account, to some extent at least, for the confidence and favour bestowed upon him from the first by the queen. As early as June 1514, she nominated him Abbot of Aberbrothock, the most valuable of the Scottish abbacies, and in September of that year, a month after her marriage, she commissioned him to act as her representative with plenary powers before the Lords of Council.

But trouble was already in the air, and the high hopes of the house of Douglas were fated to bring more than disappointment upon the poet. The hasty and ill-managed marriage of Queen Margaret to so powerful a noble as Angus had at once excited the alarm of the Scottish peers. "It was investing the house of Douglas with almost royal dignity, and the experience of the last hundred years had shown only too well how insolent, daring, and ambitious that house could be." That this apprehension was not altogether unfounded may be gathered from one fact. James Beaton, Archbishop of Glasgow and Chancellor of Scotland, having spoken strongly against the royal marriage, was seized by Angus at Perth and forced to

---

* Mr. Small, in an interesting note, draws attention to the fact that the present Royal Family of Great Britain derives its descent from this marriage, the issue of the union, Lady Margaret Douglas, born in 1515, having "married Matthew, fourth Earl of Lennox, whose son, Lord Darnley, husband of Queen Mary, was father of James VI."

surrender the Great Seal, which was then handed to the keeping of Gavin Douglas. For some months thereafter, though the Lords of Council immediately ordered him to restore the sign of authority, the poet appears to have held the office, or at least the title, of Chancellor. The popular feeling of the time is indicated by the statement in a contemporary diary that " all the court was rewlit by the Erle of Angus, Mr. Gawin Dowglass, and the Drummonds,* but nocht weill." Moved by their apprehensions, the Lords declared that by her marriage the queen had forfeited the guardianship of her son James V.; and they determined to recall the Duke of Albany, grandson of James II. and cousin of James IV., from France to the regency of Scotland.

Meanwhile, the archbishopric of St. Andrews having become opportunely vacant, the queen had nominated Gavin Douglas to the primacy, recommending him to Pope Leo the Tenth as second to none in learning and virtue. But the canons, partaking the spirit of the times, elected John Hepburn, their prior, to the see, and the latter, laying siege to the archiepiscopal castle, expelled the retainers of Douglas, who had taken possession. Nor did the Earl of Angus, with a succour of two hundred horse, manage to reinstate his uncle. Hepburn was in turn ousted by Andrew Foreman, Bishop of Moray, who had obtained the papal bulls for his own appointment, and by bestowing the priory of Coldingham on the brother of Lord Hume, had prevailed upon that nobleman to support him with

* The mother of Angus was a daughter of Lord Drummond.

ten thousand men-at-arms.   Douglas, however, actuated
by a spirit of decency which appears to have been rare
in his time, withdrew from the disgraceful rivalry.   His
moderation, nevertheless, seemed likely to go without
reward, for the abbacy of Aberbrothock, which he
had considered secure, was confirmed to his rival,
Archbishop Beaton.

Even this was not the last of the poet's troubles just
then.   In January, 1515, the bishopric of Dunkeld
became vacant.   Once more the queen named Douglas
for preferment ; and in this case, by the aid, it is
supposed, of her brother Henry VIII., obtained the
papal confirmation of her choice.   But the Earl of
Athole had induced the canons to postulate his
brother, Andrew Stewart, and, the Duke of Albany
having now arrived from France, Douglas was sum-
moned before the Lords of Council, found guilty of
negotiating for benefices at the papal court, and forth-
with consigned to prison.   The offence with which he
was charged was one forbidden by several old Scottish
statutes, and the revival of these now sufficiently
served Albany's purpose, which was to weaken the
queen's party by removing from it one of its most able
adherents.   For more than twelve months Douglas
was confined under charge of his former rival, Hepburn,
in the castles of St. Andrews, Dunbar, and Edinburgh,
and from some of his letters extant, he appears to
have chafed considerably at his imprisonment.   The
indignity was also deeply felt by his friends.   Fortune,
however, turned presently with a suddenness charac-
teristic of the times.   The imprisonment of so noble a

prelate brought about a certain revulsion of popular feeling in the country. The Pontiff was not slow to threaten with excommunication the troublers of his bishop, and Albany began to fear that, for his severity in this and other matters, he might have to reckon with the queen's brother, Henry VIII. Douglas was accordingly released from imprisonment, reseated as a lord of council, consecrated, first by Archbishop Beaton at Glasgow, and afterwards by the primate, Foreman, at St. Andrews,* and assisted to wrest his episcopal palace from Stewart by force of arms.

The poet was now deeply loaded with debt, but he set about the discharge of his duties to his bishopric and the state with diligence and success. He finished the bridge at Dunkeld begun by his predecessor, Bishop Brown; and in May, 1517, he was one of the three ambassadors to France whose mission resulted in the memorable treaty of Rouen.

So important was this treaty, which bound Scotland and France in a league of mutual defence against England, that the vacillating Albany, heartily sick of the troubles of his regency, made the signing of it an excuse for visiting his vast estates on the Continent. His absence was the signal for immediate anarchy at home. The Archbishops of St. Andrews and

---

* In 1489, when James IV., in one of his accesses of religious feeling, had caused himself to be enrolled as a canon of Glasgow cathedral, an Act of the Scottish Parliament had erected Glasgow into an archbishopric, with the Bishops of Dunkeld, Dunblane, Galloway, and Argyle as suffragans, and the Act had been confirmed by a Bull of Pope Innocent VIII. But the measure had been strongly opposed by Foreman, and he refused to recognise the consecration of Douglas of Glasgow.

Glasgow, and the Earls of Arran, Angus, Argyle, and Huntly had been named as a commission of regency, but the power of Angus so overshadowed the others that in 1520 a conspiracy was formed by them to seize him in Edinburgh. The chief of this conspiracy was James Hamilton, Earl of Arran, and he and the chiefs of his faction met in the house of Archbishop Beaton at the foot of Blackfriars Wynd, to arrange the execution of their plot. On the opposite side of the same street stood the palace of the bishops of Dunkeld, and while the conspirators were still deliberating, Douglas was announced. Beaton received his suffragan apart, when the latter tendered an offer from his nephew to retire with his friends from the city if allowed to do so in safety. After urging the keeping of the peace, Douglas reminded the archbishop that it was his duty as a churchman to preserve order. Mediation, however, was vain. The Hamiltons, being the more numerous party, felt sure of their object ; and accordingly Beaton made excuses to Douglas, and, protesting that he was ignorant of Arran's intentions, ended his disavowal with the words, " Upon my conscience, I cannot help what is about to happen." As he spoke the archbishop solemnly laid his hand upon his heart, when Douglas heard the clink of mail under the priestly vestment. " My lord," he exclaimed indignantly, " I perceive your conscience is not good, for I hear it clattering " (*Anglice*, telling tales). And immediately betaking himself to his nephew, he bade him defend himself like a man. " As for me,"

he said, " I will go to my chamber and pray for you."
Angus at once took possession of the High Street,
which could then be approached only by steep narrow
closes on each side ; and when the Hamiltons pre-
sently rushed to the attack they found themselves
overborne in these narrow entries by the long lances
of their opponents. The result was a complete
victory for the party of Angus, seventy of the
Hamiltons being left dead on the street ; and while
Home of Wedderburn, coming with eight hundred
borderers to assist Angus, burst with sledge-hammers
through one of the city gates, Arran and his son fled
out of another upon a coal-horse from which they had
thrown the load. Archbishop Beaton himself, who
had taken an active part in the fight, was pursued to
the high altar of the Church of the Blackfriars, and
was on the point of being slain, the rochet being torn
from his back, when he was saved by the interposition
of Gavin Douglas.

For many years this fight was remembered in Edin-
burgh by the significant name of *Clean-the-Causeway.*

Had Angus, now at the summit of power, been as
true to the queen as Gavin Douglas had proved true
to him the rest of the poet's days might have been
spent in the honourable administration of his diocese.
But when Margaret returned from her brother's court,
whither she had fled to escape the severity of Albany,
she had grave charges to bring against her husband.
Not only had he forsaken her when she lay ill with
typhus at Morpeth, but he had appropriated her
Ettrick Forest rents, worth 4000 merks yearly, and,

worst of all, he had been guilty of abducting Lady
Jane Stuart, a daughter of the house of Traquair,
whom he was keeping at Douglas Castle. The
queen's love for her husband was now changed into
hate, she meditated a divorce, and in November,
1521, she procured the return of Albany with a strong
French armament and ample munitions of war.
Before this display of force Angus fled to the Kirk of
Steyll, now Ladykirk, in Berwickshire, and despatched
Bishop Douglas to the English court with counter
charges of infidelity against Margaret.

The effort to enlist Henry's interest against his sister
entirely failed, and in turn Douglas had the mortifica-
tion to learn that the Regent had deprived him of his
bishopric and other benefices. But the keenest stroke
was to come when he heard that Angus, his stronghold
of Tantallon having been seized by Albany, had for-
saken his own cause, and was treating with the Regent
for pardon and permission to retire to France.

It is not too much to say that this final blow,
striking his most vital sense, the honour of the house
of Douglas, broke the poet's heart. A last letter
exists written by him from a London inn to Cardinal
Wolsey, which reveals his anguish of mind. He
writes of himself as a " desolatt and wofull wycht,"
and refers to "thair ontreuth that causit me labour
for the wele of thair Prince, and thair securite, quhilk
now has wrocht thair avne confusioun and perpetuall
schayme." For some months he remained in London,
on intimate terms with Wolsey and Wolsey's friend,
Polydore Virgil the historian. Had he lived he
might still, despite the intrigues of his rival Beaton,

have re-entered Scotland as Archbishop of St. Andrews; for the primacy presently became vacant by the death of Foreman, and Angus soon returned to the north with greater influence than ever. But the plague struck him down. He died in September, 1522, at the house of his friend Lord Dacre, and was buried by his own desire in the Hospital Church of the Savoy, by the side of the Bishop of Leighlin.

Of the facts of Douglas's life it is somewhat difficult now to judge, so wide is the difference between the habit of thought of his time and ours. Dr. Merry Ross has blamed the poet for his constant efforts to promote the interests of his family, but the censure seems hardly just. It is never a difficult task to take exception, and it seems only fair to remark of Douglas that while his faults were those of the best men of his time, his virtues were many and were exceptional. In each of his high offices he is known to have scrupulously fulfilled his duty, and the fact remains that with many opportunities of enriching himself, he died poor. The picture of him given, with the intuition of genius, by Sir Walter Scott in "Marmion," seems the fittest and truest.

> A bishop by the altar stood,
> A noble lord of Douglas blood,
> With mitre sheen, and rocquet white;
> Yet showed his meek and thoughtful eye
> But little pride of prelacy;
> More pleased that, in a barbarous age,
> He gave rude Scotland Virgil's page,
> Than that beneath his rule he held
> The bishopric of fair Dunkeld.*

* Canto vi., st. 11.

Of Douglas's longest original work, " The Palice of Honour," no manuscript is known to exist. The earliest texts are an edition printed in London about 1553 by William Copland, and an Edinburgh edition of 1579. The latter was reprinted at Perth in 1787, and by Pinkerton in 1792, before its reproduction in facsimile by the Bannatyne Club in 1827. The poem of " King Hart " and some verses by Douglas on " Conscience" are contained in the Maitland MS. (1555-1585) in the Pepysian Library at Cambridge, and the former was printed by Pinkerton in his *Ancient Scottish Poems* in 1786. No fewer than five MSS. of the translation of the *Æneid* have come down to modern times. Of these, one in the library of Trinity College, Cambridge, written about 1525, claims to be the " first correck coppy nixt eftir the Translatioun wryttin be Master Matho Geddes " the Bishop's chaplain, and it has some marginal notes in Douglas's own writing. The Elphynstoun MS., used by Mr. Small, and the Ruthven MS., which belonged to the ill-fated Earl of Gowrie, are in the University Library, Edinburgh. There is a manuscript at Lambeth Palace, and one is preserved in the library of the Marquis of Bath at Longleate, Wilts. The first printed edition was a mutilated one by William Copland in 1553; there was the famous Edinburgh folio edited by Thomas Ruddiman in 1710; and in 1839, upon the basis of the Cambridge MS., was produced the sumptuous edition of the Bannatyne Club. The first complete edition of the poet's works, in four volumes, was edited in an entirely satisfactory manner by Mr. John Small, M.A., in 1874.

" The Palice of Honour" is an allegorical composition in the fashion of Douglas's time, a Gothic structure, as Dr. Irving says, in which "ancient and modern usages, classical and Christian subjects, are almost constantly blended together, and a nymph of Calliope's train expounds the scheme of human redemption." The poet in a garden, of a May morning, falls into a swoon and sees pass him in succession the courts of Minerva, Diana, and Venus. Venus has him seized and is about to condemn him for contumely, when the court of the Muses arrives, and upon Calliope's intercession and his own composition of a lay in praise of the goddess of love he is set free. In the Muses' train he visits the Castalian fount, hears recited the long roll of the deeds of ancient heroes, and at last reaches the mountain on whose summit glitters the magic palace. Close to the summit he finds his path crossed by a fearful ditch, deep as Hell, wherein, amid boiling pitch, brimstone and lead, welter those wretches who have been tempted from pursuit of honour by pleasure and sloth. Carried across by his guardian nymph, he is shown a vision first of the storm-tossed world, then of the wonderful Palace of Honour, and again, in Venus' mirror, the most remarkable actions recorded in history. The inhabitants of the Palace are next passed in review—those who during their lives have followed the laws of truth, fidelity, and valour. The nymph then conducts him to a delightful and wonderful garden, but in attempting to gain access by

the bridge of a single tree, he falls into the moat and
awakes.   The composition is in a strictly conventional
vein, hardly ever rising above the level of laboured
prose, though the verse is full of sweetness, with an
occasional vigorous touch, and there is throughout an
exuberant if somewhat diffuse richness of detail.   It
must remain chiefly remarkable as proof of the wide
classical learning of its author.   There seems ample
room for the belief, moreover, that Bunyan got from
the " Palice of Honour" a large part of the suggestion
of his *Pilgrim's Progress.*

"King Hart," though in the same conventional
vein of allegory, exhibits riper powers than Douglas's
earlier work.   So vivid, indeed, sometimes become
the circumstances and characters that the reader
forgets the allegory, and catches fire at the story itself.
The narrative is full of action, the personifications are
natural and real as life, and the plot has strong human
interest, while the allegory is original, consistent
throughout, and forcible.   In all respects this
must be reckoned a greater performance than its
more famous sister piece.   As a study of the growth
and decline of an emotion it will, behind its archaic
method, bear comparison with some of the best
analytical novel-writing of the present day.

But the work to which Douglas must owe his
enduring fame is his latest and longest, the translation
of Virgil's *Æneid.*   Here he was away from the fatal
atmosphere of convention ; the nature of the task set
a bound to his discursive bent ; and amid the variety
of the great epic he struck at last upon the true

medium for his genius. His was the earliest metrical translation of a classic into the English or Scottish language, and its appearance, marking the dawn of the Renaissance in the north, gave the first sign that the middle ages were past. From the intrinsic beauty and worth of the performance, notwithstanding the antique language in which it appears, this must continue to rank among the greatest translations of the Augustan poet. It is true that here and there Douglas reads certain anachronisms into the classic, the Sybil becomes a nun, Æneas a "gentle baron," and so on, while at times, in portraits of men and women and in descriptions of nature, he is tempted to add deft touches of his own; but the work is that of one who knew the original language thoroughly, and who brought to its rendering an ample and richly varied phraseology of his own. Douglas's *Æneid* was the first work which carried Scottish literary influence to the south of the Tweed, and its immediate result was the Earl of Surrey's translation of the second and fourth books of the *Æneid* into English. It is a testimony to the excellence of the Scottish poet's work that Surrey embodied in his version many expressions and even whole lines of the northern translator.

To each of the twelve books of the *Æneid*, and to the additional book by Mapheus Vegius of the fifteenth century, which he included, Douglas wrote an appropriate prologue, and it is in these prologues that his finest work is seen. Here the Scottish genius for natural description appears. The colour, says Mr. Stopford Brooke, is superb, while of the landscape

of the poet he adds, "there is nothing like it in
England till Thomson's *Seasons*, and Thomson was a
Scotchman." Mr. Small, drawing attention to "the
dreary picture of winter in the seventh prologue, the
glowing description of May in the twelfth, and the
beauties of an evening in June in the thirteenth,"
gives it as his opinion that in these are to be found
"descriptive passages equal, if not superior, to any
which exist in the whole range of Scottish poetry."
Here are lively touches of fancy, and rural imagery
homely and real, and here, at his truest and best,
Douglas touches home to the heart of poetry when he
speaks with his own lips of the things that his own
eyes saw.

The translation was made by Douglas at the
request of his cousin Lord Sinclair, and at its conclu-
sion he bade farewell to poetry—

> And will direct my labours euermoir
> Vnto the common welth and Goddis gloir.

What he might have done in the nine remaining
years of his life, had his resolution and his fortunes
been different, it is idle to imagine. What he has
done assures him, if not, indeed, a "monument
more lasting than brass," at least a laurel that will
live as long as the great deeds which have given
lustre to the Douglas name. In "The Court of
Venus," written about 1560, Rolland describes him—

> Bischope and als ane honest Oratour,
> Profound Poet and perfite Philosophour ;
> Into his days abone all buir the bell,
> In sic practikis all vtheris did precell.

HONOUR.

*The " ballad," curious for its plethora of rhymes, with which
" The Palice of Honour" concludes.*

HIE Honour! sweit heuinlie flour degest¹, ¹ grave.
Gem verteous, maist precious, gudliest;
   For hie renoun thou art guerdoun conding², ² condign, fit.
Of worschip kend³ the glorious end and rest, ³ Of worth ascer-
                                  tained.
But⁴ quhome in richt na worthie wicht may lest. ⁴ Without.
  Thy greit puissance may maist auance all thing,
  And powerall to mekill auaill⁵ sone bring, ⁵ poor folk to
                                  much conse-
                                  quence.
I thé requeir, sen thow but peir art best,
  That efter this in thy hie blis we ring⁶. ⁶ reign.

Of grace thy face in euerie place sa schynis
That sweit all spreit baith heid and feit inclynis
  Thy gloir afoir for till imploir remeid.
He docht⁷ richt nocht, quhilk⁸ out of thocht thé tynis⁹! ⁷ avails.
                                  ⁸ who.
                                  ⁹ loses.
Thy name but blame, and royal fame, diuine is;
  Thow port, at schort,¹⁰ of our comfort and reid¹¹ ¹⁰ gate, in short.
                                  ¹¹ counsel.
  Till bring all thing till glaiding efter deid;
All wicht but sicht of thy greit micht ay crynis¹², ¹² diminishes,
                                  shrinks.
                                ¹³ shining one.
  O schene¹³! I mene¹⁴ nane may sustene thy feid¹⁵. ¹⁴ bemoan.
                                  ¹⁵ feud.

Haill, rois maist chois til clois thy fois greit micht !
Haill, stone quhilk schone vpon the throne of licht !
 Vertew, quhais trew sweit dew ouirthrew al vice,
Was ay ilk day gar[1] say the way of licht,
Amend, offend, and send our end ay richt !
 Thow stant, ordant as sanct, of grant maist wise
Till be supplie[2], and the hie gre[3] of price.
Delite the tite me quite of site to dicht[4],
 For I apply schortlie to thy deuise.

[1] Was always each day causing.

[2] succour.
[3] degree, prize.
[4] Extend thee soon to wipe me quit of shame.

KING HART.

[King Hart, personifying the heart of man, is represented in the pride of youth, guarded in his seemly castle by the five senses, and attended by a court of youthful qualities, such as Strength and Wantonness.]

KING HART into his cumlie castell strang
  Closit about with craft and meikill vre[1],   1 much labour.
So semlie wes he set his folk amang
  That he no dout had of misaventure;
  So proudlie wes he polist, plane and pure,
With youthheid and his lustie levis grene,
  So fair, so fresche, so liklie to endure,
And als so blyth as bird in symmer schene.

For wes he never yit with schouris schot[2],   2 with sorrows
                                            assailed.
  Nor yet ourrun with rouk[3] or ony rayne: 3 over-run with
                                            moisture.
In all his lusty lecam[4] nocht ane spot,   4 his fair body.
  Na never had experience into payne;
  Bot alway into lyking, nocht to layne[5],   5 in pleasure, to
                                            say truth, *lit.*
Onlie to love and verrie gentilnes   not to lie.
  He wes inclynit cleinlie to remane
And wonn[6] vnder the wyng of Wantownness.   6 dwell.

[Close by stands the delightful palace of Dame Pleasance, and one day surrounded by her handmaids, Beauty, Kindness, Mirth, and others, she appears with all her forces near the castle of King Hart. Alarm is brought by the watchmen to the hall where the king is sitting, whereupon]

Youthheid vpstart and cleikit[1] on his cloik,
    Was browdin[2] all with lustie levis grene;
"Ryse, Fresche Delyte! lat nocht this mater soke[3];
    We will go se quhat may this muster mene.
So weill we sall ws it copé[4] betwene,
Thair sall nothing pas away vnspyit;
    Syn[5] sall we tell the king as we have sene,
And thar sall nothing trewlie be denyit."

Youthheid furth past, and raid on Innocence,
    Ane mylk-quhyt steid that ambilit as the wynd;
And Fresche Delyt raid on Benevolence,
    Throw-out the meid that wald nocht byd[6] behind.
The bemes bricht almost had maid thame blind
That fra fresche Bewtie spred vnder the cloude.
    To hir thay socht[7], and sone thai culd hir find;
No saw thai nane never wes half sa proude.

The bernis[8] both wes basit of the sicht,
    And out of mesour marrit in thair mude[9]:
As spreitles folkis on blonkis hvffit on hicht[10]
    Both in ane studie starand still thai stude.
Fayr-Calling freschlie on hir wayis yuid[11]
And both thair reynyeis cleikit in hir handis,
    Syn to hir castell raid as scho war woude[12],
And festnit vp thir folkis in Venus' bandis.

[Other messengers whom the king sends out are captured in
turn, and at last he himself, exasperated, issues forth to fight.
Pleasance then arranges her troops in order of battle, and,
defeating and wounding the king, casts him into a dungeon in
her palace. Here his malady is made worse by the fact that
from his dungeon he can see and hear the mirth in the queen's
hall. Meanwhile Jealousy and Prodigality are his attendants].

Marginal glosses:
1 hooked.
2 broidered.
3 soak, rest.
4 share.
5 Afterwards.
6 abide.
7 made way.
8 barons.
9 marred in mood, disconcerted.
10 on white steeds paused on high.
11 went.
12 mad.

Discretioun wes as than bot young of age,

    He sleipit with Lust quhair-euer he micht him find :

And he agane wes crabbit at the page.

    Ane ladill full of luif, stude him behind,

    He swakit in his ene[1] and maid him blinde.   [1] dashed into his eyes.

[Business, Noble Bearing, and Disport strive to make interest with Dame Pleasance, but, laughing, she bids them attend their master. Presently, however, the imprisoned courtiers of King Hart make fatal interest with one of the queen's handmaids.]

This wourthy King in presoun thus culd ly

    With all his folk, and culd thair nane out brek.

Full oft thai kan vpone Dame Pietie cry,

    "Fair thing! cum doun a quhyle and with ws speik.

    Cum! farar[2] way ye micht your harmes wreik[3]   [2] A further, another. [3] your hurts avenge.

Than thus to murdour ws that yoldin ar.

    Wald ye ws rew, quhair-euir we micht our reik[4]   [4] reach over, attain to.

We suld men be to yow for euirmare."

Than answert Danger and said, "That were grete doute,

    A madin sweit amang sa mony men

To cum alane, but[5] folk war hir about ;   [5] unless.

    That is ane craft myself culd never ken[6]."   [6] a trick I could never take; cognizance of.

    With that scho ran vnto the Lady kene[7];   [7] intrepid.

Kneland, "Madame," scho said, "keip Pietie fast !

    Sythen[8] scho ask, no licence to her len[9].   [8] Although. [9] lend.

May scho wyn[10] out scho will play yow a cast[11]."   [10] get. [11] trick.

[Alas! then came a night when Danger slept.]

The dure on chare it stude; all wes on sleip ;

    And Pietie doun the stair full sone is past.

This Bissines hes sene, and gave gud keip[12];   [12] heed.

    Dame Pietie hes he hint[13] in armeis fast.   [13] seized.

He callit on Lust, and he come at the last ;

His bandis gart[1] he birst in peces smale :

Dame Pietie wes gritlie feirit and agast.

Be that wes Confort croppin in our the wall.

[1] caused.

[King Hart and his court, set free, proceed to storm the palace, and at last the queen, reduced to straits, throws herself upon his courtesy.]

So sweit ane swell as straik vnto his hart

Quhen that he saw Dame Plesance at his will.

" I yeild me, schir ! and do me nocht[2] to smart !"

The fayr Quene said vpone this wyss him till.

" I sauf youris, suppois it be no skill[3].

All that I haue, and all that myne may be,

With all my hairt I offer heir yow till,

And askis nocht bot ye be trew till me."

[2] make me not.

[3] I saved your (life), though it be no argument.

Till that [quhilk] Loue, Desyre, and Lust devysit

Thus fair Dame Plesance sweitlie can assent.

Than suddandlie Schir Hart him now disgysit,

On gat his amouris clok or euer he stent[4].

Freschlie to feist thir amouris folk ar went.

Blythnes wes first brocht bodwarde[5] to the hall :

Dame Chastite, that selie innocent,

For wo yeid wode, and flaw out our[6] the wall.

[4] ere ever he stretched.

[5] as messenger.

[6] went mad, and flew out over.

The lustie Quene, scho sat in middes the deiss ;

Befoir hir stude the nobill wourthy King.

Servit thai war of mony diuerss meiss[7],

Full sawris[8] sweit and swyth[9] thai culd thame bring.

[7] messes.

[8] savours.
[9] quickly.

Thus thai maid ane [richt] mirrie marschalling ;

Bewtie and Loue ane hait burde¹ hes begun ;   ¹ a hot tussle.

   In wirschip of that lustie feist so ding²   ² worthy.

Dame Plesance has gart perce Dame Venus' tun.

[The second canto paints a sadder picture. Seven years of
wedded bliss have flown, when one morning a stranger, Age,
knocks at the gate.]

At morrowing tyde, quhen at³ the sone so schene⁴   ³ that.
      ⁴ fair.

   Out raschit⁵ had his bemis frome the sky,   ⁵ dashed.

Ane auld gude-man befoir the yet⁶ was sene,   ⁶ gate.

   Apone ane steid that raid full easalie.

   He rappit at the yet, but courtaslie,

Yit at the straik the grit dungeoun can din⁷ ;   ⁷ the donjon-
      tower
      resounded.

   Syne at the last he schowted fellonlie⁸,   ⁸ violently.

And bad thame rys, and said he wald cum in.

Sone Wantownnes come to the wall abone⁹,   ⁹ above.

   And cryit our¹⁰, " Quhat folk are ye thair out ? "   ¹⁰ over.

" My name is Age," said he agane full sone,

   " May thow nocht heir? Langar how I culd schout ! "

   " What war your will?" " I will come in, but dout."

" Now God forbid ! In fayth ye cum nocht heir !

   Rin on thy way, [or] thow sall beir ane route¹¹,   ¹¹ blow.

And say the portar he is wonder sweir¹²."   ¹² obstinate, *lit.*
      lazy.

[At this news the courtiers begin to take flight. Youthheid is
the first to go ; and here, says Merry Ross, " even allegory
cannot chill the tenderness of the king's farewell."]

" Sen thou man pas¹³, fair Youthheid, wa is me !   ¹³ Since thou
      must go.

   Thow wes my freynd, and maid me gude seruice.

Fra thow be went never so blyth to be

   I mak ane vow, [al]thocht that it be nyce¹⁴.   ¹⁴ foolish.

Of all blythnes thy bodie beiris the pryce[1].

To warisoun[2] I gif thé, or thow ga[3],

This fresche visar, wes payntit at devyce[4].

My lust[5] alway with thé se that thow ta[6].

"For saik of thé I will no colour reid

    Nor lusty quhyte vpone my bodie beir,

Bot blak and gray; alway, quhill[7] I be deid,

    I will none vther wantoun wedis weir.

Fayr-weill, my freynd! Thow did me never deir[8].

Vnwelcum Age, thow come agane my will!

    I lat thé wit I micht thé weill forbeir.

Thy warisoun suld be [richt] small but skill[9]."

[After Age enter Conscience, Reason, and Wit. Reason
removes the film from the eyes of Discretion, and reads aloud
the conditions of his own service.]

Ressoun rais vp, and in his rollis he brocht.

    "Gif I sall say, the sentence sall be plane;

Do never the thing that ever may scayth thé ocht[10];

Keip mesour and trouth, for thairin lyes na trayne[11].

Discretioun suld ay with King Hart remane.

Thir vthir young folk-seruandis ar bot fulis.

Experience mais[12] Knawlege now agane,

And barnis[13] young suld lerne at auld mennis sculis.

"Quha gustis[14] sweit, and feld nevir of the sowre,

Quhat can [he] say? How may he seasoun[15] juge?

Quha sittis hate, and feld nevir cauld ane hour,

Quhat wedder is thairout vnder the luge[16]

How suld he wit¹? That war ane mervale huge! ¹ know.

To by richt blew², that nevir ane hew had sene!   ² To buy true
blue.

   Ane servand be, that nevir had sene ane fuge³! ³ bundle.

Suppois it ryme it accordis nocht all clene.

"To wiss⁴ the richt and to disvse the wrang,   ⁴ understand.

   That is my scule to all that list to leyr⁵."   ⁵ that choose to
learn.

[But as the lighter courtiers, Strength, Worth in War, and the
rest, depart, Dame Pleasance herself grows cold to the king, his
caresses become irksome, and at last she bids him farewell.
Then King Hart returns to his own castle, kept by Heaviness.
Here, before long, he is besieged by the forces of Decrepitude,
led by Headache, Cough, and Palsy; and finally, being mortally
wounded, he prepares for death by making his will and
testament.]

DIDO'S HUNTING PARTY.

From the Fourth Book of the Æneid.

BE this the queyn with havy thochtis onsound
In every vane nurisis the greyn wound.
Smyttin so deip with the blynd fyre of lufe,
Hir trublit mynd gan fro all rest remufe.
Compasing the gret prowes of Enee,

The large wirschip feill syse[1] remembris sche
Of his lynage and folkis; for ay present
Deip in hir breist so wes his figur prent[2]
And all his wordis fixt, that, for besy thocht,
None eis hir membris nor quyete suffir mocht[3].

Sum-tyme the quene Enee[4] with hir did leid
Throw-out the wallis onto euery steid[5],
The tresour all and riches of Sydony
Schawing to him; and offerit all reddy
The cetie of Cartage at his commandment.
Begyn scho wald to tell furth hir intent,
And in the myd word stop and hald hir still
And quhen the evin coyme it wes hir will
To seik wayis hym to feist, as sche did air[6],
And, half myndles, agane sche langis sair

For tyll inquyre and heir the sege of Troy,
And in a stair[1] behaldis hym for joy.   1 gaze.
Eftir all wes voydit, and the lycht of day
Ay mair and mair the mone quenchit away,
And the declyning of the sternis brycht[2]   2 the bright stars.
To sleip and rest perswadis euery wycht,
Within her chalmer allane scho langis sair,
And thocht all waist for lak of hir lufair.
Amyd ane woid bed scho hir laid adoun,
And of him absent thinkis scho heris the soun[3];   3 sound.
His voce scho heris, and him behaldis sche,
Thocht[4] he, God wait, fer from her presence be.   4 Though.
And sum-tyme wald scho Ascanius, the page,
Caucht[5] in the figur of his faderis ymage   5 Catch.
And in hir bosum brace, gif scho tharby
The luif vntellable mycht swyk[6] or satisfy.   6 assuage.
The werk and wallis begovn ar nocht upbrocht;
The younkeris deidis of armes exercis nocht;
Nodir[7] fortreis nor turratis suir of weir[8]   7 Neither.
   8 sure turrets of war.
Now graith[9] thai mair; for all the werk, but weir,   9 prepare.
Cessis and is stoppit, baith of pynnakles hye
And byg towris, semyt to ryse in the skye.*

Furth of the see, with this, the dawing springis.
As Phebus rais, fast to the yettis thringis[10]   10 eagerly to the gates throng.
The chois galandis, and huntmen thaim besyde
With ralis and with nettis strang and wyde
And hunting speris stif with hedis braid.

* Each book of the *Æneid* was divided by Douglas into
chapters, and the two passages above, descriptive of Dido's
passion, are included from the first and second chapters of Book
IV. as introducing the incidents of the hunt in chapter four.

From Massylyne horsmen thik thiddir raid,

With rynning hundis, a full huge sort,

¹ tarrying at the gate. Noblis of Cartage, hovand at the port[1],

The quene awatis that lang in chalmer dwellis.

Hir fers steid stude stamping, reddy ellis,

[2] champing. Rungeand[2] the fomy goldin bitt jingling,

Of goldin pall wrocht his riche harnissing.

And scho, at last, of palice ischit out,

[3] company. With huge menze[3] walking hir about;

[4] embroidered. Lappit in ane brusit[4] mantill of Sydony,

[5] twisted. With gold and perle the bordour all bewry[5],

[6] quiver. Hingand by hir syde the cais[6] with arrowis ground;

Hir brycht tressis envolupit war and wound

[7] coif, hood. Intill a kuafe[7] of fyne gold wyrin threid;

[8] purple attire. The goldin buttoun claspit hir purpour weid[8].

And furth scho passit with all hir company.

[9] gathered about. The Troiane peple forgadderit[9] by and by

Joly and glaid the fresche Ascanius ying;

Bot first of all, most gudlie, hym-self, thar king

[10] without doubt. Enee, gan entir in falloschip, but dout[10],

[11] joined. And vnto thaim adionyt[11] his large rowt.

Lyk quhen Apollo list depart or ga

Furth of his wintring realm of Lisia

And leif the flude Exanthus for a quhile,

[12] visit. To vesy[12] Delos his moderis land and ile,

Renewand ringis and dancis, mony a rowt,

Mixt togiddir, his altaris standing abowt,

The peple of Crete and thaim of Driopes

And eik the payntit folkis Agathirces,

[13] guise, manner. Schowtand on ther gise[13] with clamour and vocis hie,

Apon thi top, Mont Cynthus, walkis he,

His wavand haris, sum-tyme, doing down thring[1]   [1] thronging down.

With a soft garland of lawrere[2] sweit smelling,   [2] laurel.

And wmquhile[3] thaim gan balmyng and anoynt   [3] formerly.

And into gold addres at full gude poynt[4];   [4] in good order.

His grundin dartis clattering by his syde,

Als fresch, als lusty[5] did Eneas ryde,   [5] desirable.

With als gret bewtie in his lordlie face.

And eftir thai ar cumin to the chace,

Amang the montanis in the wild forrest,

The ryning hundis of cuplis sone thai kest,

And our the clewis and the holtis belyf[6]   [6] over the dells and the woods quickly.

The wild bestis dovn to the daill thai drive.

Lo, ther the rais[7], rynning swyft as fyre,   [7] roes.

Drevin from the hychtis[8] brekkis out at the swyre[9].   [8] heights. [9] gorge.

Ane-vther part, syne[10] yonder mycht thow see   [10] presently.

The hirdis of hartis, with ther heidis hie,

Ourspynnerand[11] with swyft cours the plane vaill,   [11] fleeting over.

The hepe of dust wpstouring[12] at thair taill,   [12] upstorming.

Fleand the hundis, leiffand the hie montanis.

And Ascanyus, the child, amyde the planis,

Joyus and blyth, his stertling[13] steid to assay,   [13] restless.

Now makkis his renk[14] yondir, and now this way,   [14] course.

Now prekis furth by thir and now by thaim[15],   [15] by these and those.

Langing, amang faynt frayit[16] beistis vntame,   [16] affrighted.

The fomy bair doun from the hillis hycht,

Or the dun lyon discend recontir he mycht.

In the meyn-quhile the hevinnis all about

With fellon noyis gan to rummyll and rowt[17];   [17] roar.

1 blast.

A bub[1] of weddir followit in the taill,

2 mixed.

Thik schour of rane myddillit[2] full of haill.

3 scatters far and near.

The Tyrian menye skalis wydequhair[3]

And all the galandis of Troy fled heir and thair,

And eik with thaim the yong Ascanius,

Nevo to King Dardane and to Venus.

4 places.

For feir to diuers stedis[4] throw the feildis

5 corners and shelters.

Thai seik to haldis, housis, hirnis, and beildis[5].

6 suddenly.

The riveris rudlie ruschit our hillis bedene[6].

Within a cave is enterit Dido queyn,

And eik the Troiane duke, all thaim allane,

By aventure as thai eschewit the rane.

Erth, the first modir, maid a takin of wo,

7 marriage-goddess.

And eik of wedlok the pronuba[7] Juno,

8 the air showed knowledge.

And of thair cupling wittering schew the air[8];

9 lightning.

The flamb of fyreflaucht[9] lychtnyt heir and thar,

10 without lies, in truth.

And on the hillis hie toppes, but les[10],

11 named.

Sat murnyng nymphis, hait[11] Oreades.

This was the foremast day of hir glaidnes

And first morow of hir wofull distres;

12 fashion.

For nother the fassoun[12] nor the maner sche

Attendis now, nor fame, ne honestie,

Nor from thens-furthwart Dido ony moir

Musis on luif, secret, as of befoir,

13 calls.

Bot clepis[13] it spousage, and with that fair name

Clokit and hyd hir cryme of oppyne schame.

WINTER.

Prologue to the Seventh Book of the Æneid.

As brycht Phebus, schene souerane[1], hevynnis e,

The opposit held of his chymmis hie[2],

Cleir schynand bemys, and goldin symmeris hew,

In lattoun[3] colour altering haill[4] of new,

Kithing no syng[5] of heyt be his visage,

So neir approchit he his wynter staige ;

Redy he was to entir the thrid morne

In cloudy skyis vndir Capricorne.

All-thocht[6] he be the hart and lamp of hevin

Forfeblit wolx his lemand giltly lewyne[7]

Throw the declyning of his large round speir.

The frosty regioun ringis[8] of the yeir,

The tyme and sessoune bitter cald and paill,

Thai schort days that clerkis clepe brumaill.

Quhen brym[9] blastis of the northyne art[10]

Ourquhelmit had Neptunus in his cart,

And all to schaik the levis of the treis,

The rageand storm ourwalterand wally seis[11],

Reveris ran reid on spait[12] with watteir broune,

And burnis hurlis all thair bankis downe,

And landbrist rumland rudely wyth sic beir[13],

[1] shining sovereign.
[2] mansions high.
[3] mixed metal, prob. brass.
[4] wholly.
[5] Showing no sign.
[6] Although.
[7] Very feeble waxed his glowing gilded levin.
[8] reigns.
[9] fierce.
[10] direction.
[11] over-riding wavy seas.
[12] flood.
[13] breakers rumbling with such noise.

So loud ne rummist wyld lioun or beir.

¹ dolphins (sea-swine) or whales.

Fludis monstreis, sic as meirswyne or quhailis[1]

² send down.

For the tempest law in the deip devallyis[2].

Mars occident, retrograide in his speir,

Provocand stryff, regnit as lord that yeir.

Rany Orioune wyth his stormy face

Bewalit of the schipman by his rays,

³ Untoward.

Frawart[3] Saturne, chill of complexioune,

Throw quhais aspect derth and infectioune

Bene causit oft, and mortale pestilens,

⁴ the degrees of his ascent.

Went progressiue the greis of his ascens[4];

And lusty Hebe, Junois douchtir gay,

⁵ spoiled.

Stud spulyeit[5] of hir office and array.

⁶ soaked in water moist.

The soill ysowpit into wattir wak[6],

⁷ mists.

The firmament ourkest with rokis[7] blak,

⁸ dun grew.

The ground fadyt, and fauch wolx[8] all the feildis,

⁹ covered smooth with snow.

Montayne toppis sleikit wyth snaw ourheildis[9],

On raggit rolkis of hard harsk quhyne stane

¹⁰ stony cliffs shone.

With frosyne frontis cauld clynty clewis schane[10].

Bewtie wes lost, and barrand schew the landis

With frostis haire ourfret the feildis standis.

¹¹ blasts.
¹² piercing.

Soure bittir bubbis[11] and the schowris snell[12]

Semyt on the sward ane similitude of hell,

Reducyng to our mynd, in every steid,

Goustly schaddois of eild and grisly deid,

¹³ Thick foggy shadows darkened.
¹⁴ threw.

Thik drumly scuggis dirknit[13] so the hevyne.

Dym skyis oft furth warpit[14] feirfull levyne,

¹⁵ cruel blasts.

Flaggis of fyir, and mony felloun flawe[15],

¹⁶ showers.
¹⁷ biting.

Scharp soppis[16] of sleit and of the snypand[17] snawe.

¹⁸ dreary.

The dowy[18] dichis war all donk and wait,

¹⁹ flooded with torrent.

The law vaille flodderit all wyth spait[19],

The plane streits and every hie way
Full of fluschis, doubbis, myre, and clay.
Laggerit leys wallowit[1] farnys schewe,
Broune muris kithit thair wysnit[2] mossy hewe,
Bank, bra, and boddum[3] blanschit wolx and bair,
For gurll[4] weddir growyt bestis haire.
The wynd maid wayfe[5] the reid weyd on the dyk;
Bedovin in donkis deyp wes every syk[6].
Our craggis and the front of rochis seyre[7]
Hang gret isch-schoklis lang as ony spere.
The grund stude barrand, widderit, dosk, and gray;
Herbis, flouris, and gersis wallowit away[8].
Woddis, forestis, wyth nakyt bewis blout[9],
Stud strypyt of thair weyd in every hout[10],
So bustuysly[11] Boreas his bugill blew,
The deyr full dern[12] dovn in the dalis drew.
Smal byrdis, flokand throw thik ronnis[13] thrang,
In chyrmyng and with cheping[14] changit thair sang,
Sekand hidlis and hirnys[15] thaim to hyde
Fra feirfull thudis of the tempestuus tyde.
The wattir lynnis routtis[16], and euery lynde[17]
Quhyslyt and brayt of the swouchand[18] wynde.
Puire laboraris and byssy husband men
Went wayt and wery draglyt in the fen.
The silly scheip and thair lytill hyrd gromis
Lurkis vndir le of bankis, wodys, and bromys;
And wthir dantit[19] gretar bestial
Within thair stabillis sesyt[20] into stall,
Sic as mulis, horsis, oxin, and ky[21],
Fed tuskit baris, and fat swyne in sty,
Sustenit war by mannis gouernance

[1] Bemired leas withered.
[2] showed their withered.
[3] bottom.
[4] stormy.
[5] wave.
[6] rill.
[7] many.
[8] grasses withered away.
[9] boughs bare.
[10] wood (holt).
[11] rudely.
[12] secretly.
[13] shrubs.
[14] twittering and chirping.
[15] hiding-places and corners.
[16] roar.
[17] lime-tree.
[18] soughing.
[19] daunted.
[20] secured.
[21] kine.

On hervist and on symmeris purviance.

¹ far and near.
² shrill.

Widequhair¹ with fors so Eolus schouttis schyll²
In this congelit sessioune scharp and chyll,

³ cool.

The callour³ air, penetrative and puire,

⁴ Dazing, stupe-
   fying.

Dasyng⁴ the bluide in every creature,

⁵ genial hot fires.

Maid seik warm stovis and beyne fyris hoyt⁵,

⁶ under-vest.

In double garmont cled and wyly-coyt⁶,
Wyth mychty drink and meytis confortive,
Agayne the stormé wyntre for to strive.

⁷ Refreshed.
⁸ basked.

Repaterit⁷ weill and by the chymnay beykyt⁸

⁹ stretched.

At evin be tyme dovne a bed I me streikit⁹,

¹⁰ Wrapped.

Warpit¹⁰ my heid, kest on claythis thrinfauld,
For till expell the perrellus peirsand cauld.

¹¹ then prepared.

I crocit me, syne bownit¹¹ for to sleip

¹² heed.

Quhair, lemand throw the glas, I did tak keip¹²
Latonia, the lang irksum nycht,

¹³ glances.

Hir subtell blenkis¹³ sched and wattry lycht
Full hie wp quhyrlyt in hir regioune,
Till Phebus rycht in oppositioune,
Into the Crab hir propir mansioune draw,
Haldand the hycht allthocht the son went law.
Hornit Hebawde, quhilk clepe we the nycht owle,
Within hir caverne hard I schout and yowle.

¹⁴ distorted.

Laithlie of forme, wyth crukit camschow¹⁴ beik,

¹⁵ horrible.
¹⁶ uncanny.

Vgsum¹⁵ to heir was hir wyld elriche¹⁶ screik.
The wyld geis claking eik by nychtis tyde

¹⁷ Over.

Attoure¹⁷ the citie fleand hard I glyde.

¹⁸ grave, deep.

On slummyr I slaid full sad¹⁸, and slepit sownd
Quhill the oriyont wpwart gan rebound.

Phebus' crownit byrd, the nychtis orloger,
Clappand his wyngis thryse had crawin cleir.
Approching neir the greiking[1] of the day,   [1] graying, dawn.
Wythin my bed I waikynnit quhair I lay.
So fast declinis Synthea the mone,
And kais keklis[2] on the ruiff abone[3].   [2] daws cackle.
                                                              [3] above.
Palamedes byrdis crouping in the sky,
Fleand on randoune[4] schapin lik ane Y,   [4] in flight.
And as ane trumpat rang thair vocis soun,
Quhais cryis bene prognosticatioun
Off wyndy blastis and ventositeis.
Fast by my chalmir, in heych wysnit treis[5],   [5] high withered
The soir gled[6] quhislis loud wyth mony ane pew,   trees.
Quhairby the day was dawin, weil I knew.   [6] sorrel hawk.
Bad beit the fyire, and the candill alycht,
Syne blissit me, and, in my wedis dycht,
Ane schot-wyndo[7] vnschet a lytill on char,   [7] A projected
Persawit the mornyng bla, wan, and har[8],   window.
                                                              [8] livid, wan, and
Wyth cloudy gum and rak[9] ourquhelmit the air,   grey.
                                                              [9] mist and cloud.
The soulye stythlie hasart, rowch, and hair[10],   [10] The soil hard-
Branchis brattlyng, and blayknit schew the brays[11],   frosted, misty,
                                                                  and gray.
With hyrstis harsk of waggand wyndilstrays[12],   [11] bleak appeared
                                                                  the hills.
The dew-droppis congelyt on stybill and rynd,   [12] bare spots
And scharp hailstanis, mortfundit[13] of kynd,   rough with
                                                                  wagging dried
Hoppand on the thak and on the causay[14] by.   grasses.
                                                              [13] cold as death.
The schot I clossit and drew inwart in hy[15],   [14] thatch and
Chiverand for cauld, the sessoun was so snell,   causeway.
                                                              [15] in haste.
Schup[16] with hait flambe to fleme[17] the fresyng fell,   [16] addressed me.
And as I bownit[18] me to the fyre me by   [17] drive away.
                                                              [18] addressed.
Bayth wp and downe the hous I did aspy,
And seand Virgill on ane lettrune[19] stand,   [19] writing table.

1 seized.

To writ anone I hynt[1] ane pen in hand,
For till performe the poet grave and sad,

2 ere then.

Quham sa fer furth, or than[2], begun I had,

3 became
annoyed some-
what.

And wolx ennoyit sum-deyll[3] in my hart,
Thair restit vncompleittit so gret ane part,
And til myself I said in guid effect,

4 must.

"Thow man[4] draw forth, the yok lyis on thi nek."
Wythin my mynd compasing thocht I so,
"Na-thing is done quhill ocht remanis to do."

5 chance.

For byssines quhilk occurrit on cace[5]

6 Overturned.

Ourvoluit[6] I this volume lay ane space,

7 though.
8 chose.

And, thocht[7] I wery was, me lyst[8] nocht tyre,

9 to leave over.

Full laith to leve our[9] werk swa in the myre,

10 stop.

Or yit to stynt[10] for byttir storme or rane.
Heyr I assayit to yok our pleuch agane,

11 one-fold,
honest.

And, as I culd, with afauld[11] diligence
This nixt buike following of profund sentence
Has thus begoune in the chyll wyntir cauld,

12 out-field and
in-field.

Quhen frostis days ourfret bayth fyrth and fauld[12].

MORNING IN MAY.

*Prologue to the Twelfth Book of the Æneid.**

DYONEA, nycht hyrd, and wach of day,
The starnis chasit of the hevin away,
Dame Cynthea dovn rolling in the see,
And Venus lost the bewte of hir e,
Fleand eschamyt within Cylenyus cave.
Mars onbydrew[1] for all his grundin glave[2],
Nor frawart[3] Saturn, from his mortall speyr,
Durst langar in the firmament appeir,
Bot stall abak yond in his regioun far,
Behynd the circulat warld of Jupiter.
Nycthemyne, affrayit of the lycht,
Went vndir covert, for gone was the nycht,
As fresch Aurora, to mychty Tythone spous,
Ischit of hir safron bed and evir[4] hous
In crammysin[5] cled and granit violat,
With sanguyne cape and selvage purpurat[6],
Onschot the windois of hyr large hall,
Spred all wyth rosys and full of balm ryall,
And eik the hevinly portis crystallyne

[1] withdrew.
[2] sharpened sword.
[3] untoward.

[4] ivory.
[5] cramoisie, crimson cloth.
[6] purple edge.

* In 1752 two English versions of this prologue appeared, one in the *Scots' Magazine* by Jerome Stone, schoolmaster of Dunkeld, and another by Francis Fawkes. Of the latter, Mr. Small quotes two fine passages in his introduction to Douglas. Warton also gives a prose paraphrase of the prologue in his *History of English Poetry*.

Vpwarpis braid[1], the warld to illumyn.

The twinkling stremowris of the orient

Sched purpour sprangis[2] with gold and asure ment ,

Persand the sabill barmkyn[4] nocturnall,

Bet doun the skyis clowdy mantill wall[5].

Eous the steid with ruby hamis reid

Abuf the seyis lyftis furth his heid

Of cullour soyr[6], and sum-deill brovn as berry,

For to alichtyn and glaid our emyspery,

The flambe owtbrastyng at his neys-thyrlys[7].

Sa fast Phaeton wyth the quhip him quhirlys

To roll Apollo his faderis goldin chair

That schrowdyth all the hevynnis and the ayr,

Quhill[8] schortly, with the blesand torch of day,

Abilyeit[9] in his lemand[10] fresch array,

Furth of hys palyce ryall ischyt Phebus

Wyth goldin crovn and vissage gloryus,

Crysp hairis, brycht as chrysolite or topace,

For quhais hew mycht nane behald his face,

The fyry sparkis brastyng fra his ene

To purge the ayr and gylt the tendyr grene,

Defundand[11] from hys sege[12] etheriall

Glaid influent aspectis celicall[13]

Before his regale hie magnificens

Mysty vapour vpspringand, sweit as sens[14],

In smoky soppis[15] of donk dewis wak[16]

Moich hailsum stovis ourheildand the slak[17].

The aureat fanys[18] of hys trone souerane

With glytrand glans ourspred the occiane,

The large fludis lemand all of lycht

Bot with a blenk[19] of his supernale sycht.

Marginal glosses:

[1] Opened up wide.
[2] sprays, streaks.
[3] mingled.
[4] rampart.
[5] screen wall.
[6] sorrel, reddish.
[7] nostrils.
[8] Till.
[9] Habited.
[10] flaming.
[11] Pouring out.
[12] seat.
[13] heavenly.
[14] incense.
[15] clouds.
[16] wet.
[17] Moist wholesome vapours covering the valley.
[18] The golden vanes.
[19] glance.

For to behald, it was a gloir to se
The stabillit[1] wyndis and the cawmyt see[2],

The soft sessoun, the firmament serene,
The lowne[3] illumynat air, the fyrth amene,
The syluer-scalit fyschis on the greit[4]
Ourthwort[5] cleir stremis sprynkland[6] for the heyt,
Wyth fynnis schynand brovn as synopar[7],
And chyssell talis, stowrand[8] heyr and thar.
The new cullour alychtnyng all the landis,
Forgane thir stannyris[9] schane the beryall strandis,
Quhill the reflex of the diurnal bemis
The bene bonkis[10] kest ful of variant glemis,
And lusty Flora did hir blomis spreid
Vnder the feit of Phebus sulyart[11] steid.
The swardit soyll enbrovd with selcouth[12] hewis
Wod and forest obumbrat[13] with thar bewis,
Quhois blissfull branchis, porturat on the grund,
With schaddois schene schew rochis rubycund.
Towris, turattis, kyrnellis[14], pynnaclis hie
Of kirkis, castellis, and ilke[15] fair cite,
Stude payntit, euery fyall, fane, and stage[16],
Apon the plane grund by thar awin vmbrage.
Of Eolus north blastis havand no dreyd,
The sulye[17] spred hyr braid bosum on breid,
Zephyrus' confortabill inspiratioun
For till ressaue law in hyr barm[18] adoun.
The cornis croppis[19] and the beris new brerd[20]
Wyth glaidsum garmond revesting the erd,
So thik the plantis sprang in euery pece
The feyldis ferleis[21] of thar fructuus flece.
Byssy dame Ceres and provd Pryapus,

[1] stilled.
[2] calmed sea.

[3] still.

[4] sand.

[5] Athwart.
[6] darting.

[7] cinnabar.

[8] storming.

[9] Opposite this gravel.

[10] The pleasant banks.

[11] glittering.

[12] strange.

[13] shadowed.

[14] battlements.

[15] each.

[16] tower, vane, and storey.

[17] soil.

[18] bosom.

[19] tops.
[20] leaf.

[21] marvel.

Reiosyng of the planis plenteus,

¹ Furnished.   Plenyst¹ sa plesand and maist propirly

By nature nurist wondir nobilly.

On the fertill skyrt lappis of the ground,

² Stretching broad.   Streking on breid² ondyr the cirkill rovnd,

³ pleasant.   The variant vestur of the venust³ vaill

⁴ turfy furrow.
⁵ sward.   Schrowdis the scherald fur⁴, and euery faill⁵

⁶ leaves.   Ourfret with fulyeis⁶ of figuris full diuers

⁷ dispersed.   The spray bysprent with spryngand sproutis dispers⁷.

For callour humour on the dewy nycht,

⁸ Restoring.
⁹ grasses.   Rendryng⁸ sum place the gers⁹ pilis thar hycht

Als far as catal, the lang symmeris day,

Had in thar pastur eyt and knyp away;

And blisfull blossummis in the blomyt yard

Submittis thar hedis in the yong sonnis salfgard.

¹⁰ rampart.   Ive levis rank ourspred the barmkin¹⁰ wall,

The blomyt hawthorn cled his pikis all.

¹¹ buds.   Furth of fresch burgionis¹¹ the wyne-grapis ying

Endlang the treilyeis dyd on twystis hing.

¹² locked.   The lowkyt¹² buttonis on the gemmyt treis

Ourspredand leyvis of naturis tapestreis;

Soft gresy verdour eftir balmy schowris

On curland stalkis smyling to thar flowris.

Behaldand thame sa mony diuers new,

¹³ sky-coloured.
¹⁴ dark brown (brunette).   Sum pers¹³, sum paill, sum burnet¹⁴, and sum blew,

¹⁵ grey.
¹⁶ rose-red.   Sum grece¹⁵, sum gowlis¹⁶, sum purpour, sum sangwane,

¹⁷ reddish.   Blanchit or brovne, fawch¹⁷ yallow mony ane,

¹⁸ degree.   Sum hevynly cullorit in celestiall gre¹⁸,

¹⁹ deep wavy sea.   Sum wattry hewit as the haw wally see¹⁹,

²⁰ divided.   And sum depart²⁰ in freklys red and quhyte,

Sum brycht as gold with aureat levis lyte,

The dasy dyd on breid hir crownell[1] smaill,   [1] spread abroad her coronet.

And euery flour onlappit[2] in the daill,   [2] unfolded.

In battill gyrs burgionys the banwart[3] wyld,   [3] In rank grass buds the banewort.

The clavyr, catcluke, and the cammamyld;

The flour-de-lice furth spred his hevinly hew,

Flour dammes[4], and columby blank and blew;   [4] damask rose.

Seyr[5] downis smaill on dent-de-lion sprang,   [5] Many.

The ying grene blomyt straberry levis amang.

Gymp gerraflouris[6] thar royn[7] levys vnschet,   [6] Dainty gillyflowers. [7] vermilion.

Fresche prymros, and the purpour violet.

The roys knoppis, tetand[8] furth thar heyd,   [8] rose-knobs peeping.

Gan chyp, and kyth[9] thar vermel lippis red;   [9] show.

Crysp scarlet levis sum scheddand, baith attanis

Kest fragrant smell amyd from goldin granis.

Hevinly lylleis, with lokerand[10] toppis quhyte,   [10] curling.

Oppynnit and schew thar creistis redymyte[11],   [11] ornate.

The balmy vapour from thar sylkyn croppis

Distylland hailsum sugurat hunny droppis;

And syluer schakaris[12] gan fra levis hyng   [12] thin hanging plates.

Wyth crystal sprayngis[13] on the verdour ying: [13] sprays.

The plane pulderyt[14] with semely settis[15] sovnd,   [14] powdered. [15] shoots.

Bedyit[16], full of dewy peirlis rovnd,   [16] dipped in water.

So that ilk burgioun, syon[17], herb, and flour   [17] each bud, shoot.

Wolx all enbalmyt of the fresch liquour,

And bathit hait did in dulce humouris fleit[18],   [18] float.

Quharof the beis wrocht thar hunny sweit,

By michty Phebus operatiounis

In sappy subtell exalatiounis.

Forgane[19] the cummyn of this prince potent   [19] Against.

Redolent odour vp from rutis sprent[20],   [20] sprang.

Hailsum of smell as ony spicery,

Tryakle, droggis, or electuary,

Seroppis, sewane[1], sugour, and synamome,

Precyus invnctment, salve, or fragrant pome[2],

Aromatik gummis, or ony fyne potioun,

Must, myr, aloes, or confectioun ;

Ane paradice it semyt to draw neyr

Thyr galyart[3] gardyngis and ilke greyn herbere[4].

Maist amyabill walxis the amerant medis.

Swannys swouchis[5] throw-out the rysp[6] and redis,

Our al thir lowys[7] and the fludis gray

Seyrsand by kynd[8] a place quhar thai suld lay.

Phebus red fowle hys corall creist can steyr[9],

Oft streking[10] furth hys hekkyll, crawand cleir,

Amyd the wortis and the rutis gent[11]

Pykland[12] his meyt in alleis quhar he went,

Hys wifis, Toppa and Pertelok, hym by,

As byrd al tyme that hantis[13] bygamy.

The payntit povne[14], pasand with plomys gym[15],

Kest vp his taill, a provd plesand quheil rym,

16 Dressed in
his feather
covering.
17 Portraying.
18 brushwood.
19 branches.
20 Many.
Yschrowdryt in hys fedramme[16] brycht and schene,

Schapand[17] the prent of Argus' hundreth ene.

Amang the brounis[18] of the olyve twestis[19]

Seyr[20] small fowlis wirkand crafty nestis

Endlang the hedgeis thyk and on rank akis[21],

Ilk byrd reiosyng with thar myrthfull makis[22].

In corneris and cleir fenystaris[23] of glas

Full byssely Aragne wevand was,

To knit hyr nettis and hir wobbys sle,

Tharwith to caucht the myghe[24] and littill fle.

So dusty puldyr vpstowris[25] in euery streyt,

Quhill corby[26] gaspyt for the fervent heyt.

Vnder the bewys beyn[1] in lusty valis,   [1] pleasant boughs.
Within fermans[2] and parkis cloys of palys,   [2] enclosures.
The bustuus bukkis rakis[3] furth on raw;   [3] bold bucks range.
Heyrdis of hertis throw the the thyk wod schaw,
Baith the brokettis[4], and with brayd burnyst tyndis;   [4] two-year-olds.
The sprutlyt[5] calvys sowkand the reid hyndis,   [5] speckled.
The yong fownis followand the dun dayis,
Kyddis skippand throw ronnis[6] eftir rayis.   [6] brushwood.
In lyssouris[7] and on leys littill lammis   [7] pastures.
Full tait and trig socht[8] bletand to thar dammis.   [8] tight and neat, made their way.
Tydy ky lowys[9], veilys by thame rynnis;   [9] kine low.
All snog and slekyt worth thir bestis skynnis.
On salt stremis wolx Doryda and Thetis;
By rynnand strandis Nymphis and Naedes,
Syk as we clepe[10] wenchis and damysellis,   [10] Such as we name.
In gresy gravis[11] wandrand by spring wellis,   [11] In grassy groves.
Of blomyt branchis and flowris quhite and rede
Plettand thar lusty chaiplettis for thar hede.
Sum sing sangis, dansis ledys, and rovndis[12],   [12] round (dances).
Wyth vocis schill[13], quhill all the daill resovndis.   [13] clear.
Quharso thai walk into thar caraling
For amorus lays doith all the rochis ryng.
Ane sang, "The schip salis our the salt fame
Will bring thir merchandis and my lemman hame!"
Sum other singis, "I wil be blyth and lycht,
Myne hart is lent apon sa gudly wycht!"
And thochtfull luffaris rowmys to and fro,
To leis[14] thar pane and plene[15] thar joly wo   [14] lose. [15] pour forth.
Eftyr thar gys[16], now singand, now in sorow,   [16] After their guise.
With hartis pensyve, the lang symmeris morow.
Sum ballettis lyst endyte of his lady,

Sum levis in hoip, and sum aluterly[1]
Disparyt is, and sa quyte owt of grace;
His purgatory he fyndis in euery place.
To pleis his luife sum thocht to flat and fene[2],
Sum to hant[3] bawdry and onlesum mene[4];
Sum rownys[5] to hys fallow, thame betwene,
Hys mery stouth and pastans[6] lait yistrene.
Smyland sayis ane, " I couth in previte
Schaw thé a bowrd[7]." "Ha, quhat be that?" quod he.
" Quhat thing?—That moste be secret," sayd the
      tother.
" Gude Lord! mysbeleif ye your verray brother?"
" Na, neuyr a deill[8], bot harkis quhat I wald;
Thou mon be prevy." " Lo, my hand vphald!"
" Than sal thou walk at evin." Quod he, "Quhiddyr?"
" In sik[9] a place heyr west, we bayth togiddyr,
Quhar scho so freschly sang this hyndir[10] nycht;
Do chois thé ane and I sal quynch the lycht."
" I sal be thar, I hope," quod he, and lewch[11];
" Ya, now I knaw the mater weill enewch."
Thus oft dywulgat is this schamefull play,
Na-thing according to our hailsum May,
Bot rathyr contagius and infective,
And repugnant that sessoun nutrytive
Quhen new curage kytlis[12] all gentill hartis,
Seand throu kynd[13] ilk thyng springis and revertis.
Dame Naturis menstralis, on that other part,
Thayr blyssfull bay[14] entonyng euery art[15],
To beyt[16] thar amouris of thar nychtis baill[17],
The merll, the mavys, and the nychtingale
With mery notis myrthfully furth brest[18],

[1] entirely.
[2] flatter and feign.
[3] practise.
[4] unlawful means.
[5] whispers.
[6] stolen pleasure and pastime.
[7] jest.
[8] whit.
[9] such.
[10] latter.
[11] laughed.
[12] tickles.
[13] Seeing by nature.
[14] melody.
[15] direction.
[16] amend, abate.
[17] sorrow.
[18] burst.

Enforsing thame quha mycht do clynk it best.
The cowschet crowdis and pirkis on the rys[1];
The styrlyng changis diuers stevynnys nys[2];
The sparrow chyrmis in the wallis clyft;
Goldspynk and lyntquhyte fordynnand the lyft[3];
The gukgo galis[4], and so quytteris[5] the quaill,
Quhill ryveris rerdyt[6] schawis and euery vaill,
And tender twystis[7] trymlyt on the treis
For byrdis sang and bemyng of the beis;
In wrablis dulce[8] of hevynly armonyis
The larkis, lowd releschand[9] in the skyis,
Lovys thar lege[10] with tonys curyus
Baith to Dame Natur and the fresch Venus,
Rendryng hie lawdis in thar obseruance,
Quhais suguryt throtis mayd glayd hartis dans;
And al small fowlys singis on the spray.
"Welcum, the lord of lycht and lamp of day!
Welcum, fostyr of tendir herbys grene!
Welcum, quyknar of florist flowris schene!
Welcum, support of euery rute and vane[11]!
Welcum, confort of alkynd fruyt and grane!
Welcum, the byrdis beyld[12] apon the breyr!
Welcum, maister and rewlar of the yeyr!
Welcum, weilfar of husbandis at the plewis!
Welcum, reparar of woddis, treis, and bewis[13];
Welcum, depayntar of the blomyt medis!
Welcum, the lyfe of euery thing that spredis!
Welcum, stourour[14] of alkynd bestiall!
Welcum be thi brycht bemys, glading all!
Welcum celestiall myrrour and aspy,
Atteching[15] all that hantis[16] sluggardy!"

[1] The ring-dove coos and perches on the twigs.
[2] delicate sounds.
[3] make the heaven resound.
[4] calls.
[5] twitters.
[6] made murmurous.
[7] twigs.
[8] warbles sweet.
[9] letting go (their song).
[10] Praise their liege.
[11] fibre.
[12] shelter.
[13] boughs.
[14] bestirrer, ruler.
[15] Reproving.
[16] practise.

And with this word, in chalmer quhair I lay,
The nynt morow of fresche, temperat May,
On fut I sprent[1] into my bayr sark[2],
Wilfull for till compleyt my langsum[3] wark
Twichand the lattyr buke of Dan Virgill,
Quhilk me had tareyt al to lang a quhile,
And to behald the cummyng of this kyng[4]
That was sa welcum tyll all warldly thyng,
With sic tryumphe and pompos curage glayd,
Than of his souerane chymmis[5], as is sayd,
Newly arissyn in hys estayt ryall,
That, by hys hew, but orleger[6] or dyall,
I knew it was past four houris of day,
And thocht I wald na langar ly in May
Les Phebus suld me losanger[7] attaynt.
For Progne had or than[8] sung hyr complaynt,
And eik hir dreidful systir Philomene
Hir lais endit, and in woddis grene
Hyd hir-selvin, eschamyt of hyr chance[9];
And Esacus completis his pennance
In riveris, fludis, and on euery laik;
And Peristera byddis luffaris awaik.
"Do serve my lady Venus heyr with me!
Lern thus to mak your obseruance," quod she.
"Into myne hartis ladeis sweit presens
Behaldis how I beinge[10] and do reuerens."
Hir nek scho wrinklis, trasing mony fold,
With plomis glitterand, asur apon gold,
Rendring a cullour betwix grene and blew
In purpour glans of hevinly variant hew.
I meyn our awin native bird, gentill dow,

Syngand in hyr kynd "I come hidder to wow,"
So pryklyng hyr grene curage for to crowd[1]   coo.
In amorus voce and wowar soundis lowd,
That, for the dynning of hir wanton cry,
I irkyt of my bed and mycht nocht ly,
Bot gan me blys, syne in my wedis dres,
And, for it was ayr morow, or tyme of mes[2],   [2] early morn, ere
                                                          time of mass.
I hynt a scriptour[3] and my pen furth tuike.   [3] seized a pen-
                                                          case.
Syne thus begouth of Virgill the twelt buike.

EVENING AND MORNING IN JUNE.

*From " The Proloug of the Threttene Buik of Eneados ekit to
Virgill be Mapheus Vegius."*

Towart the evin, amyd the summyris heyt,
Quhen in the Crab Appollo held his sete,
Duryng the joyous moneth tyme of June,
As gone neir was the day, and suppar done,

¹ quickly.

I walkit furth abowt the feildis tyte¹

² Which then.

Quhilkis tho² replenist stude full of delyte,
With herbis, cornis, catale, and frute treis,

³ store.

Plente of stoyr³, byrdis and byssy beis

⁴ green.

In amerant⁴ medis fleand est and west,
Eftir laubour to tak the nychtis rest.

⁵ glanced on the heaven.

And as I blynkyt on the lift⁵ me by,

⁶ became.

All byrnand reid gan walxin⁶ the evin sky;

⁷ all, whole.

The son, enfyrit haill⁷ as to my sycht,
Quhirlit about his ball with bemis brycht,
Declynand fast towart the north in deyd;
And fyry Phlegon, his dym nychtis steid,

⁸ dipped, plunged.

Dowkyt⁸ his heid sa deip in fludis gray
That Phebus rollis doun vnder hell away,
And Esperus in the west wyth bemis brycht
Vpspringis, as for-ridar of the nycht.

⁹ meadows.

Amyd the hawchis⁹ and euery lusty vaill

The recent dew begynnis doun to scaill[1],   1 scatter.
To meys[2] the byrnyng quhar the son had schine,   2 allay.
Quhilk tho was to the neddir warld decline.
At euery pilis[3] point and cornis croppis[4]   3 hair's.
                                                               4 tips.
The techrys stude as lemand beriall droppis[5]   5 The dew stood
And on the hailsum herbis clene, but wedis[6],   like burning
                                                                beryl drops.
Lyke crystall knoppis[7] or small siluer bedis.   6 free from weeds.
                                                               7 knobs.

The lycht begouth to quynkill out and faill,
The day to dyrkyn[8], decline, and devaill[9];   8 darken.
                                                               9 descend.
The gummis[10] rysis, doun fallis the donk rym[11],   10 mists.
                                                               11 dank rime.
Baith heyr and thair scuggis[12] and schaddois dym.   12 clouds.
Vpgois the bak[13] wyth hir pelit[14] ledderyn flycht ;   13 bat.
                                                               14 naked.
The lark discendis from the skyis hycht,
Singand hyr compling sang[15] eftyr hyr gys[16],   15 even-song.
                                                               16 guise.
To tak hyr rest, at matyn hour to rys.
Owt our the swyre[17] swymmis the soppis[18] of mist,   17 gorge.
                                                             18 clouds.
The nycht furthspred hyr cloke with sabill lyst[19],   19 edge.
That all the bewtie of the fructuus feyld
Was wyth the erthis vmbrage clene ourheild[20].   20 covered over.
Bath man and beste, fyrth[21], flude, and woddis wild   21 pasture-land.
Involuit in the schaddois warrin sild[22].   22 were hidden.
Still war the fowlis fleis[23] in the ayr,   23 Silent were the
                                                                birds' flights.
All stoyr[24] and catall seysit[25] in thair lair,   24 store.
                                                             25 secured.
And euery thing, quharso thame likis best,
Bownis[26] to tak the hailsum nychtis rest   26 Makes ready.
Eftir the day's laubour and the heyt.
Closs warrin all and at thar soft quyet,
But sterage[27] or removing, he or sche,   27 Without stir.
Ouder[28] best, byrd, fysch, fowle, by land or se ;   28 Either.
And schortlie euery thing that dois repare

In firth or feyld, flude, forest, erth, or ayr,
Or in the scroggis¹ or the buskis ronk,
Lakis, marrasis, or thir pulis donk,
Astabillit liggis² still to slepe, and restis;
Be the small birdis syttand on thar nestis;
The litill midgeis, and the vrusum³ fleyis,
Laboryus emmotis⁴, and the byssy beyis,
Als weill the wild as the taym bestiall,
And euery othir thingis gret and small,
Owtak⁵ the mery nychtgaill, Philomene,
That on the thorn sat syngand fra the splene⁶.
Quhais myrthfull notis langing for to heyr,
Ontill a garth vndir a greyn lawrer⁷
I walk onon and in a sege⁸ down sat,
Now musand apon this and now on that.
I se the poill and eik the Ursis brycht,
And hornyt Lucyne, castand bot dym lycht
Becaus the symmyr skyis schayn sa cleyr :
Goldin Venus, the mastres of the yeir,
And gentill Jove, with hir participate,
Thar bewtuus bemis sched in blyth estayt ;
That schortly, thar as I was lenyt doun,
For nychtis silens, and this byrdis sovn,
On sleip I slaid.

1 stunted shrubs.
2 lies.
3 restless.
4 ants.
5 except.
6 from the heart.
7 laurel.
8 seat.

[In a dream Mapheus Vegius, author of the additional book
appended to the work of Virgil, appears to the poet and induces
him, partly by argument, partly by twenty blows with a cudgel,
to include that book in his translation.]

                  And I for feir awoik,
And blent⁹ abowt to the north-est weill far,
Saw gentill Jubar schynand, the day star,

9 glanced.

And Chiron, clepit the sing[1] of Sagittary,   [1] called the sign.
That walkis the symmirris nycht, to bed gan cary.
Yondyr dovn dwynis[2] the evin sky away,   [2] wanes, declines.
And vpspryngis the brycht dawing of day
Intill ane other place nocht far in sundir,
That to behald was plesans and half wondir,
Furth quynching gan the starris, one be one,
That now is left bot Lucifer allone.
And forthirmore, to blason this new day,
Quha mycht discrive[3] the byrdis blyssfull bay[4]?   [3] describe.
                                                               [4] melody.
Belyve[5] on weyng the bissy lark vpsprang   [5] Immediately.
To salus[6] the blyth morrow with hir sang.   [6] salute.
Sone our the feildis schinis the lycht cleyr,
Welcum to pilgrym baith and lauborer.
Tyte on his hynis gaif the greif[7] a cry,   [7] Quickly on his
                                                               hinds gave the
"Awaik on fut, go till our husbandry!"   steward.
And the hird callis furth apon his page,
"Do drive the catell to thar pasturage!"
The hynnis wyfe clepis[8] vp Katheryn and Gill;   [8] calls.
"Ya, dame," sayd thai, God wait[9], wyth a gude will.   [9] God knows.
The dewy grene, pulderit[10] with daseis gay,   [10] powdered.
Schew on the sward a cullour dapill gray;
The mysty vapouris springand vp full sweit,
Maist confortabill to glaid all mannis spreit;
Tharto, thir byrdis singis in the schawis[11],   [11] coverts
As menstralis playng, "The joly day now dawis!"